CW00689819
RORER
Telecom

Welcome To Kurdistan!

The Kurdistan Region of Iraq is one of the most fascinating tourist destinations in the world. As the "Cradle of Civilization" it is home to more archeological and historic sites than any other region on earth. It boasts the oldest continuously inhabited city in the world as well as its oldest bridge and aqueduct ruin, Neanderthal caves and countless citadels, shrines, churches, mosques and ancient temples dot its landscape.

But Kurdistan is more than mere ancient history. It is a vibrant democratic and modern society whose citizens are renowned for their hospitality and multi-cultural and religious diversity.

For those wishing to enjoy dramatic scenery, Kurdistan's vast number of lakes and rivers, and flowering mountains are a visual delight and a photographer's paradise. One can take a ride up to snow-covered peaks on one of the longest teleferics in the world. There is no end to the pleasures and exciting things to do and see. One can shop in modern malls or ancient bazaars and there are culinary delights at every turn.

In 2014 Erbil was named the Arab Capital of Tourism, a singular honor for a non-Arab city. It won out over Dubai, Sharjah and the Saudi resort of Taif. Nearly 3 million people a year visit the region and the number is growing. Five star hotels and resorts as well as economic accommodations abound.

We are certain that once you experience this fascinating land you will come to regard it as many others do... **The Unbelievable Kurdistan!**

Nechirvan Barzani
Prime Minister
Kurdistan Regional Government

First Edition
2015-2016

Published by
Kurdistan Iraq Tours
A Division of The Other Iraq Tours LLC

Erbil, Kurdistan Region of Iraq / Delray Beach, Florida USA

Principles:
Harry Schute / Dr. Douglas Layton

Copyright © 2015 World Impact Press LLC
All rights reserved. No part of this publication may be reproduced, distributed, or transmitted in any form or by any means, including photocopying, recording, or other electronic or mechanical methods, without the prior written permission of the publisher, except in the case of brief quotations embodied in critical reviews and certain other noncommercial uses permitted by copyright law. For permission requests, write to the publisher, addressed:

Attention: Permissions Coordinator
World Impact Press LLC
324 SW 3rd Ave / Delray Beach, FL 33444
info@kurdistantourquide.com

Publisher's Cataloging-in-Publication Data
KURDISTAN TOUR GUIDE
ISBN 978-0-9962667-0-3-52495

Registered Domains:
kurdistantourquide.com - kurdistantourquide.net
kurdistantourquide.info - kurdistantourquide.org
kurdistantourism.com - tourkurdistan.com
tourkurdistan.info - tourkurdistanquide.com

Project Editor/Art Director:
Dr. Douglas Layton

Historical Research:
Benjamin Kweskin / Tara Sinclair

Contributing Articles :
Ancient History
from the Pen of Dr. Douglas Layton

Art of Kurdish Music
from the Pen of Chopy Fatah

Artists, Poets and Writers of Kurdistan
from the Pen of Dr. Douglas Layton and Qadir Qachagh

Battle of Gaugemela
from the Pen of Harry Schute

Classical Music of Kurdistan
from the Pen of Adan Karim

Cuisine Of Kurdistan
from the Pen of Chiman Zebari

Horses of Kurdistan
from the Pen of Karwan Barzani

Flowers and Fauna of Kurdistan

Plant Diversity in Kurdistan
from the Pen of Sarbagh Salih

Kurdish Cinema
from the Pen of Jano Rosebiani

Kurdish Women: Noble Ambitions and Bright Future
from the Pen of Pakshan Zangana

Peshmerga
from the Pen of Muhsin Khalidi

Preserving Nomadic Cultural and Heritage of Kurdistan
from the Pen of Anne - Marie Deisser

Security
from the Pen of Harry Schute

Project Photographer / David Parks/Faris Saadi

Contributing Photographers:
Dr. Douglas Layton - Stafford Clarry - Balin Zrar - Musleh Akraey - Shivan Harkey - Saman Muhamad Aziz - Salami Jan - Rauuf Shekh - Jameel - Naisih Ali Khayat - Muhamad - Aziz Jaf - Karzan Karo -

Graphic Design:
Cat Yayın Tasarım, Tülay Yılgör- Istanbul, TURKEY
www.catyayintasarim.com.tr
Joshua Lamothe - USA

Cover:
Design: Dr. Douglas Layton /
Photography: David Parks, Stafford Clarry /
Model: Paria Pourmozafari

Printing: Platin Group / Sadettin Sarıkaya - Istanbul, TURKEY / platin.sadettin@gmail.com

Kurdistan Project Coordinator: Balin Zrar
Marketing Director / Tara Sinclair
Istanbul Coordinator / Mystic Art and Design, Gürsel Bulut / gurselbulut@yahoo.com

Ordering Information:
Quantity sales. Special discounts are available on quantity purchases by corporations, associations, and others. For details, contact the publisher at the address above.

1. KURDISTAN, TOURISM, IRAQ, HISTORY, MIDDLE EAST, KURDISH COOKING, MEDIAN EMPIRE, NEANDERTHALS, ARCHEOLOGY, KURDISH MUSIC

Disclaimer: The publishers have made every effort to ensure the accuracy of the information in this book prior to going to press. However, they do not accept any responsibility for any loss, injury or inconvenience resulting from the use of information contained in this guide.

CONTENTS*

*See inside flap for color code

Letter from the Editor

Kurdistan is too vast a land to be contained in one simple volume but we have done our best to include those elements most likely to pique the interest of an adventurous soul. While there are a few "brief" companion Guides available, this is the first truly comprehensive Tour Guide to the Kurdistan Region of Iraq.

In January of 1992, I paid what I thought would be a short two week visit that somehow turned into 22 years and counting. I have visited most if not all of the sites listed—many on numerous occasions. Yet, I am forever amazed as I learn new and interesting things about the places I've been and discover from friends and fellow wanderers facts of which I was not aware.

One could spend a lifetime merely investigating the myriad caves of Kurdistan—some dating to the Neanderthal era. I have often stood on the site of Alexander the Great's historic battle with the Ruler of Persia, Darius III. Realizing the site has never been excavated I wonder what wondrous artifacts must lie beneath this battlefield where as many as a million men fought for the future of the known world and the title *Lord of the Earth*. This is truly a fresh and largely unexplored region—the "cradle of civilization" which any serious traveler should not miss.

When asked what I hold to be Kurdistan's most valuable treasure the answer is simple – its people. They are ever ready to host a guest and show them around this incredible land. It will not take you long to discover as I and many others have—that Kurdistan is truly an amazing adventure.

But beware! Short adventures in this captivating "land between the rivers" can easily turn into a lifetime of exploration.

KURDISTAN QUICK GUIDE

Visas

Citizens of the United States and North America, Schengen and all EU countries as well as New Zealand and Australia will be granted a ten day entry permit at the airport upon arrival. Stays over ten days require an approximate $45 exit fee upon departure and stays over fifteen days require registration with the Foreigners Registration Office located at 100 Meter Road, next to the Erbil International Airport.

All other countries require an Iraqi visa prior to entry into Kurdistan, which can be obtained through the nearest Iraqi Embassy or Consulate. The process normally takes a minimum of two weeks.

For assistance in locating the nearest location for obtaining a visa you can contact the regional Kurdistan Regional Government (KRG) office nearest you. While these offices do not issue visas directly they can assist in this and other issues pertaining to your visit to Kurdistan.

For a list of KRG Diplomatic offices see:

http://en.wikipedia.org/wiki/

List_of_diplomatic_missions_of_Iraqi_Kurdistan
http://dfr.gov.krd/p/p.aspx-?p=40&

For a list of Iraqi

Consulates see:
http://www.mofa.gov.iq/en/DiplomaticMissions/dm1.aspx

Local Consular Representatives

In case you need to locate your local consulate such as in the case of a lost passport or emergencies please see the following sites for local addresses and information:
http://kurdistaniraqtours.com/new/about-kurdistan/consular-representatives

Currency

The currency of Kurdistan is the Iraqi Dinar (IQD). The rate of exchange varies and for up to date information please check at the airport upon arrival or at your hotel or any of the many banks in each city. As an example the rate of exchange in December 2014 was roughly 1220 IQD to $1

The US Dollar and sometimes the Euro as well as a few other currencies are also often accepted at larger establishments such as hotels and major restaurants. US dollars are accepted at some smaller shops. However credit cards are not accepted at most locations other than major hotels. ATM machines are uncommon yet they do exist in some banks and shopping malls but will dispense currency only in Iraqi Dinars and function sporadically. Traveler's checks are generally not accepted. To be sure you will have suf-

ficient funds for your visit it is recommended to carry sufficient cash. US Dollars are the most accepted currency. For a currency calculator see: http://kurdistaniraqtours.com/about-kurdistan

Voltage: 220v

Both UK three-pronged and European two-pronged plugs are in use. Visitors are advised to take a universal adapter with them just in case. Adaptor plugs are available in most major hotels but it is good idea to bring adaptors with you. Your local travel store or shops at most airports will have the appropriate adaptor.

Transportation

Flights: The Kurdistan Region has two international airports: Erbil International Airport and Sulaymani International Airport. Most flights operating from Europe and the Middle East fly directly to Kurdistan. Several IATA member scheduled carriers fly to Erbil, and more IATA airlines are expected to soon begin flights there. Several charter companies also operate flights to Erbil or Sulaymani. There are numerous airlines that travel regularly to both the capital Erbil and Sulaymani. For up to date information see:

http://erbilairport.com/Main/Main.aspx

http://www.sul-airport.com/

Overland Route To The Kurdistan Region Of Iraq

Overland entry into the Kurdistan Region is possible through Turkey & Iran. The suggested route is to fly to Istanbul Ataturk Airport and then take a two-hour domestic flight to Diyarbakir in eastern Turkey. Turkish visas can be obtained for most nationalities on arrival at Istanbul Airport. Baggage may have to be retrieved from the International Terminal and checked in at the Domestic Terminal. At Diyarbakir Airport taxis can be hired to drive to the Ibrahim Khalil/ Habur border crossing point, Turkey's border with the Kurdistan Region in Iraq. Many drivers make this journey frequently and are familiar with the route. It is advisable to settle the fare beforehand but a typical price is $150 USD. You should check that the driver has the necessary paperwork to take passengers over the border. Because of the trip time it is advisable to begin the overland journey in the early morning, staying overnight in Diyarbakir if necessary. It is not advisable to travel at night. After crossing the border at Ibrahim Khalil, another taxi can take you to your destination within the Kurdistan Region. Some buses have permission to travel onward in Kurdistan as well. The approximate journey time from Diyarbakir to the border is 4 hours; then from the border to Dohuk is one and a half hours; to Erbil four hours; and to Sulaymani six hours.

There are alternative routes via Iran but these are less frequently travelled and not as safe as traveling through Turkey. Haji Omran is the most frequently used border from Iran with the closest city being Mahabad and Piranshahr where a taxi may be hired to take you to the Iran/Kurdistan, Iraq border.

Taxis

There are many taxis in nearly every city of Kurdistan. Some of them will take you longer distances (city-to-city). It is customary to settle the cost for the destination prior to getting inside. Inside the city fares may range from 1000 IQD to 7,000 IQD depending on the destination but few trips will cost more than 5000 IQD (approximately $4 USD). Transport one way between the major cities is approximately:

• Erbil to Duhok IQD10000 per person
• Erbil to Sulaymani IQD15000 per person
• Erbil to Kirkuk IQD10000 per person

This cost is for a shared taxi with four persons. The rental for a private taxi is roughly four times this amount but sometimes a cheaper rate can be negotiated. There are taxi stands in the center of most cities that specialize in "intra city" transport. Be sure to

agree on a price before departure.

Buses

There are buses that travel both within and between cities. Normally foreigners do not choose this option but it is certainly safe to do so and if you are on a tight budget it is an option. Cost is nominal (1000-2000 IQD). There is a regular bus service between Erbil, Sulaymani and Kirkuk.

Private car rental

There are currently no self-drive short-term rental facilities due to insurance issues but these matters are being addressed and it is envisioned that in the near future this service will be available. Long-term self-drive rentals are available from several agencies – some internationally known. Most short-term car rentals come with a driver and costs vary depending on the type of vehicle. Costs can range from $50-100 USD per day and $1000 – 2000 per month. When traveling outside the city and overnighting the client will normally be expected to pay for an inexpensive hotel and food for the driver.

Day Tours

Day tours are available through *Kurdistan Iraq Tours* for $270 per day, which includes up to three persons. Lunch is not included but may be taken along the way at local restaurants or a pack

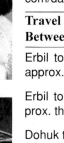

lunch can be taken along. The only restriction is that the trip must be able to be completed in daylight hours. Destinations are custom designed but for a sample of sites and itineraries, see:http://kurdistaniraqtours.com/day-tour

Travel & Distance Between Major Cities

Erbil to Sulaymani - 170 km, approx. three and half hours

Erbil to Dohuk - 245 km, approx. three hours

Dohuk to Sulaymani - 340 km, approx. five hours

Internet Connection, Mobile Phones

Many hotels in the Kurdistan Region offer Internet connection in the rooms and/or in their business centers, and most also offer wireless connections. Several local Internet service providers offer Internet connection to offices and homes for a monthly fee. The speed is slower than normally experienced in some locales, but connections are fairly reliable. As many international mobile operators have roaming agreements with Kurdistan Region's operators, foreign mobile phones often work. Please check with your mobile operator for call and SMS charges. It is advisable to buy a local SIM card (if you wish to save on local call charges) and insert it into an unlocked handset, and buy mobile cred-

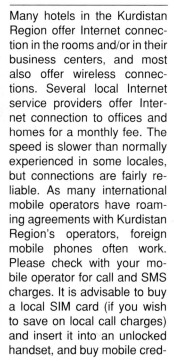

it top-up cards. Korek, Asiacell and Zain, the Kurdistan Region's largest mobile phone service operators, have roaming agreements with several foreign operators, including European, US and UK companies. If you wish to use your mobile locally please check with your mobile phone service operator whether it has a roaming agreement with Korek, Asiacell or Zain.

Postal And Freight Services

Letters and packages can be sent by normal post from the Kurdistan Region abroad, but at present they cannot be sent from abroad directly to the Kurdistan Region. The issue is that zip codes have not been assigned as yet and many residences and businesses have no clearly marked number or street making regular delivery impractical. This is changing but will take time. FedEx and DHL offer airfreight services to and from Kurdistan, please contact them for details. The post office in Erbil is temporarily located near the Citadel, close to the old court building. You must ask in the area for the exact location, as the street and number is not clearly marked. Sometime this year the office is scheduled for relocation to a more permanent and accessible location. The Post office in Sulaymani is located on Mawlawi Street (no number displayed) and the one in Duhok is located at Barzani Street across from Azadi Hospital.

The Arabic word for post, which is also used in Kurdish, is 'maqtab al-bareed'. Postcards can be obtained in some major hotels and in the bazaar.

Local Customs And Dress

Dress: Kurds tend to dress smartly and conservatively, and it is advisable for visitors to do the same. Skirts should fall below the knee and shoulders should be covered, and suits or smart dress should be worn at business meetings. There is no need for women to wear headscarves, as many Kurdish women do not. Men are advised not to wear shorts or sleeveless shirts. When entering Mosques or temples head coverings are required and shoes are to be left at the door.

Customs: The Kurds are very hospitable and it is not unusual to be invited to dine or enjoy tea in private homes. It is considered impolite to refuse hospitality but if circumstances do not permit or if you wish to decline the common response is "I apologize", which can mean one has a previous engagement but is in fact a polite way of decline.

When entering a house it is customary to allow the host to precede you through the door although they may seem at first to insist you precede them. In other circumstances your host will insist you enter first and it is not uncommon for Kurds to wait as long as necessary for you to oblige.

When sitting in the presence of others it is considered very impolite to point the sole of your foot toward another person. Shoes are often left at the door when visiting in homes and the host will often supply slippers to wear inside.

Men generally shake hands when greeting and some women do as well but some (particularly more observant Muslims) may feel uncomfortable with this and a verbal greeting suffices.

Climate

Average rainfall is 375-724mm (14-28 Inches) The climate of the Kurdistan Region is semi-arid continental: very hot and dry in summer, and cold and wet in winter. Spring is the most beautiful season in Kurdistan and the time when Kurds celebrate Newroz, the Kurdish New Year, on the Spring or Vernal Equinox. Mean high temperatures range from 13-18 degrees Celsius (55 – 64 F) in March to 27-32 degrees Celsius (80- 90F) in May. The summer months from June to September are very hot and dry. In July and August, the hottest months, mean highs are 39-43 degrees Celsius (102-109 F), and rarely but sometimes reach nearly 50 degrees Celsius (122 F). Autumn is dry and mild, and like

spring is an ideal time of year to travel in the Region. Average temperatures are 24-29 degrees Celsius (75-84 F) in October, cooling slightly in November. Winters are mild, except in the high mountains. Mean winter high temperatures are 7-13 degrees Celsius (44-55 F), and mean lows are 2-7 degrees Celsius (35-44 F).

Time Difference

The Kurdistan Region and the rest of Iraq are three hours ahead of Greenwich Meantime (GMT).

Emergency Numbers:

All Cities
Police: 104

Fire: 115

Ambulance: 122

General Board of Tourism, Erbil: +964 750 777 9788, +964 770 777 9788

Email: info@kurdistantour.net

Assistance For Journalists And Business Travelers

Journalists, delegations and travelers visiting for official or business purposes can contact the KRG for advice on arranging meetings and hiring drivers, fixers, interpreters and security. Please contact:
The KRG Department of Foreign Relations, Erbil: dfr@krg.org

KRG Representation to the UK, London: uk@krg.org

KRG Representation to the US, Washington DC: us@krg.org

Health

There are no known major health threats in Kurdistan. Vaccinations are not required for entry. While the water supply is treated, as with most foreign travel, it is recommended that visitors drink bottled water during their stays. Most restaurants are clean and safe to eat in but sidewalk vendors should be frequented with caution. Travel insurance including emergency evacuation is recommended. While Kurdistan has an ever-increasing number of modern medical facilities, the Region is still developing in this sector and sometimes the best care is found in other surrounding countries. Private air transportation is very limited and expensive. Be sure to bring an ample supply of any special prescription medicines as these may or may not be available locally.

Local Food & Drink

Kurdish cuisine is based on lamb, chicken, rice and bread, and usually employs many fresh herbs and vegetables. Fish served in restaurants is often barbecued over an open fire to make a traditional Iraqi dish called *Mazgouf*. Fresh fruit or Baklava, a Middle Eastern flaky pastry and nut dessert, is usually served after the main course. While many types of fruit and vegetables are available throughout the year, seasonal and local products, such as wild asparagus, native rhubarb, green almonds and buffalo yoghurt, are highly prized and enjoyed. Black tea with sugar is the most popular beverage both inside and outside the home. Drinking alcohol in moderation is acceptable in some restaurants and hotels. Drunken and loud behavior is frowned upon. (See article on Kurdish Cuisine)

National Holidays Observed By KRG Council Of Ministers In 2014:

(Ministries and government offices are closed. Businesses may also close. Please note that if the national holiday falls at the weekend (Friday or Saturday), then the next working day is taken off as the national holiday and government offices are closed).

• 1st January: New Year's Day

• 6th January: Army Day

• 24th January: Mouloud (Prophet Mohammad's Birthday) *

• 5th March: Uprising Day (Liberation of Ranya City)

• 11th March: Liberation of Erbil City

• 14th March: Mullah Mustafa Barzani's Birthday

• 21st - 23rd March: Newroz Kurdish New Year (Spring equinox)

• 9th April: Baghdad Liberation Day (fall of Saddam Hussein's regime)

• 1st May: Labour Day

• 14th July: Republic Day

• 7th – 9th August: Eid-al-Fitr Feast*

• 14th - 17th October: Eid al-Qurban Feast *

• 4th November: Muharram (Islamic New Year) *

• 13th November: Ashura *

• 25th December: Christmas Day

• 31st December: Iraq Day (tentative- TBA)

Other important dates

(These are working days at the KRG Council of Ministers, and businesses are open. Special events take place around the Region to mark these dates).

• 8th February: Ramadan Revolution Day

• 10th February: Kurdish Authors Union Day

• 18th February: Kurdish Students Union Day

• 1st March: Commemoration of Mustafa Barzani's Death

• 7th March: Liberation of Sulaymani City

• 8th March: Women's Day

• 13th March: Liberation of Duhok City

• 16th March: Halabja Day

• 20th March: Liberation of

Kirkuk City

• 1st April: Assyrian New Year

• 14th April: Commemoration of Anfal genocide against the Kurds

• 16th April: Remembrance of Chemical Attack on Balisan and Sheikh Wasan

• 17th April: FAO Day (Food and Agricultural Organization – focus on nutritional needs)

• 25th April: Anniversary of First Cabinet of Kurdish Government (1993)

• 13th June: Sulaymani City Fallen and Martyrs Day

• 8th August: Ceasefire Day (end of Iran-Iraq War)

• 9th July: Start of Ramadan, month of fasting (estimated) *

• 16th August: Establishment of the Kurdistan Democratic Party Day

• 3rd October: Iraqi Independence Day (National Day)

• 11th December: Establishment of Kurdish Women's Union

* Follows the Muslim calendar, Islamic holiday dates are estimated only.

Languages

Kurdish, the most widely spoken language in the Kurdistan Region, is part of the Indo-European family of languages. The Kurdistan Region's official languages for government purposes are Kurdish and Arabic. However, English is widely spoken and education in the fields of Engineering and Medicine are in English. There are also a number of English language Universities and many young people speak English well.

The two most widely spoken dialects of Kurdish are Sorani and Badini (Kurmanji). Other dialects spoken by smaller numbers are Hawrami (also known as Gorani) and Zaza. The Sorani Kurdish dialect uses Arabic script while the Kurmanji Kurdish dialect is written in Latin script. Sorani is most prevalent in Erbil and Sulaymani Governorates, while Badini (Kurmanji) is primarily spoken in Duhok Governorate and some parts of Erbil Governorate. As the Region's Kurdish-language media has developed nearly all people in the Kurdistan Region can speak or understand both of the major dialects. The Kurdistan Regional Government's policy is to promote the two main dialects in the education system and the media.

Here are a few simple phrases to get you by until you master the language

Note: The spellings used here are transliterations to English, to make it easier for non-Kurdish speakers to read the pronunciation.

English	Sorani Kurdish	Badini (Kurmanji) Kurdish
Hello	Rozh-bash	Rozh-bash
Good morning	Beyanee-bash	Beyanee-bash
Welcome! (On arrival)	Be kher bi (t)	Be kher hati
Goodbye	Khwa-hafees	Khwa-hafees
Thank you	Supas	Supas/Mamnoon
You're welcome	Ser chaw / Sha-ee neeya	Ser Chaava
How are you?	Chonee?	Chaawayi?
Are you well?	Bashee?	Bashee?
I'm fine, thank you	Bashem, supas	Bashem, supas
What's your name?	Naw-et cheeya?	Nav-ey ta cheeya?
My name is John	Naw-em John-ah	Nav-ey min John-ah
What would you like to drink?	Chee dakhoy?	Chi vadkhui?
Tea (without sugar)	Chai (bey shakir)	Chai (bey shakir)
Please	Zahmat Nabe	Bey Zahmat
Where is the bazaar?	Bazaar le chweya?	Bazaar la kidareya?
Where is the Khanzad Hotel?	Otel Khanzad la chweya?	Otel Khanzad la kidareya?
Yes	Aa / Balay	Aa / Balay
No	Na	Na
OK	Bale	Bale/Arey

Is it safe to travel in Kurdistan?

(see article on Security by Colonel Harry Schute)

Generally speaking the Kurdistan Region of Iraq is a very safe place to visit. There have been surprisingly few major incidents since the Gulf War and to date no loss of foreign life due to any terrorist activity. Kurdistan has its own security, military and police force and the autonomous government prides itself on its record of safety. The region is unlike the rest of Iraq in this regard and is widely known in media and political circles as "The Other Iraq". It has often been said that the Kurdistan Region of Iraq is safer than New York, Paris or London all of which have suffered enormous security problems in the past. It should also be noted that personal attacks such as muggings, etc. are virtually unknown in Kurdistan. However, as is the case in all countries, visitors are advised to mind their personal belongings and keep valuables in the hotel safe when possible. It is not advisable to trek or camp in remote areas without being accompanied by a trained guide as there are mine fields in some areas and in some cases (such as with Iran) borders are not clearly demarcated.

KURDISTAN SECURITY

By Colonel (retired) Harry Schute
Senior Security Advisor
Ministry of Interior
Kurdistan Regional Goverment

When people think of anywhere in Iraq – to include Kurdistan – they generally do not think anything positive about the security situation. At least that's the perspective they would have based on what they are hearing from the evening news. They may have heard something here or there about how Kurdistan is somehow, "different," but in the end it probably all blurs together. The fact is; security in Kurdistan is *very* different.

Since the beginning of the Iraq War in 2003, Kurdistan was an active participant and ally in assisting the U.S. led coalition to defeat the regime of Saddam Hussein, as well as providing active support during the fight against terrorists and insurgents in the ensuing years. In spite of the proximity of Kurdistan to active hot spots in places like Mosul, the Kurdistan Regional Government's security forces have done a very good job in providing security along the internal border and throughout Kurdistan. They well understand who the enemy is, and through excellent methods of intelligence, proactive security efforts and a supportive population, have been able to set the conditions for Kurdistan to be a safe haven.

Through the years, tens of thousands have fled from other parts of Iraq to Kurdistan because they could find security. At the same time, tens of thousands have travelled to Kurdistan from other parts of Iraq and regional countries to find peace and tranquility, whether that is in the modern shopping malls and hotels, or to put their feet in the green grass of a rolling hill, or in the waters of a mountain stream.

We have also seen extensive investment and development, not only from regional countries, but also from Europe, America and elsewhere. Those businesses and investors know that in the eight years of the Coalition presence in Kurdistan, that not a single soldier had been lost, nor has a westerner been kidnapped or lost in a terror attack. They know that the people of Kurdistan greatly treasure those who come to their aid and to work with them, and would give themselves before they would allow any harm to those guests. They know that the people of Kurdistan are looking to the rest of the world to grow and develop, and not to bankrupt ideologies of hate.

Of course the region and the world face new challenges today from the likes of a new breed of radical Islamic extremist terrorists. People in cities like Paris, Ontario, London, and Madrid, New York and elsewhere have all learned this sad reality too well. Even with these challenges, the Kurdistan Security Forces continue to hold the line by holding terrorists at bay. It is through the hard work and sacrifice of those security forces that Kurdistan remains stable, remains secure and remains open to welcome all tourists, business people and others who come in peace.

Tailored security solutions for regional issues

- Experienced security consultancy

- Crisis and evacuation planning

- Security threat assessments

- Comprehensive facility protection

- Training and awareness briefing

- Security infrastructure procurement support

www.vscsecurity.com

ANCIENT & MODERN HISTORY

Zagros Mountains

Ancient History
Excerpt from "Searching for Democracy" (1992)
By Dr. Douglas Layton

"Roughly five thousand years ago the people who inhabited the land we now call Kurdistan were tribal groups divided by geography, language and war. The tribes of the Zagros Mountains and surrounding areas came to be known as Lullubi, Kassites, and Hurrians to name but a few. The ancient Greek historian Herodotus mentioned the Bousae, Paretaceni, Strouchates, Arizante, Boudii, and Magi as parts of a group of tribes, which ultimately united under the name, Medes. The Medes later came to dominate a region, which stretched from Athens to India.

Prior to that time another tribe, the Quti, or Gutium, seemed to be especially powerful, surviving as a semi-developed state for nearly one hundred years. They are most likely associated with the land of Karda or Qarda, first mentioned on a Sumerian clay tablet of the third millennium BC. Alexander the Great reportedly referred to these people as Qarduk when he passed through this land and Pliny wrote of "the people formerly called Carduchi but now Cordueni."

Some historians maintain the Quti were led by ruthless dictators, but there is strong evidence suggesting otherwise, I. M. Diakonoff, in the *Cambridge History of Iran*, said the Quti were most likely ruled by "tribal chieftains elected for a term." If so, this mountain tribe would have been among the first of the world's people to taste democracy as a form of government.

It is certain, however, that the Medes migrated from a point further east into the Zagros Mountains and managed to unite the tribes of the region into a single people using democratic principles as well as military prowess as their means. It was they who formed the people of the region into a full-fledged nation in approximately 727 BC, which, at its peak ruled a vast empire swallowing and sometimes assimilating such kingdoms as the Urartians and Mannaeans. It can be said, with few exceptions, the people we now call Kurds find their ancestry from the nation of the Medes.

There is a great deal of discussion on the subject. Though some come to different conclusions, there is no proof the Kurds are not the descendants of the Medes and much that they are.

Persepolis

The historian Darmatesta in his book *Iranian Studies* supported this contention, as did Arnold Wilson in *Mesopotamia: Clashes of Loyalty 1918-1920* who wrote, "The Kurdish nation is a direct descendent of

Sloane described the Kurds as "the sons of the Medes." The evidence supporting the ancestry of the Kurds, as Medes is so great that, for the authors, the fact is fairly well established and we feel free to exchange

Median Empire

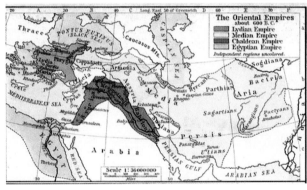

the Medians, and their language is one of the Western Iranian languages." In *The Historians History of the World*, Professor Cyes concluded, "The Medes were no other than Kurdish tribes whose linguistic affiliation was Aryan, Indo-European." Vladamir Minorisky agreed in *The Kurds, Encyclopedia of Islam*, and E.

the words Kurd and Mede without reservation.

Significantly, the Kurds themselves believe the Medes to be their ancestors. When Kurds established a television station in Europe, they referred to it as Med (Mede) TV. The Kurdish Poet Dildar wrote what became his people's unofficial

national anthem, proclaiming, "We are the Medes!" The Kurds of the world seem united on this point.

In time, the term *Medes* fell into disuse and the label Kurd (possibly related to Qurti or Karduchi) once again identified this mountain people. The fact remains, however, that the Medes so fully succeeded in imposing their language, culture, and physical characteristics on the ancient Kurds that one became synonymous with the other.

The nations in which the Kurds live today would sorely like to disallow the Kurds this heritage as they prefer to treat them not only as a people without a nation but a people without a history. The Kurds have a vibrant past claiming cultural achievements unknown to other people of the age. While we most often think of the Kurds as a group of warlike clans, the Sumerians referred to them as "painters of pottery" and Merhdad Izady, former professor of Near Eastern

History at Harvard University, maintained in *The Kurds: A Concise Handbook*, that the Kurds were the first to engage in agriculture, metallurgy, common weaving, and the firing of pottery.

It is also evident that the Medes (actually six tribes that united for common cause) were among the first peoples to utilize democracy as a form of government. Diakonoff wrote, "One gets the impression that while among their western neighbors discord and the shortsighted and grasping policy of individual rival princelings predominated, the Medes were united in a single tribal union headed by a common military leader. He says, "The division of the tribes appears to have gradually lost its former important social role with the Medes, for otherwise the Assyrian sources would have given it more attention. But presumably the tribal union of the Medes was not merely nominal. It is to this nation that the Medes must have owed the possibility of collective action."

Khanis

While neighboring Mannaeans, Sumerians, and even the Old Hittite Kingdom were experimenting with democratic principles, ruling with counselors and primitive senates in oligarchies, it was the Medes who successfully realized the region's first vast empire based at least in part on democratic principles. Perhaps Medes learned of democracy from others beyond the Zagros or saw it practiced by their predecessors,

Peter Paul Ruben's/ Daniel in the Lion's Den/ Washington National Gallery

the Quti. Whatever the progression of events, the Medes felt a compelling need to unite and either could not or did not wish to accomplish this goal by purely military means. They offered the surrounding tribes a chance to participate in the governing of the land where they lived. These tribes were inclined to accept this offer due to the brutal attacks of the Assyrians, Urartians, and Mannaeans who mercilessly destroyed villages, consigned adults to harsh slavery, burned living children, and skinned captured leaders alive.

Although there are many differences between the resulting government and that of today's democracies there are also striking similarities including "republics" such as America. America's government is not a "pure democracy" in the sense that a majority rules, but it is a "rule of law" based on principles generally accepted as true by all the people in the land. It is the law that protects the minority and binds the people. The Medes and later the Medo-Persians employed this same form of government (republic) in a more limited manner and gave the world what came to be known as "The Law of the Medes and Persians." This law is discussed on several occasions in ancient manuscripts including the Bible and Torah.

The Persians who later conquered Ecbatana (Hamadan), then capital of the Medes in 550 BC, extended to the Medes a continuing participation in government through a more southern seat of power, Babylon. One of the best-known rulers of this vast Medo-Persian empire was Darius who was renowned for his subjugation to the rule of law elaborated upon in the famous story of the Jewish prophet Daniel and the Lions den (Daniel's tomb is located in the Kurdish city of Kirkuk).

Unfortunately the democratic experience of the Medes was diluted rather than strengthened over time and eventually democratic values gave way to totalitarianism. Diakonoff suggested that the ancient organs of self-government—councils of elders, popular assemblies etc.—most likely collapsed because greedy military leaders seized Assyria's great wealth for themselves rather than sharing it for the good of the nation. In spite of the ultimate failure of Me-

dian democracy, they once ruled the world, and the question—"What made the Medes great?"— Can be answered in two succinct points.

First, the Medes were brilliant warriors. They were renowned for their horsemanship and were the first to use "guerrilla warfare." These fearless fighters, then as now, were called Pesh Merga or "those ready to die." The Assyrians often referred to the Medes as "The strong ones."

Zoroastrian Symbol

Second, the Medes employed a system of government that enticed their enemies to join them rather than fight. It was an early form of democracy, the heretofore-unique concept that people should not be ruled merely by the sword but by the law. Diakonoff said of Median local government, "The most powerful person-

age bore no higher title than 'Lord of the township' and was obliged to reckon with organs of self-government of the type of a council of elders and a popular assembly which may have elected him or confirmed his rank."

Today's democracies owe a debt of gratitude to these forebears of modern government. Even though

Ancient Star of David

democratic principles have been refined and polished over the centuries, "the rule of law" remains, without doubt, the foundation of all successful democracies in the world."

Note from the author: "*On the issue of Kurds as descendants of the Medes, there are some modern historians that maintain there are linguistic evidences calling this conclusion into question. To simply sum up the argument they maintain that the Kurdish language is more akin to the Southern Persian dialects than the original Northern dialects of the Medes. However,* most linguists see a direct derivation from Median to Parthian and from Parthian to Kurdish. All three languages belong to the Northwest Iranian group of the wider Iranian language family—only from different time-frames. Median is classified as Northwestern Old Iranian. Parthian was Northwestern from the Middle Iranian Period. Kurdish is a Neo Iranian language from the Northwestern Branch. These dissenters also do not consider a practical issue; namely that the Medes were conquered by the Persians and relocated from their original northern capital of Ecbatana (Hamadan) to a southern redoubt in Babylon. The mother of the great Persian King Cyrus was a Mede. Rather than destroy Media, the Persians incorporated it into what became known as the Medo-Persian Empire. It would be without precedent that a people would live in a region for hundreds of years and not be influenced by the local dialects just as people who were born in the northern reaches of United States but live their entire lives in the South end up using colloquialisms."

Exploring the ruins of 17th Century Madrassa

Archeology

Iraq has long been regarded as the nation with more archeological and historical sites than any country in the world. It is easy to conceive this, as it was the cradle of civilization. The Kurdistan Region rests along a series of mountain ranges and encompass-

The Gate of Amediye / Assyrian Carvings

es a significant portion of what has traditionally been called "The land between the rivers" and "The birthplace of civilization." Home to well over one thousand known archeological sites, the Region's top historic attractions are the Erbil citadel and Shanidar Cave.

The Erbil citadel is widely recognized as the world's oldest continually inhabited city. There are other cities that may be as old (such as nearby Damascus in Syria and Mardin in Turkey) but none have been continuously inhabited as is the case with Erbil (Hawler). The fortress stands atop more than 30 meters (98 ft.) of successive settlements dating back earlier that

6,000 BC. Currently undergoing a comprehensive restoration, including extensive mapping for future archeological excavation, the site is now a UNESCO World Heritage site. While renovation is being undertaken a few families have been left inside the Citadel (Qala) in order to preserve the designation of "oldest inhabited city."

Throughout its exceptionally long history of inhabitation, the Erbil citadel has survived through the reign of a long list of classical civilizations including: Sumerians, Assyrians, Akkadians, Babylonians, Persians and Greeks, and the site is likely to produce a trove of artifacts from these and other eras once excavations develop.

Just south of the Erbil Citadel, located in Minaret Park, is another of Erbil's significant historical sites. The Choli Minaret, also known as the Mudhafaria minaret, was built in 1190 AD during the reign of King Muzaffar al-Din Abu Sa'eed al-Kawkaboori. The minaret stands 36 metres (118 ft.) and is inscribed with Kufic calligraphy; excavations of the surrounding area have revealed the foundations of a mosque from the same time period. The local reference to it as "Choli" indicates its position in relation

Choli Minaret

to the city at the time—i.e. far away.

In addition to the city's own record, historians believe that the epic Battle of Gaugamela, in which Alexander the Great defeated

Battle of Gaugamela

the Persian King Darius III in 331 BC, was fought just 32 km. (20 miles) to the west of Erbil. The precise site of the battle has never been unquestionably ascertained and the area has never been excavated.

While some may find the

actual site to be somewhat unremarkable, Shanidar cave has produced Iraq's only Neanderthal remains, showing evidence of humanoid inhabitation in the Region for more than 60,000 years. A Columbia University team from the United States between 1957 and 1961 excavated the cave. The site produced ten skeletons dating between 60,000 and 80,000 years old, and one of these along with casts of the others are now on display at the Smithsonian Institution in Washington, DC. Recently the site has been improved and a statue erected to Ralph Solecki who discovered the cave in 1951.

Yezidi Pilgrims at Lalish

A large number of undeveloped archeological sites exist throughout the Kurdistan Region. From partially unearthed remains of Sumerian buildings revealing specimens of their famous cuneiform writing to relatively recent remnants of Ottoman rule, the Region is bursting with historical significance.

The importance of the region's historic import has only recently been revealed as prior to 2008 there had been no significant investigation of the region's known "tels" (man made hills indicating the remains of ancient civilizations). Now that Kurdistan has become an autonomous region with a democratically elected government intent on discovering and preserving its heritage there has been one significant find after another.

For details of current digs see:

Chaldean Monk at the Mar Mattai Monastery

http://kurdistaniraqtours.com/new/blog/amazing-archeological-finds-kurdistan-region-iraq

Modern History and Geography

General Information

• With a population of 5.2 million and increasing, the three main governorates of Erbil, Sulaymani, and Duhok recently joined by a fourth—Halabja—cover approximately 40,000 sq. km. (15,444 sq. mi.) - larger than the Netherlands and four times the area of Lebanon. This does not include areas such as Kirkuk and other disputed territories now administered by the Kurdistan Regional Government. Eventually many of these areas will no doubt become permanent and official fixtures in the Kurdistan Region of Iraq—especially Kirkuk.

• The Region is geographically diverse, from hot and dry plains to cooler mountainous areas with natural springs and snowfall in the winter.

• Foreign guests are warmly welcomed. Among the growing number of visitors are international media and business people as well as those returning from the Kurdish Diaspora.

• Not a single US or coalition soldier died in Kurdistan during the Iraq war, nor has a single foreigner been kidnapped in the areas administered by the Kurdistan Regional Government (KRG). With the cooperation of citizens, the Kurdistan Region's security forces have kept the area safe and stable. Security responsibility was formally transferred from the Multinational Forces to the KRG in May 2007.

• The capital and the seat of the Kurdistan Regional Government is Erbil, a city known in Kurdish as Hawler. The Citadel in Erbil is considered the world's oldest continuously inhabited settlement. The next largest cities are Sulaymani and Dohuk. Please note that Slemani is the KRG's offi-

Traditional Kurdish Dress

cial English spelling, but it can also be found with other spellings such as Sulaimani, Suleimani, Sulaimaniyah, and Suleimaniah.

• The Kurdistan Regional Government exercises executive power according to the Kurdistan Region's laws as enacted by the democratically elected Kurdistan Parliament. Prime Minister Nechirvan Barzani who as-

Tribal Kurd

sumed office in the spring of 2014 leads the current government.

• Iraq's Constitution recognizes the Kurdistan Regional Government and the Kurdistan Parliament as the region's formal institutions and the Peshmerga forces as the Region's legitimate security guard.

• The current coalition government consists of several political parties that reflect

Young Yezidi Girl

the diversity of the Region's population, which includes Chaldeans, Assyrians, Syriacs, Turkmen, Yezidis, Arabs and Kurds living together in harmony. At least 30 percent of the seats of Parliament are reserved for women unlike any other government in the Middle East which is indicative of the liberal nature of the society.

• More than sixty-five percent of destroyed villages have been rebuilt since being razed during the Anfal campaign perpetrated by Saddam Hussein's regime in the 1980s.

Celebrating Newroz

• The Kurdish language is of Indo-European origin and among the family of Iranian languages, such as Persian and Pashto, and is distinct from Arabic. The two main dialects are Sorani and Bahadini (Kurmanji). Some small tribes speak Zaza and Hawrami (Gorani).

• The Kurdistan Region has at least a dozen public universities and even more licensed private universities. Some of them use English as the main language of teaching and examination, most notably the University of Kurdistan Hawler (UKH) and the American University of Iraq – Sulaimani (AUI-S).

• A new, liberal foreign investment law was ratified in June 2006, providing incentives for foreign investors such as the possibility of owning land, up to ten-year tax holidays, and easy repatriation of profits.

• To rapidly benefit from its oil and gas resources, the KRG has signed dozens of production sharing contracts with companies from over twenty countries.

Halgurd

• The Kurdistan Region has international airports in Erbil and Sulaymani, with direct flights to and from Europe and the Middle East. A new international airport is under construction in Duhok.

Geography

The Kurdistan Region is an autonomous region in Federal Iraq. The Kurdistan Region currently comprises the four governorates of Erbil, Sulaymani, Duhok and recently Halabja. It borders Syria to the west, Iran to the east and Turkey to the north, where fertile plains meet the Zagros Mountains.

The Tigris, Greater Zab and Lesser Zab rivers traverse the Region. The mountains of the Kurdistan Region have an average height of about 2,400 metres (7,875 ft.) rising to 3,000-3,300 metres (9850 - 10,800 ft.) in

places. The highest peak, Halgurd, is near the border with Iran and measures just fewer than 4,000 metres (13,125 ft.) The highest mountain ridges contain the only forestland in the Region although historians note the entire region was once forested with various species especially cedars.

On the craggy slopes of the Kurdistan Region, you will find trees, birds and wild goats. On the mountain ridges grow small oaks, junipers and mountain herbs. Poplars grow in the stream valleys and eucalyptus can be found in watered areas on the plains.

A wide variety of rare birds can be seen

year round in many areas especially in the mountains of Barzan, which has been declared a Wildlife Preserve by the President, Masoud Barzani.

Kurdistan Region

Area:
40,643 square kilometers (15,692 sq. mi.)
Population: 5.2 million

Capital city: Erbil (also known as Hewler)

The people living in the Kurdistan Region are predominantly Kurds as well as Assyrians, Chaldeans, Turkmen, Armenians and Arabs.

The Region has a young and growing population, with thirty-six percent aged 0-14 years, and only four percent aged over 63. The median age in Kurdistan is just over 20, meaning more than fifty percent are less than 20.

The Kurdistan Region's demography has changed considerably in the last few decades mainly because of forced migration by the previous Iraqi government, which is one of the main reasons for the movement from the countryside to towns and cities. By 2001, at least 600,000 people were internally displaced mainly because of

the previous Iraqi regime's policies since the 1970s. This included more than 100,000 people expelled in November 1991 alone from Kirkuk by the Iraqi government. According to a UNDP survey, sixty-six percent of people living in Duhok Governorate have been forced to change their residence due to war at any point in their lives, while the figures in Sulaymani and Erbil are thirty-one percent and seven percent respectively.

Traditionally, the majority of people in the Kurdistan Region lived in villages and survived on farming and animal husbandry of mainly sheep and goats thanks to the land's fertile soil. The Region was known as the breadbasket of Iraq. Today this trend has been reversed, with the majority living and working in the three main cities of Erbil, Duhok and Sulaymani.

In the 1980s Saddam Hussein's regime destroyed over 4,000 villages and forcibly moved their residents to collective towns. Many of these villages have now been rebuilt. The Kurdistan Regional Government, with the support of UN agencies and NGOs, after 1991 rebuilt 2,620 of some 4,000 destroyed villages.

Government

The Kurdistan Regional Government (KRG) exercises executive power according to the Kurdistan Region's laws as enacted by the democratically elected Kurdistan National Assembly. Prime Minister Nechirvan Barzan who assumed office on 7 May 2006 leads the current government.

The Kurdistan Regional Government (KRG) was formed in 1992 by the Kurdistan National Assembly, the first democratically elected parliament in Kurdistan (and in Iraq) following the no-fly zone designed to protect the Kurdistan Region from the violence of Iraq's former Ba'ath regime.

The KRG developed experience and expertise throughout successive cabinets, especially after the fall of the former regime in 2003. In 2006, two separate KRG cabinets unified to form the fifth Cabinet, led by current Prime Minister Nechirvan Barzani. The fifth Cabinet embarked upon a number of unprecedented projects and policies that were not possible in previous years.

These included the construction of international airports, a proactive oil and gas policy, reconstruction of the Region's infrastructure, the promotion of relations with members of the

Mullah Mustapha Honor Guard

international community, and greater funding for social and economic projects within the Region. The sixth Cabinet, led by Dr. Barham Salih, built upon the successes of the fifth Cabinet, promoting a number of important domestic issues related to housing, higher education, and government transparency. The seventh Cabinet has achieved some key strategic successes, none more important than developments in the field of oil and gas and a rapid influx of foreign investment.

Previous cabinets have overseen groundbreaking improvements in the delivery of basic services for citizens, including provision of electricity, infrastructure development, improvement in the provision of health and education, and an unprecedented growth in per capita GDP and standards of living.

Kurdish Parliament

President Barzani with Former
Secretary of Defense Robert Gates

Chronology of Key Events – Ancient to 2014

• 60-80,000 years ago: Evidence of Neanderthal people living in Shanidar Cave near the Great Zab River in Erbil Governorate.

• 30-300,000 years ago: Evidence of Old Stone Age (Middle Paleolithic) people living in six caves near the village of Hazar Merd, southwest of Sulaymani.

• 9,000 BC: At Karim Shahir near Chemchemal, the earliest evidence of wild wheat and barley cultivation and domesticated dogs and sheep.

• 6,750 BC: At Jarmo village near Chemchemal, evidence of the oldest known permanent farmed settlement of mud houses, with wheat grown from seed and herds of goats, sheep and pigs.

• 4,000 BC: Evidence that Arbela was settled, making it one of the oldest, continuously inhabited sites in the world. Excavation is difficult because the modern city lies on top of the ancient town.

• 612 BC: After the Babylonians destroyed the Assyrian capitals of Ashur and Nineveh, the Assyrian empire city of Arbela, becomes part of the Babylonian empire.

• 539 BC: After Persian leader Cyrus the Great takes over Babylon, Arbela joins the vast Achaemenid or ancient Persian Empire.

• 331 BC: Alexander the Great and Darius III of Persia fight the Battle of Gaugamela, also known as the Battle of Arbela, about 50 kilometers (30 miles) north-west of Erbil. In the aftermath, his Army's officers murder Darius and Alexander goes on to conquer the Persian Empire including Babylon and extends his empire to the Punjab in India.

• 6-700 AD: Arabs conquer Kurdistan Region and convert many to Islam.

• 1100s–1800s: In this period several semi-independent principalities, the Ardalan, Botan, Badinan, Baban and Soran, ruled the Kurdistan Region.

• Early 1500s: The Kurdistan Region becomes the main focus of the rivalries between the Ottoman and Persian empires.

• 1534-1918: Region is part of the Ottoman Empire.

Kurdish Dress from Ottoman Era

• 1514: After Turkish Sultan Selim I defeats the Shah of Persia, Kurdish scholar Idriss Bitlissi persuades the Sultan to give back to the Kurdish Princes their former rights and privileges in exchange for their commitment to guard the border between the two empires. The principalities in the Kurdistan region enjoyed wide autonomy until the early 19th century.

• 1784: Prince Ibrahim Pasha Baban founds the city of Sulaymani making it the capital of the Baban Emirate.

Dress of the late 1800s

• 1847: Collapse of Botan, the last independent Kurdish principality, which included the towns of Amadiye and Akre.

• 1914-1918: World War I.

• 1917: Britain seizes Baghdad.

• 1918: Sheikh Mahmoud Barzinji becomes governor of Sulaymani under British rule.

He and other Kurdish leaders who want Kurdistan to be ruled independently of Baghdad rebel against the British. He is defeated a year later.

•1920 - Britain creates state of Iraq with League of Nations approval.

• 1920 - Great Iraqi Revolution - rebellion against British rule.

• 1921 - Faysal, son of Hussein Bin Ali, the Sharif of Mecca crowned Iraq's first king.

• 1923: The Treaty of Lausanne between Turkey and the allied powers invalidates the Treaty of Sevres, which had provided for the creation of a Kurdish state.

• 1925: After sending a fact-finding committee to Mosul province, the League of Nations decides that it will be part of Iraq, on condition that the UK hold the mandate for Iraq for another 25 years to assure the autonomy of the Kurdish population. The following year Turkey and Britain signed a treaty in line with the League of Nation's decision.

• 1932 - Iraq becomes an independent state.

1939-1945 - World War II. Britain re-occupies Iraq.

• 1946-1947: The Republic of Mahabad, which was officially known as the Republic of Kurdistan was established in Iran. While short lived, it was the only time that Kurds had truly established their own independent state.

• 1958 - The monarchy is overthrown in a military coup led by Brigadier Abd-al-Karim Qasim and Colonel Abd-al-Salam Muhammad Arif. Iraq is declared a republic.

• 1963 - Prime Minister Qasim is ousted in a coup led by the Arab Socialist Baath Party. Arif becomes president.

• 1963 - The Baathist government is overthrown by a group of officers led by Arif.

1966 - After Arif is killed in a helicopter crash on 13 April, his elder brother, Major General Abd-al-Rahman Muhammad Arif, succeeds him as president.

• 1968 - A Baathist led-coup ousts Arif. Revolution Command Council (RCC) takes charge with General Ahmad Hasan al-Bakr as chairman and country's president.

• 1970: The Kurdistan Democratic Party, led by Mustafa Barzani, reaches an agreement with Baghdad on autonomy for the Kurdistan region and political representation in the Baghdad Government. By 1974, key parts of the agreement are not fulfilled, leading to disputes.

• 1971-1980: The Iraqi Government expels more than 200,000 Faili (Shia) Kurds from Iraq.

• 1972 - Iraq nationalizes the Iraq Petroleum Company (IPC).

• 1974 - Iraq grants limited autonomy to Kurdish region.

• 1975: The Iraqi Government signs the Algiers Agreement with Iran, in which they settle land disputes in exchange for Iran ending its support of the Kurdistan Democratic Party and other concessions.

• 1979 - Saddam Hussein succeeds Al-Bakr as president.

• 1980-1988 - Iran-Iraq war.

• 1981 June - Israel attacks an Iraqi nuclear research center at Tuwaythah near Baghdad.

• 1983: 8,000 boys and men from the Barzani clan

Halabja Memorial Cemetery

disappear under the Iraq Government. In 2005, 500 of them are found in mass graves near Iraq's border with Saudi Arabia, hundreds of kilometers from the Kurdistan Region. The discovery of the remains of the Barzani Kurds is chronicled in the award-winning documentary "Saddam's Road to Hell."

• 1987-1989: The Iraqi Government carries out the genocidal Anfal campaign against Kurdish civilians,

Halabja Memorial

including mass summary executions and disappearances, widespread use of chemical weapons, destruction of some 4,500 villages and of the rural economy and infrastructure. Residents are forcibly removed to collective towns. An estimated 200,000 are killed in the campaign. On 16 and 17 March 1988, Iraqi Government airplanes drop chemical weapons on the town of Halabja. Between 4,000 and 5,000 people, almost all civilians, are killed.

• 1990 - Iraq invades Kuwait, prompting what becomes known as the First Gulf War. A massive US-led military campaign forces Iraq to withdraw from Kuwait in February 1991.

• 1991: The people in the Kurdistan Region rise up against the Iraqi Government days after the Gulf War ends. Within weeks the Iraqi military and helicopters suppress the uprising. Tens of thousands of people flee to the mountains, causing a humanitarian crisis. The US, UK and France declare a no-fly zone at the 36th parallel. The establishment of a safe haven prompts the return of refugees. Months later, Saddam Hussein withdraws the Iraqi Army and his administration and imposes an internal blockade on Kurdistan. The KRG begins to rebuild the villages destroyed during the Anfal campaign.

Gulf War

George Bush in Kuwait in April.

• 1991 April - Iraq subjected to weapons inspection program. Mid-March/early April - Southern Shia and northern Kurdish populations - encouraged by Iraq's defeat in Kuwait - rebel, prompting a brutal crackdown. A UN-approved safe-haven is established

Operation Provide Comfort

in northern Iraq to protect the Kurds. Iraq ordered to end all military activity in the area.

• 1992 August - A no-fly zone, which Iraqi planes are not allowed to enter, is set up in southern Iraq, south of latitude 32 degrees north. The Iraqi Kurdistan Front, an alliance of political parties, holds parliamentary and presidential elections and establishes the Kurdistan Regional Government.

• 1993 June - US forces launch a cruise missile attack on Iraqi intelligence headquarters in Baghdad in retaliation for the attempted assassination of US President

• 1994: Power-sharing arrangements between the Kurdistan Democratic Party (KDP) and the Patriotic Union of Kurdistan (PUK) fall apart, leading to conflict and two separate administrations in Erbil and Sulaymani respectively.

• 1995 April - UNSC Resolution 986 allows the partial resumption of Iraq's oil exports to buy food and medicine (the "oil-for-food program").

• October - Saddam Hussein "wins" a referendum allowing him to remain president for another seven years.

• 1996 August - After call for aid from KDP, Iraqi forces launch offensive into northern no-fly zone and briefly occupy Erbil.

• September - US extends northern limit of southern no-fly zone to latitude 33 degrees north, just south of Baghdad.

• 1998: The PUK and KDP sign the Washington Agreement, ending their internecine conflict.

Coalition Forces Protect Kurdistan

• October - Iraq ends co-operation with UN Special Commission to Oversee the Destruction of Iraq's Weapons of Mass Destruction (UNSCOM).

• December - After UN staff is evacuated from Baghdad, the US and UK launches a bombing campaign, "Operation Desert Fox", to destroy Iraq's nuclear, chemical and biological weapons programs.

• 1999 February - Grand Ayatollah Sayyid Muhammad Sadiq al-Sadr, spiritual leader of the Shia community is assassinated in Najaf.

• December - UNSC Resolution 1284 creates the UN Monitoring, Verification and Inspection Commission (UNMOVIC) to replace UNSCOM. Iraq rejects the resolution.

• 2001 February - Britain, US carry out bombing raids to try to disable Iraq's air defense network. The bombings have little international support.

• 2002 - US President George W Bush tells skeptical world leaders at a UN General Assembly to confront the "grave and gathering danger" of Iraq.

• UN weapons inspectors return to Iraq backed by a UN resolution, which threatens serious consequences if Iraq is in "material breach" of its terms.

• March - Chief weapons inspector Hans Blix reports that Iraq has accelerated its cooperation but says inspectors need more time to verify Iraq's compliance.

• March - UK's ambassador to the UN says the diplomatic process on Iraq has ended; arms inspectors evacuate; US President George W Bush gives Saddam Hussein and his sons 48 hours to leave Iraq or face war.

• 2003: The *Peshmerga*, Kurdistan's official armed forces, fight alongside the coalition to liberate Iraq from Saddam Hussein's rule.

• March - US-led invasion topples Saddam Hussein's government, marks start of years of violent conflict with different groups competing for power.

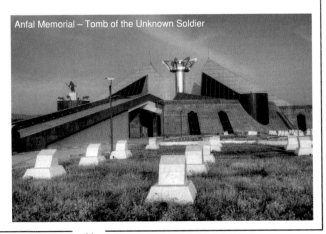

Anfal Memorial – Tomb of the Unknown Soldier

• July - US-appointed Governing Council meets for first time. Commander of US forces says his troops face low-intensity guerrilla-style war. Saddam's sons Uday and Qusay killed in gun battle in Mosul.

• August - Suicide truck bomb wrecks UN headquarters in Baghdad, killing UN envoy Sergio Vieira de Mello. Car bomb in Najaf kills 125 including Shia leader Ayatollah Mohammed Baqr al-Hakim.

• 14 December - Saddam Hussein captured in Tikrit.

• 2004 March - Suicide bombers attack Shia festivalgoers in Karbala and Baghdad, killing 140 people.

• April-May - Shia militias loyal to radical cleric Moqtada Sadr take on coalition forces. Hundreds are reported killed in fighting

Saddam Hussein on Trial

during the month-long US military siege of the Sunni Muslim city of Falluja. Photographic evidence emerges of abuse of Iraqi prisoners by US troops.

• June - US hands sovereignty to interim government headed by Prime Minister Iyad Allawi.

• August - Fighting in Najaf between US forces and Shia militia of radical cleric Moqtada Sadr.

• November - Major US-led offensive against insurgents in Falluja.

Downtown Erbil and Citadel

• 2005 30 January - Some eight million vote in elections for a Transitional National Assembly.

2005 28 February - At least 114 people are killed by a car bomb in Hilla, south of Baghdad, in the worst single such incident since the US-led invasion.

• April - Amid escalating violence, parliament selects Kurdish leader Jalal Talabani as president. Ibrahim Jaafari, a Shia, is named as prime minister.

• 2005 May onwards - Surge in car bombings, bomb explosions and shootings: Iraqi ministries put the civilian death toll for May at 672, up from 364 in April.

• June - Masoud Barzani is sworn in as regional president of Iraqi Kurdistan.

wave of sectarian violence in which hundreds of people are killed.

• 22 April - Newly re-elected President Talabani asks Shia compromise candidate Nouri al-Maliki to form a new government, ending months of deadlock.

• May and June - An average of more than 100 civilians per day are killed in violence in Iraq, the UN says.

• 7 June - Al-Qaeda leader in Iraq, Abu Musab al-Zarqawi, is killed in an air strike.

• November - Iraq and Syria restore diplomatic relations after nearly a quarter century. More than 200 die in car bombings in the mostly Shia area of Sadr City in Baghdad, in the worst attack on the capital since the US-led invasion of 2003.

• August - Draft constitution is endorsed by Shia and Kurdish negotiators, but not by Sunni representatives.

• October - Voters approve a new constitution, which aims to create a federal democracy.

• December - Iraqis vote for the first, full-term government and parliament since the US-led invasion.

• 2006: At the start of the year, the PUK and KDP agree to unify the two administrations. On 7 May, Prime Minister Nechirvan Barzani announces a new

Kurdish Cultural Museum / Duhok

unified cabinet.

February - A bomb attack on an important Shia shrine in Samarra unleashes a

• December - Saddam Hussein is executed for Crimes Against Humanity.

• 2007 January - US President Bush announces a new Iraq strategy; thousands more US troops will be dispatched to shore up security in Baghdad. UN says more than 34,000 civilians were killed in violence during 2006; the figure surpasses official Iraqi estimates threefold.

• February - A bomb in Baghdad's Sadriya market kills more than 130 people.

It is the worst single bombing since 2003.

• March - Insurgents detonate three trucks with toxic chlorine gas in Falluja and Ramadi, injuring hundreds.

• April - Bombings in Baghdad kill nearly 200 people in the worst day of violence since a US-led security drive began in the capital in February.

• August - Truck and car bombs hit two villages of Yezidi Kurds, killing at least 250 people - the deadliest attack since 2003. Kurdish and Shia leaders form an alliance to support Prime Minister Maliki's government but fail to bring in Sunni leaders.

• September - Controversy over private security contractors after Blackwater security guards allegedly fire at civilians in Baghdad, killing 17.

• October - The number of violent civilian and military deaths continues to drop, as does the frequency of rocket attacks.

• December - Britain hands over security of Basra province to Iraqi forces, effectively

President Masoud Barzani

marking the end of nearly five years of British control of southern Iraq.

• 2008 January - Parliament passes legislation allowing former officials from Saddam Hussein's Baath party to return to public life.

• March - Iranian President Mahmoud Ahmadinejad visits. Prime Minister Maliki orders crackdown on militia in Basra, sparking pitched battles with Moqtada Sadr's Mehdi Army. Hundreds are killed.

• September - US forces hand over control of the western province of Anbar - once an insurgent and Al-Qaeda stronghold - to the Iraqi government. It is the first Sunni province to be returned to to the Shia-led government. Iraqi parliament passes provincial elections law. Issue of contested city of Kirkuk is set aside so elections can go ahead elsewhere.

• November - Parliament approves a security pact with the United States under which all US troops are due to leave the country by the end of 2011.

• 2009 January - Iraq takes control of security in Baghdad's fortified Green Zone and assumes more powers over foreign troops based in the country. PM Nouri al-Maliki welcomes the move as Iraq's "day of sovereignty".

One fourth of Iraq's oil found in Kurdistan

• March - US President Barack Obama announces withdrawal of most US troops by end of August 2010. Only 50,000 of 142,000 troops are to stay on into 2011 to advise Iraqi forces and protect US interests, leaving by end of 2011.

• June - US troops withdraw from towns and cities in Iraq, six years after the invasion, having formally handed over security duties to new Iraqi forces.

• July - New opposition forces make strong gains in elections to the regional parliament of Kurdistan, but the governing KDP and

Baghdad kill at least 155 people, in Iraq's deadliest attack since April 2007.

• December - The al-Qae-

Prime Minister Nechirvan Barzani

da-linked Islamic State of Iraq claims responsibility for suicide bombings in Baghdad that kill at least 127 people, as well as attacks in August and October that killed 240 people. Tension flares with Tehran as Iranian troops briefly occupy an oilfield in Iraqi territory.

ing a delay in campaigning. "Chemical" Ali Hassan al-Majid, a key figure in Saddam Hussein's government, is executed.

• March - Parliamentary elections. Nine months pass before a new government is approved.

• August - Seven years after the US-led invasion, the last US combat brigade leaves Iraq.

• September - Syria and Iraq restore diplomatic ties a year after breaking them off.

• October - Church in Baghdad seized by militants. 52 people killed in what is described as worst single disaster to hit Iraq's Christians in modern times.

• November/December - Parliament reconvenes after long delay, re-appoints Jalal Talabani as president and Nouri al-Maliki as prime minister. A new government includes all major factions.

• 2011 February - Oil exports from Iraqi Kurdistan resume, amid a lengthy dispute between the region and the central government over contracts with foreign firms.

• April - Army raids camp of Iranian exiles, killing 34. Government says it will shut Camp Ashraf, home to

PUK alliance retains a reduced majority. Masoud Barzani (KDP) is re-elected in the presidential election.

• October - Two car bombs near the Green Zone in

• 2010 January - Controversy as candidates with alleged links to Baath Party are banned from March parliamentary polls. A court later lifts the ban, prompt-

thousands of members of the People's Mujahedeen of Iran.

• December - US completes troop pullout. Unity government faces disarray. Arrest warrant issued for vice-president Tariq al-Hashemi, a leading Sunni politician. Sunni bloc boycotts parliament and cabinet.

2012 - Bomb and gun attacks target Shia areas throughout the year, sparking fears of a new sectarian conflict. Nearly 200 people are killed in bombings targeting Shia Muslims in the immediate wake of the US withdrawal.

1.4 million IDPs and Refugees flee ISIS

• March - Tight security for Arab League summit in Baghdad. It is the first major summit to be held in Iraq since the fall of Saddam Hussein. A wave of pre-summit attacks kills scores of people.

• April - Oil exports from Iraqi Kurdistan halted amid row with central government over contracts with foreign firms.

• November - Iraq cancels a $4.2bn deal to buy arms from Russia because of concerns about alleged corruption within the Iraqi government.

• December - President Jalal Talabani suffers a stroke. He undergoes treatment in Germany and makes some progress through the winter and spring.

• 2013 September - Fugitive Vice-President Tariq al-Hashemi is sentenced to be hanged for murder. He sought refuge in Turkey after being accused of running death squads.

• April - Troops storm a Sunni anti-government protest camp in Hawija near Kirkuk, leaving more than 50 dead and prompting outrage and clashes in other towns. Insurgency intensifies, with levels of violence matching those of 2008. By July the country is described as being a full-blown sectarian war zone with the notable exception of Kurdistan.

Hundreds of thousands of children displaced

• July - At least 500 prisoners, mainly senior al-Qaeda members, escape from Taji and Abu Ghraib jails in a mass breakout.

September - Regional parliamentary elections in Iraqi Kurdistan, won comfortably by Kurdistan Democratic Party. Series of bombings hits Kurdistan capital Erbil in the first such attack since 2007. Al-Qaeda-affiliated Islamic State of Iraq says it was responding to alleged Iraqi Kurdish support for Kurds fighting jihadists in Syria.

• October - Baghdad Parliamentary elections set for April 2014. Government says October is deadliest month since April 2008, with 900 killed.

Christian IDP – Ankawa

• December - At least 35 people killed in twin bombing of Baghdad churches on Christmas Day.

• 2014 January - Pro-al-Qaeda fighters infiltrate Fallujah and Ramadi after months of mounting violence in mainly Sunni Anbar province. Government forces recapture Ramadi but face entrenched rebels in Fallujah.

• April - Prime Minister Al-Maliki's coalition wins a plurality at first parliamentary election since 2011 withdrawal of US troops, but falls short of a majority.

• June - Sunni rebels led by the Islamic State of Iraq and the Levant (ISIL or ISIS) surge out of Anbar Province to seize Iraq's second city of Mosul, moving on to the oil refinery center of Baiji. Tens of thousands flee amid reports of atrocities. The US and other nations including some in the Middle East offer assistance.

• July – as International support for the Kurdish effort to repel ISIS increased the success of the effort was telling. In the months of July through December the region returned to a state of normality as far as local life is concerned. There is no longer a threat of ISIS capturing any part of Kurdistan and in fact the Kurds have expanded their regional hold to include areas that were previously in dispute –including the oil region of Kirkuk and Garmian Administration.

• August – Prime Minister Maliki, a long-standing obstacle to Iraqi unity resigns and a new more moderate government is formed under the leadership of Haidar al-Abadi. The Kurds play a major role in the new government including the post of Minister of Finance held by former Foreign Minister Hoshyar Zebari. The presidency as has been long-standing custom remains in the hands of the Kurds in the person of Fuad Masum.

• September – More than 1.2 million refugees and Internally Displaced Persons (IDPs) are hosted in Kurdistan putting enormous strain on the regional budget.

• November – an agreement was reached between the Kurds and Baghdad resolving long standing disputes over the national budget and the sale of oil. This has increased the level of economic and social stability in Kurdistan. While there had been talk of an Independent Kurdistan throughout the months of August to October, that discussion has been tabled in favor of focus on totally defeating ISIS and creating a more stabile political atmosphere in Iraq as a whole.

Abu Bakr al-Baghdadi – Self Proclaimed Caliph of ISIS

The Future

One thing is certain—the Kurds now find themselves in a stronger position politically and economically than ever before in their long and often tumultuous history.

While the Kurds have certainly had a turbulent and often violent past, close examination of Iraq's modern history points out a striking difference between the modern Kurdistan Region of Iraq (KRI), which has maintained stability and relative security and the rest of Iraq ruled by Baghdad, which continues to exhibit instability, chaos and little security. Almost all of the recent violence described in the above timeline occurred in the areas south of Kurdistan. For this and other reasons, many governments have issued two separate travel advisories for Iraq and the *Kurdistan Region of Iraq (KRI).*

The *(KRI)* has for the past ten years oft been referred to in media and many government communiqués as "The Other Iraq." While there have been isolated incidences of violence in Kurdistan, on the whole the region has remained remarkably secure and attempts by entities such as ISIS to disrupt the region have been quickly repelled. (See Article on Security by Colonel Harry Schute).

No power on earth can stifle the aspirations of the approximately forty million Kurds (located in Iraq, Turkey, Iran, Syria and Armenia) indefi-

An ancient poet holds the future of Kurdistan

nitely and today the Kurds enjoy a degree of freedom and self-rule that they have fought and struggled to regain for centuries. This is especially true of the Kurds who reside in Iraq who now exercise democratic values once again as a federally autonomous region with their own freely elected Parliament and President. After centuries of political subjugation, the Iraqi Kurds have once again established the "rule of law" as their guiding light to the future and have the autonomy to develop their society in its own unique manner. The Kurdish example in Iraq will no doubt lead to more freedom in other areas where Kurds are in a majority. The region is not only politically stable, but also economically prosperous. There has been a great deal of discussion about the future possibility of independence or some type of UAE type confederation for the three main regions of Iraq (Kurdish, Sunni and Shia) but for now the Kurds are focused on creating a more stable atmosphere for the whole of Iraq leaving the ultimate disposition of the nation to a future consideration.

The Kurds have fashioned a prosperous economy and vibrant democracy born of an incredible history and ancient culture. Most believe that Kurdistan is on the threshold of its greatest era and the realization of many of its people's historic dreams. Considering its vast wealth of civilization's treasures, Kurdistan has been noted by the likes of National Geographic Magazine as one of the top twenty places in the world to visit.

RELIGIONS OF KURDISTAN

As a whole, the Kurdish people are adherents to a large number of different religions and creeds, perhaps constituting the most religiously diverse people of West Asia. The region is well known for its moderate religious practices and religious tolerance and it is not unusual to find Muslim and Christian or Yezidi villages that have coexisted in proximity for thousands of years. The Kurdish Regional Government enforces religious freedom and there is no mandatory religious education in schools. Radical practices such as honor killings are outlawed although there are still isolated incidents in some—mostly remote—village areas.

The dominant religion is Sunni Islam, adhered to by the majority of its inhabitants. These include Kurds, Iraqi Turkmen, and Arabs, belonging mostly to

Lalish

the Shafi'i school of Sunni Islam. There are also a number of Shia Kurds often referred to as Feyli who reside primarily in border areas with Iran and in southern cities such as Khanaqin in the Garmian Administrative region. Most Assyrians in the region (of which there is a considerable minority) adhere to an orthodox form of Christianity. Chaldeans are another prominent Christian sector

representing the Eastern Rite Catholic Church. They are related to Rome but enjoy a great deal of liberty in the appointment of local Church hierarchy. There is a smaller minority of Armenians in the region but a fairly large number of Kurds who reside in Armenia itself.

Yezidis make up a significant minority; Kaka'i (Yarsan), Mandaean, and Shabak religions are also followed to a lesser extent. While the claim is sometimes disputed, the Yezidis are often linked to the ancient Zoroastrian religion, which was the national religion of the Median Empire from c. 700 - 500 BC. There are many similarities but Yezidis claim their religion predates Zoroastrianism. For more see the section on Lalish. Shabak draw from Christian, Yezidi and Islamic elements, often performing pilgrimages to Shia

Jalil Khayat Mosque

Mar Mattai Monastery

and Yezidi shrines. While some Shabak refer to themselves as Shia they are an independent faith. Mandaeans are a gnostic sect who revere some of the prophets of the Bible while rejecting others. They are also mentioned as a "people of the book" in certain Hadith (sayings of Mohammed). Some believe they find their origins in the Sabians and due to difficulties in Iraq, most have relocated to Syria, Jordan and Iran.

Prior to the conquest of Iraqi Kurdistan by Muslims in the 7th Century, the predominant religion of the region was Christianity with the Christian kingdom of Adiabene located in what is today modern Erbil as its most famous center. It is a commonly held tradition that the Magi of Christmas fame originated their journey to Bethlehem from the formerly Jewish city of Amediye. One of the prominent sub tribes of the Medes was the Magi and the area had many practicing Chaldeans who were originators of modern astronomy lending credibility to the "star story". Amadiye was also a center of Judaism and many were looking for signs of the Messiah predicted in the Torah and

Ancient Hebrew Text

Bible. No one knows for certain if this legend is truth or myth but it is interesting to note that the colorful locals adhere to the story and Amadiye is a must see site in Kurdistan if one is interested in the historical religions of the region.

Prior to the Christian era there were a large number of Jews in the region, especially during the Adiabene Empire, for a brief time a Jewish Kingdom. The Jews of Kurdistan are thought to be the descendants of those Jews (Israelites) that were deported from Israel by the Assyrian Empire in the 8th century BC. The Jews of Kurdistan migrated to Palestine during previous centuries but the overwhelming majority of the Kurdish Jews fled to Israel together with Iraqi Jews in Operation Ezra and Nehemiah during 1950–1952. There are some 200,000 Kurdish Jews, residing in Israel. Especially in the area of the Galilee Kurdish Jews still celebrate Newroz (the Kurdish New year) wearing traditional costumes with billowing pants for the men and some of the neighbors refer to the celebration fondly as "pajama day". If one enters the Iraqi Souk in Jerusalem and shouts "Biji Barzani" (long live Barzani referring to Mullah Mustapha Barzani the father of the modern Kurdish movement) he will be greeted in return with shouts of the same. Additionally, the first female Rabi in history was a Kurd, Asenath Barzani. Erich Brauer in his book *The Jews of Kurdistan* makes a strong case that the "Lost Tribes of Israel" are in fact remnants of the Diaspora who did not return to Palestine but remained in the land they had become accustomed to over their centuries long stay—a logical conclusion supported by many fascinating facts.

Kurdistan has sometimes been referred to as "The Other Holy Land." It is home to numerous historic Mosques, temples and Madrassa ruins, churches and monasteries dating from the 3rd Century AD as well as the ruins of ancient synagogues. Here one will find the tombs of famous religious leaders from the Islamic faith and of the ancient Yezidis as well as prophets from the Torah and Old Testament such as Nahum in the city of al Qosh and the tomb/shrine of Daniel, which is a prominent feature of the skyline of Kirkuk.

Kurdistan is truly a land of many faiths.

A fascinating adventure to—THE OTHER HOLY LAND!

Young Yezidis

NEWROZ

NEWROZ (NOWROZ)

Newroz means "new-day". It is the Kurdish New Year, a pre-Islamic holiday and the most important festival in Kurdish culture. Newroz marks the first day of spring or Equinox and the beginning of the year in the Persian calendar. It is celebrated on the day of the astronomical Northward equinox, which usually occurs on March 21 or the previous/following day depending on where it is observed. The celebrations usually last a week.

It is a time for entertainment, games, singing, dancing, family gatherings, eating special foods, poetry readings, fireworks, music, and wearing bright, colorful, and traditional clothing. Historically the day celebrates the deliverance of the Kurds from a tyrant, and it is seen as another way of demonstrating support for Kurdish nationalism.

Celebrations continue throughout the evening across Kurdistan from Sulaymani to Zakho and every place in between; one can always see and often join the colorful vibrant celebrations along roadsides, in parks and city centers.

The festivities in Akre in Duhok Governorate are perhaps the most well

known throughout Kurdistan. Young boys climb up Mount Qeli every March 20 and light torches on this mountain as well as the adjacent mountain located behind old city and a former Jewish neighborhood.

Story of Zahhak

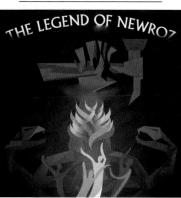

Newroz is a time of recounting a famous story of an evil king who had serpents growing from his shoulders and whose rule lasted 1,000 years. During this time, two young men were sacrificed daily and their brains were offered to Zahhak's serpents. As a result of this evil, there was no spring each year. However, the man who was in charge of sacrificing the two young men every day would instead kill only one man a day and mix his brains with that of a sheep in order to save the other man.

As discontent grew, a nobleman named Kawa, a blacksmith who had lost six sons to Zahhak planned a revolt. The young men who had been saved from the fate of being sacrificed (ancestors of the Kurds) were militarily trained by Kawa and marched to Zahhak's Castle (Mount Qeli) where Kawa killed the king with his hammer and he became a renowned and kind ruler. The day of this victory (March 20), Kawa and his men set fire to the hillsides to celebrate and spring returned the next day.

Fire

Fire plays a predominant role in the Newroz celebrations. Kurds commemorate the recounting of this famous story by lighting fires to show that it is safe and that good (light) has defeated evil (darkness).

ERBIL GOVERNORATE

MÊRGESOR
MERGASUR

SORAN
SORAN

ÇOMAN
CHOMAN

REWANDIZ
RAWANDUZ

ŞEQLAWE
SHAQLAWA

XEBAT
KHABAT

HEWLÊR
ERBIL

DEŞTÊ
HEWLÊRÊ
DASHTI
HAWLER

KOYE
KOYSINJAQ

MEXMÛR
MAKHMUR

ERBIL (Hawler)

CIHAN GROUP   DARINGROUP   KAR   KURDISTAN IRAQ TOURS   KOREK   RAMADA SULAYMANIYAH   VSC SECURITY SOLUTIONS

Downtown Erbil and Citadel

GENERAL INFORMATION

Erbil (also known as Arbil, Irbil, ancient Arbela, Hawler, Hewler) is the largest city and regional capital of the Kurdistan Region. It is also the name of the Governorate. The city is 90 km (56 mi) northeast of Mosul (an hour and a half drive, 355 km (221 mi) or nearly five hours north from Baghdad, 190 km (118 mi) or almost three hours north of Sulaymani, 160 km (99 mi) or two and a half hours southeast of Duhok, and 107 km (67 mi) one hour and forty-five minutes due north of Kirkuk.

Erbil International Airport, which opened in 2005, was the first in the Kurdistan Region and maintains relations with over 30 different carriers from all over the world.

In 1997 the population of Erbil governorate was roughly 750,000; as of 2015 its population was nearly 2,000,000.

HISTORY

Settlement in Erbil can be dated to at least 6000 BC and is considered one of the oldest continuously inhabited cities in the world. During the Middle Ages the Seljuk and later the Ottoman Empires, ruled the city and remained until the end of the First World War. In the center of the city one finds the ancient Citadel (Qala), a main focal point and one of the main centers for tourism. In July 2014 UNESCO named the Citadel of Erbil (Arbil) a World Heritage Site. A multi hundred million dollar renovation of the site is underway with the aim of meticulous-

ly returning the site to its original splendor. Many ancient and modern empires have left their mark on this city; Assyrian, Babylonians, Medes, Persians, Greeks, and Romans all played an important role in molding and shaping its identity. As the renovation proceeds the restorers are constantly

Old Erbil (Hawler)

discovering amazing archeological treasures from the past.

Following the Arab Islamic conquest in the middle of the 7th century, the city and region was largely "Islamized". Previously it had a preponderance of Christian, Jewish, and Zoroastrian communities and even afterwards it was known as a place for many Jewish synagogues and *yeshivot* (schools and centers of learning) as well as ancient Christian Churches. There was, for a brief time, a kingdom named Adiabene (Hadyab 15 AD. - 116 AD.) centered in Erbil. It was the seat of local regional Christendom though many Zoroastrians and Jews occupied it as well. Now most Christians of all denominations live in the suburb of

Ankawa, which has been swallowed by the growing city. This neighborhood is on the northwest part of the city and is very close to the airport.

Erbil is currently a booming metropolis with numerous massive building projects, planned neighborhoods, modern malls and parks, many ancient and modern historic attractions, and was the *Arab Tourism Capital of the World* for 2014.

GETTING AROUND

Taxis

Taxies are plentiful and relatively inexpensive, especially during the day and are quite easily found. Taxis from one destination to another within Erbil should cost between IQD 3,000 ($2.50) and IQD 7,000 ($6).

However, if visitors are traveling outside of Erbil the cost naturally increases depending on distance and time of day (night is usually more).

Hired Cars

There are several car rental companies, which provide a car and driver if desired. Inquire from your travel agent or hotel reception for information.

MAIN POINTS OF INTEREST

Ankawa

Northwest of downtown Erbil, this area used to be a village suburb that has largely been swallowed up by the municipality, though it mostly maintains its unique characteristics, namely the various churches, Christian schools and institutions. In recent years it has become a popular residency for the growing expatriate population and many teachers and international workers and developers choose to live in the area known for its many popular restaurants, bars, hotels, and nightclubs that serve alcohol as well as the multitude of shops that sell alcohol.

Choli (Mudhafaria) Minaret

Choli Minaret

Next to the Citadel (Qala) this is the most important landmark in Erbil. It is the last remaining part of an ancient 12th century mosque (1128-1138) during the reign of Saladin. It is named after Mudhafaria (Muzaffar) Al-Din Abu Sa'eed Al-Kawka-boori, a colleague of Saladin who married his sister. The 36 m (118 ft.) structure lies at the far end of Minaret (Minara) Park, only several blocks from the citadel. The base is octagonal and the main shaft s decorated in a beautiful glazed turquoise.

Citadel of Erbil *(See special section on the CITADEL of ERBIL)*

Qalinj Agha Hill

Underneath and adjacent to the Erbil (Hawler) Civilization Museum in south Erbil off of Kirkuk Road sits one of the most important archaeological sites in Erbil. The name of the hill, or tel is derived from Qala Anje, (the Small Mound), as opposed to Qala Gawra, or the giant Erbil Citadel (Qala) roughly one kilometer (.6 mi.) to the north.

A large mostly circular mound covering 33,000 sq. meters (355,000 sq. ft.). Qalinj Agha Hill is only 7 m (23 ft.) tall. Successive archaeological excavations claim that Qalinj Agha Hill was the site of several historical epochs through the Islamic era. It is believed this area dates back to the fifth and fourth millennium BC when the Uruk civilization reigned. King Gilgamesh from the famous book *The Epic of Gilgamesh*, ruled Uruk in the 27th century BC. Excavations revealed special gifts and toys meant to

Chaldean Church in Ankawa

accompany buried children into their afterlife. Additionally, the man-made terrace, which supports the temple, may be the oldest in the region. Some of the streets had homes that included outdoor ovens.

In the late 1960s antiquity authorities purchased the land from a local family and excavations began almost immediately. The two first official archeological excavations were overseen by Behnam Abu al-Soof who

Qaysari Bazaar

wrote two articles about his research, which were published by a respected academic archaeological journal, "More Soundings at Tell Qalinj Agha (Erbil)" (1967) and "Excavations at Tell Qalinj Agha (Erbil)" (1969) respectively. Until 2005 and even presently to a degree, there is a dearth of archaeological information available publicly or academically about the site but that will change rapidly as excavations proceed.

BAZAARS

Erbil Qaysari Bazaar

At the foot of the ancient citadel in the center of Erbil, the Qaysari Bazaar (market, souk) spreads out as far as the eye can see and beyond. It is a great place to people watch, "window shop" or shop like locals as well as enjoy Kurdish culture. It is a "must-see" for any visitor.

The first bazaar here appeared in the 13th century AD when Erbil initially began to extend past the citadel itself and became established during the beginning of the Ottoman Empire's rule of the surrounding environs. The bazaar is

in the city's main traditional market and sells anything and everything from pets to household goods, clothes, tools, food, textiles, gold, and assorted souvenirs. Restaurants and snack shops abound.

Entering Qaysari is easy since there are numerous alleys and open entrances leading to it. There are no maps to let you know where you are so getting lost is also easy but there are always hospitable locals to show the way. Some parts

Gold Bazaar in Qaysari

enclosed from above, while others are open. Like most other bazaars, shoppers walk through mazes of narrow paths between shops. For example, the northeast part of the bazaar offers shoppers fresh walnuts, locally made honey and dairy products, sheep yoghurt and many types of cheese. The western side includes many bookstalls or places to get magazines, maps, or even textbooks. The south side is filled with clothing and the east side mostly contains hardware, electronics, and (bootleg) DVDs as well as popular video games.

Some unusual aspects of the bazaar include sellers hawking traditional street food such as beets simmered in tamarind juice or fava beans flavored with sumac, a red tangy spice also popular on kebab. You can also buy any part of chicken, lamb, goat, or beef before or after you pass women's clothing stores and walk past children's books.

Ancient Christian Artifact

It is important to remember that friendly bartering is expected and if you accept the price first given, you're unlikely to walk away with any bargains. Shopkeepers are generally honest but getting the best deal is part of the experience and they are very good at haggling. When one hears "But I will lose money!" you are generally close to the real cost. However, there are a number of shops –especially gold and silver stores—where the cost is fixed or sold by weight. It is a cash culture and no credit cards are accepted. Foreign currency is often honored especially US Dollars and sometimes Euros.

For a full experience one should make time for at least one glass of boiling hot and sweet tea, a favorite drink in the Kurdistan Region. Two of the most famous teashops are Mam Khalil's teahouse or Matchko teashop. *Mastaw* (mast-ow) is a drink made from (regular) yoghurt, water, and salt, and very delicious. Other delicacies include *soujuq,* a dessert sweet on the outside and filled with walnuts, *halva*, a sesame dessert, and *naana qaysi*, a locally made fruit treat that is not as sweet as *halva.*

Good luck as you search for treasures in this ancient bazaar!

Iskan Bazaar

Where the locals (mostly men) people watch and hang out with their friends. A good place for restaurants, nargilah (water pipes), and where local street food is more varied than in other places. The long stretch of the street is actually many stores and stalls selling electronics, watches, designer clothes and sunglasses, fast food kiosks, and cafes. It is also one of the only markets that remain crowded until the late evening.

Anfal Monument

Langa Bazaar

One of the most enjoyable shopping experiences in Erbil, there is an IQD 1,000 (less than $1) area that sells clothing (some from Europe and the US) that would be quite expensive in stores. It is similar in nature to the West's "Dollar Stores". Much of the rest of the bazaar sells similar goods and materials as other bazaars and this is where people go to get the real bargains on goods of all types. It is also where there are many genuine antiques — sometimes hard to come by in Erbil.

Sheikh Allah Bazaar

East of the citadel, this bazaar is one of the most exciting parts of the citadel area. Composed of three

main streets and hundreds of stores and stalls selling wholesale and retail goods, food, household appliances and materials, cosmetics, as well as many kinds of fish, meat, fruit and vegetables and even bicycles.

MUSEUMS

Anfal Monument-Memorial/Immortal Shrine

Past Majdi Mall in Erbil, along the main Koya-Sulaymani road toward the small town of Kasnazan towers a looming monument and memorial to the Anfal Genocide that befell the Kurds under the oppressive yoke of Saddam Hussein in the 1980s. This recently completed project (2013) is a powerful testament to the resilience and survival of a long-persecuted people. It is sometimes referred to as the Tomb of the Unknown Soldier.

The structure at its base is rectangular and includes both an indoor and outdoor conference hall as well as an amphitheater and is used for official commemorative occasions such as annual events commemorating what happened on March 16, 1988 — the day the Iraqi Air Force chemically bombed the eastern city of Halabja, killing more than 5,000 civilians, the most infamous and notorious singular event to happen to Kurds during that time period.

The most impressive part of the monument are the several slanted pyramids that seemingly are coming together to form a perfect triangle but do not meet as there is still space between them. When the sun sets over the hills the monument looks like a giant torch holding up the sun—quite a breathtaking sight. Whether one is on their way east or just want to get out of the hustle and bustle of Erbil, it is an impressive site worth visiting.

Erbil Civilization Museum

**Sunday-Thursday
Hours: 9:00am-3:00pm**

Just a short walk from the ancient Citadel, Erbil's oldest museum is near the city center and opposite City Hall, on Kirkuk Rd. and Salam Barzani and Municipality Streets. It is near the Erbil International Hotel and Hariri International Stadium (where the Erbil football team plays). The museum is next to the famous and authentically Kurdish "Chwar Chra" (Four Lamps) Hotel. In addition to the museum itself there is a nice gift shop/store and an adjacent library relating to archeology. Many school trips and tour groups visit this museum and are able to take a trip back in history and learn about all the ancient cultures in the Kurdistan Region of Iraq. It is claimed that all of the museum's current artifacts are from the Kurdistan Region, as opposed to the rest of the country.

The museum was built in 1989 next to the Qalinj Agha Hill archaeological site. The museum consists of three halls, each hall containing artifacts of various time periods. The museum currently holds roughly 1,000 pieces. The relatively small number of pieces in the museum is largely attributed to the fact that most of the important archeological pieces were sent to Baghdad, and placed in the National Museum, the largest museum in the country. Until 1991, Kurds were not able to maintain any semblance of autonomy; hence most of their antiquities have been taken to Baghdad or museums outside of Iraq. However, many of the current artifacts are housed in inadequate display cases, unfortunately often mislabeled and with misspelled English. The Kurdistan Regional Government (KRG) is planning to build a modern Kurdistan National Museum to correct these inadequacies.The new museum will be built and supervised according to international standards and award-winning architects have been employed to propose designs. The location for the ambitious project – estimated budget not less than 25 million US dollars – is still to be decided upon.

Hall 1: Artifacts in this hall belong to different periods, including the Stone Age, Halaf, Arido, Ubed, Warka, and Sumerian. This hall includes exhibits from the Kurdistan Region's famous Shanidar Cave, which was excavated in the 1950s.

Hall 2: Artifacts include Urartian, Seleucids, Parthians, Babylonian, Assyrian, Saluki, Persian, Hurrians (Khurrites), and Luriakan. These items include artifacts dating back over 3,000 years.

Hall 3: Artifacts focus on Islamic civilizations; most artifacts date to the early Abbasid Age (750-1258 AD).

Syriac Heritage Museum (Ankawa)

The Syriac Heritage Museum is better known as the Ankawa Museum. The museum is located in Ankawa the Christian suburb of Erbil. The museum itself is located off of one of the main roads, near St. George's Church and City Hall. The museum is closed every weekend. Entry is free. The museum houses between 2,000 and 3,000 artifacts including: clothes, home equipment and musical instruments. Other artifacts include items having to do with wedding and family occasions, artwork, magazines, songs, records, and photos. While explanations are limited, they are available in English and Kurdish as well as Arabic and Neo-Aramaic (Syriac).

First opened in 2011, the museum focuses on Syriac-Christian (includes Assyri-

Antique Tribal Chest

Syriac Heritage Museum

an, Chaldean, and Syriac) heritage of Northern Iraq. There are three floors. The first hall includes traditional attire from different villages around the region as well as farming tools from the early 1900s. The second hall includes a moderately sized yet unique display of Christian books from the 1700s-1900s, including many different New Testaments written in Syriac. The second hall highlights examples of

legal documents from the 1900s and Christian newspapers from the region, such as the first ever printed, *Rays of Light*.

Early Syriac Bible

The third hall is dedicated for hosting cultural and heritage activities, particularly during holidays. There is a multimedia area with many videos as well as traditional music for visitors to peruse and enjoy. The 39-member staff is also very friendly and most are able to communicate in English and some other Western languages.

Much like the Kurdish Textile Museum, there is a great deal of cultural preservation and conservation. There is a workshop for repairing and preparing the belongings. There are five different sections: sewing, quilting, pottery making, and agriculture and home tools.

Families have donated eighty-five percent of the artifacts to the museum while other items are bought by the KRG. All items are then documented in a database.

The Director, Faruq Hanna Ato, began work in 2009 beginning with a vision to see cultural and historical documents brought together under one roof. He and others collected various items while visiting cities and villages where Christians live in the Kurdistan Region. The museum was opened on April 11, 2011 coinciding with the Chaldean and Assyrian New Year (Akito). The director recently stated his objectives for the museum, "I hope that before my work is done, I will be able to create academics in the fields of Archeology and folklore conservation. I want nothing more than this."

Textile Museum of Erbil Citadel

October-April:
9:00 AM- 5:30 PM
(Open every day)

May-September:
9:00 AM-7:00 PM
(Friday closed)

The brainchild and financial backer of the museum, Lolan Mustafa, is the individual mostly responsible for preparation of the museum and subsequent collection of handicrafts. He carries on a tradition handed down from his grandfather and father–collecting and preserving the ancient textile crafts of Kurdistan. The Museum is a non-profit and educational facility founded in 2004 but reestablished and reconfigured in 2014. The museum has hundreds of handicrafts as well as a well-appointed gift shop and also holds a traditional teahouse with small fare on the upper level of the museum.

A primary intention of the museum is conservation as well as preservation. There is continued educational training and collaborative efforts between domestic and international NGOs interested in cultural preservation and education.

This beautifully done museum offers visitors a glimpse of the intricate local art and skill of handicraft, as well as providing general insight into the Kurdish cultural heritage. It is viewed as both an institution of preservation for Kurdish heritage as well as an important attraction for tourists. All of the labeling is meticulously done and precise. The recently upgraded museum includes samples of traditional Kurdish costumes, tools, pots and other daily objects. There are even rare vinyl records of Kurdish music.

In 2004, Mustafa returned to Erbil from Sweden and focused on how to best utilize the increasing mass of carpets and other material he had amassed. Shortly thereafter, the Erbil Directorate of Antiquities granted him a long-term lease for what is one of the largest houses in the Citadel—the renovated mansion of Hashim Debagh who lived there in the 1930s and 1940s. Located in the southeast quarter of the Citadel; the museum is the pride and joy of many in Erbil. Devoted to textiles produced in Iraqi and Iranian Kurdistan primarily, the museum contains a colorful collection of rare carpets, clothing, and other weavings.

Antique Tribal Carpets

Phone:
+964662511660
(Lolan Mustafa)

Email Contact: info@kurdishtextilemuseum.com

Website: http://www.kurdishtextilemuseum.com/

Textile Museum Weaving Project

Kurdish weaving includes rug making, embroidering, felt making, knitting, and clothes making. The museum is much more than a collection of artifacts from the past. It is also meant to foster education and courses in sustaining the unique weaving culture. One can often see aspiring craftsmen working on looms, weaving, making felt, embroidering, and so on. At the museum you can witness tribal women weavers passing on their knowledge and skills to the younger generation, and you can even have a go yourself. All the finished articles either go on display or are sold in the museum's gift shop. The museum is happy to

Textile Museum

accept commissions and/or orders as well!

Women among the various Kurdish tribes learned to use raw materials (wool and hair from herds) as well as natural dyes from vegetables. Traditionally, weaving was widely used by the tribes to provide for daily needs. This resulted in largely self-sustained communities. This rich culture was largely destroyed during al-Anfal genocide, as many tribes fled to cities or refugee camps. Much of the culture has been lost but the museum hopes to revitalize this as well as provide an outlet for the younger generation to con-

nect with their roots.

This museum is one of the must-sees in Erbil, and since it is located within the Citadel itself it is in the most prime location. The setting is unparalleled anywhere and International visitors as well as locals are becoming more involved and excited about the museum and its stated objectives.

PARKS AND NATURE

Martyr Sami Abdulrahman Park

On the western side of Erbil is the largest public park in the Kurdistan Region, and perhaps the Middle East itself. In between Airport and Mosul Roads, the park's western side abuts the largely expat neighborhoods, appropriately called Italian and English villages. In this area you will find many nice restaurants and shops, many of which unsurprisingly cater to Westerners. South of these 'villages' are two of the cities' finest hotels; the Divan and Rotana. To the east of the park stands the heavily guarded Kurdistan Regional Government Parliament and their Council of Ministers.

This massive park is dedicated to the former Deputy Prime Minister of the KRG, Sami Abdulrahman, who was killed at the age

of 71 in a February 2004 suicide bombing. He and his wife, who is also recently deceased, were instrumental in transforming this area into a public park from its former site, which was an air force base/detention center of the Iraqi 5th Army Corps during the former regime. The park which was built during less prosperous times sometimes provoked criticism but Sami Abdulrahman often stated that if the Kurdish people forget to enjoy the beauty of their land the rest is useless. Today the park is the pride of the capital of Kurdistan and all are grateful for the dedication of the family that made it a reality. Their daughter, Bayan Sami Abdulrahman (a British citizen as well as a Kurd) currently serves as the KRG diplomatic representative to the United States in Washington, DC. after many years as the KRG representative in London.

Free to the public, and accessible through many entrances, the park is a sprawling complex of several dozen acres (more than 800 thousand sq. m; 861,118 sq. ft.) and contains two small lakes, beautifully maintained gardens, many statues, as well as the Martyrs Monument (from the 2004 blast). The 2004 Obelisk Memorial commemorates the nearly 100 people who died in the February 2004 suicide bombing. This poignant memorial includes all the names of the deceased written on it, and incorporates the powerful phrase "Freedom is Not Free." Although the founder of the park was one of the victims, his widow insisted his name be listed in alphabetical order along with all the others as he regarded himself as a servant of the people and the park as belonging to all the citizens of the city with no regard for status.

Particularly on spring and summer weekends, visitors can walk around the park and see many couples celebrating their recent nuptials with family and friends. Don't miss the music and dancing! The park also

Shanidar Park

offers its visitor's tea/snack shops, and a small restaurant that serves beer and nargilah (hookah). This park was the site of the First Erbil Freedom Day Community Run as well as annually hosting the Erbil Marathon every October which attracts many tourists and expats as well as locals.

Erbil Football Stadium

Sami Abdulrahman Park is also the location for many festivals and conferences, including the annual Erbil International Fair; various trade expositions, art exhibits, and a sports center and running/walking track. Close to the Parliament side of the park, the Zeytun Public Library, which was partially funded by the South Korean government, is an extremely modern looking building that should be open to the public soon.

As the park is quite large visitors can simply stroll along the "avenues" and enjoy the beautifully planned and displayed trees, plants, and flowers,

or they can watch their children play on a very large playground that always seems busy. For those interested in sports, there is a small lake with paddleboats and football pitches and a skateboard/BMX park. This wonderful urban space is normally full of picnickers and many locals of all ages. The park is particularly packed with young people and young couples on Friday evenings.

One of the main sources of pride for those in Erbil, the park is convenient to many hotels and other important sites like the citadel, the airport, and Ankawa neighborhood. The park grounds are meticulously maintained and there are many guards at all of the entrances for security purposes. It is somewhat easy to get lost in the park as there are not many signs but there are many people who will be able to assist you and perhaps will even personally lead you to where you need to go. It is a must-see in Erbil, and a testament that the city and society is rapidly transforming and seeks to beautify many ugly aspects of their oppressive history for future generations.

Shanidar Park

South of the citadel behind Sawwaf Mosque and across the street from Mi-

nara Park, it includes many playgrounds as well as a pond, gardens, and has a man-made cave-like structure resembling Shanidar Cave, that is used as a local art gallery.

HANARA

The recreation grounds of Hanara are 18 km (11 mi) east the Erbil's city center, and sits at an altitude of 390 m (1,280 ft.).

During the "Third Anfal" from April 7-20, 1988, the village of Hanara was largely destroyed as reported in a detailed report in *Human Rights Watch* (1993). Saddam's army came to Hanara with helicopters and fighter planes in the morning and villagers who had fled the attack came down from the hills to find nothing but smoldering rubble. Everything had been bulldozed, including the mosque.

Since then the area has been largely rebuilt and there are plans to begin construction for the Hanara Medical Centre and Sustainable Village, a modern project that will include healthcare facilities including a hospital, community development programs, and environmental protections and sustainable resources.

The area is popular for recreational purposes such as

picnics, and is frequented by tourists mostly during weekends and holidays. It is also very close to Shaklawa. The backdrop of the recreational grounds is beautiful scenery comprised of mountains and surrounded by beautiful flowers and green grassy fields where families and children can spread out and enjoy the day. Hanara is also close to the small river, Bastura Chay.

ERBIL INTERNATIONAL EQUESTRIAN RACING CLUB

Erbil International Equestrian Racing Club

Erbil now has a horse club, which is open to the public. It is located on Massif Salahadin road right next to the checkpoint. The facility, which cost more than 20 million USD, encompasses a racetrack where International races will eventually be held much as they are in nearby Jordan. At present there is an indoor jumping stadium where competition events are being held. The stable of horses is magnificent.

One can join the Club for a yearly subscription or rent horses by the hour for riding. The cost starts from $20 USD. Give it a try and have a wonder fultime. For those wishing to improve their equestrian skills there are also instructors available.

NIGHTLIFE

There are several bars and even a small slot-machine casino and American style Sport's Bar in the suburb of Ankawa where one can watch International sports events. Coffee shops abound throughout the city—both local and International—and are favorite gathering places for locals and expats alike. There is a never-ending supply of restaurants serving both local and International Cuisine and food is usually at the center of an evening out.

HOSPITALS AND CLINICS

Erbil is quickly modernizing and one result of this is increased demand for modern medical facilities. Throughout the city there are a dozen or more established public and private hospitals and numerous clinics. Many neighborhoods have small clinics as well. There is a street dubbed "Doctor's Street" and medicine and check-ups and other facilities are readily available to foreigners and locals alike. Listed are few of the better-known facilities:

Dialysis Centre

60 Meter and Malla Affendi Streets in between Saydawa and Mamostayan neighborhoods near the Langa Bazaar/Market (southeast)

Emergency Hospital

Safeen Rd and 60 Meter Rds. across the street from famous Jalil Khayat Mosque, Hawler Mall, Royal Mall, and Khanzad Family Park (center)

Emergency Medical Services

In between the Ministry of Planning and the Divan Hotel by Bakhtiari and 60 Meter Rds. (northwest)

¨Hawler Private Hospital

Barzani Nemir and Safeen Rds. North of the Citadel, south of Khanzad Family Park (center)

Hawler Teaching Hospital

Safeen Rd and 60 Meter Rds. across the street from famous Jalil Khayat Mosque, Hawler Mall, Royal Mall, and Khanzad Family Park (center)

PAR Hospital

This is perhaps the most modern of Erbil's hospitals boasting an international medical staff with over 50 consultant physicians and surgeons.
Address: 60m Street, Mamostayan Qr. Erbil, Kurdistan Region, Iraq
Tel: +964 66 210 7001 +964 66 210 7002
Web:www.parhospital.com
E-mail:info@parhospital.com

Rizgary Teaching Hospital

Peshawa Qazi and Koya Rds. between Khabat and Zanayan neighborhoods (southeast)

Rojawa Emergency Hospital

Nawroz and Qazi Muhammed Rds. in the Kurdistan neighborhood (southwest)

Sardam Private Hospital

Nawroz and Qazi Muhammed Rds. in the Kurdistan neighborhood (southwest)

Soran Private Hospital

60 Meter and Ankawa Rd. on the south end of Salahadin neighborhood (northwest)

West Eye Private Hospital

Ronaki and Gulan St. in between Ronaki and Iskan neighborhoods (southeast)

Zheen International Private Hospital

Very close to Rizgary Teaching Hospital, also on Peshawa Qazi and Koya Rds. (next to Majdi Mall southeast).

DIPLOMATIC MISSIONS

To date The Kurdistan Regional Government hosts 33 separate Diplomatic Missions, from Embassies to Consulates, to Trade Missions and the number is increasing on a regular basis. This includes all permanent members of the United Nations Security Council (UNSC). For the most updated information: http://dfr.krg.org/p/p.aspx?p=37&l=12&s=020100&r=363 / http://www.hawlergov.org/en/embassies.php

UNIVERSITIES

Erbil hosts several universities and this number is currently growing. The two most prestigious universities are The University of Kurdistan-Hawler (UKH) and Salahadin University, the oldest in the Kurdistan Region.

Cihan University

Cihan is a private institution, which also instructs in English, established in 2007. Off of Mosul Rd, and Peshawa Qazi Rd., Erbil 066; Further information, http://www.cihanuniversity.edu.iq/

Ishik University

This is a private university owned by Fezalar Educational Institution, based in Turkey, and was established in the Kurdistan Region in 2008. It is adjacent to Cihan University, off of Mosul Rd. and Peshawa Qazi Rd., http://www.ishik.edu.iq/

Lebanese French University

Much of the instruction is in French and it is considered a leading regional university. It is adjacent to Cihan and Ishik universities, off of Mosul Rd. and Peshawa Qazi Rd., http://www.lfu-bmu.net/

SABIS University

Near Ankawa St and 60 Meter St., this private university is a Lebanese-based system with some British components and taught in English. http://www.sabisuniversity.net/

Salahadin University

The oldest and largest higher education institution in the Kurdistan Region it was established in 1968 and originally based in Sulaymani but moved to Erbil in 1981. Undergraduate and graduate degrees are offered. Further information, Kirkuk Rd. and Jamal Haydary Rd, across the street from the German Consulate, Erbil; http://su.edu.iq/

The British Royal University for Science and Technology

Focusing on Science, technology, and medicine, this British-based system is an increasingly competitive private university off of Gulan St. near the famous Aras Publishing House in the Nuseran neighborhood. (http://broyalu.net/)

The University of Kurdistan-Hawler (UKH)

UKH was established in 2006. Instruction and research are held in English and the institution includes undergraduates as well as graduate students. Its first graduating class was in 2010. The University of Leicester and the University of London have close links with UKH. For further information, 30 Meter Avenue, near Kirkuk Rd. and Barzani Nemir Rd., Erbil, Iraq; www.ukh.ac/.

Arrival Hall

ERBIL INTERNATIONAL AIRPORT

Airport Code: EBL/EIA

The Erbil International Airport is situated northwest of Erbil just west of the popular expatriate community and Christian neighborhood of Ankawa. It is roughly 7 km (4 mi) from the famous Citadel. The airport, which opened in 2005 at a cost of $550 million is the first in the Kurdistan Region and maintains relations with dozens of different carriers from all over the world

The new British, Turkish, and South Korean built terminal was opened on March 3, 2010 and features one of the world's longest runways (4,800 m X 90 m (15,748 ft. x 295 ft.). It was originally built in the 1970s for the Iraqi Military and Air Force and used until 1991 when the Kurdish uprising with Western support expelled Saddam from the Region. After the 1991 Iraq War, the KRG took over the airport's administrative responsibilities.

The baggage handling system located under the main terminal is highly sophisticated and travelers are usually surprised at the speed with which their bags are delivered. It is also considered to be one of the most secure airports in the world. One should allow ample time when checking in to clear security. Three hours is wise just to be sure but generally check in can be accomplished in less than two as it is efficiently administered.

The airport includes duty-free shops, snack bars, lounge areas, baby care, prayer rooms, a clinic, ATMs, currency exchange offices, taxi information, as well as an increasingly popular VIP terminal for dignitaries and diplomats, which can be accessed for a fee. In 2006, the airport saw 164,000 visitors and in 2013 this figure jumped exponentially to over 1,200,000 visitors. The airport maintains relations with over twenty passenger airlines, five cargo airlines, and several charter airlines.

Further information
Web:
http://erbilairport.com/Main/Main.aspx
Tel: +964 66 281 0000
Email:
admin.dep@erbilairport.com

KURDISTAN IRAQ TOURS

www.kurdistaniraqtours.com

THE CITADEL OF ERBIL

GENERAL INFORMATION / HISTORY

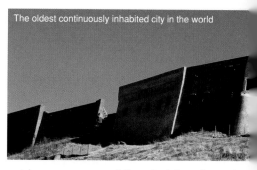
The oldest continuously inhabited city in the world

The Citadel is an archeological "tel", which is a type of earthen mound created by repeated human occupation and abandonment of a geographical site over many centuries – civilization upon civilization in this case.

It is located in the center of Erbil (locally referred to as Qala Hawler). It is believed to be the oldest continuously inhabited city in the world. There are cities in the world such as Damascus that may be as old but none have been in continuous use, as has the Qala of Erbil. In 2007, the High Commission for Erbil Citadel Revitalization (HCE-CR) began a massive restoration project and the residents were relocated and compensated with land in another area. However one family was purposely left in the city to maintain its place in history as the oldest "inhabited" city in the world. The government plans to have 50 families live in the Citadel once it is fully renovated and there will be a number of indigenous craft centers, restaurants and boutique hotels as well. Erbil Citadel was inscribed on the World Heritage List on 21 June 2014.

The earliest evidence suggests the city is at least 8000 years old. In 2006 and 2007, a team from the University of West Bohemia, together with Salahaddin University in Erbil, carried out an extensive survey and evaluation of the entire Citadel. As part of this project, geodetic measurements of the citadel were taken and these were combined with satellite imagery, regular photographic imagery and aerial photographs to create a map and digital 3D model of the citadel mound and the houses on top of it. Geophysical prospection was carried out in some areas of the citadel to detect traces of older architecture buried under the present houses. Archaeological investigations included an archaeological survey on the western slope of the citadel mound, and the excavation of a small trench in the eastern part of the Citadel. A Neo-Assyrian chamber tomb was found at the foot of the citadel mound during construction activities in 2009. The local Antiquities Service and archaeologists from the German Archaeological Institute (DAI) subsequently excavated this area. The tomb was plundered in antiquity but still contained pottery dating to the 8th and 7th centuries BC confirming the *minimum* age of the tel. Perhaps even earlier evidences will be discovered as the explorations continue. The tel is perhaps one of the most exciting investigations being undertaken by the archeological community anywhere in the world.

The Citadel at night

The Citadel appears for the first time in historical sources in the Ebla tablets around 2,300 BC, and gained particular importance during the Neo-Assyrian period. Erbil was an important center for Christianity during the Adiabene Kingdom in the first century AD.

The buildings on top of the tel stretch over a roughly oval area of 430 by 340 meters (1,410 ft. - 1,120 ft.) occupying 102,000 square meters (1,100,000 sq. ft.). The mound rises between 25 and 32 meters (82 and 105 ft.) from the surrounding plain. When it was fully

occupied, the citadel was divided in three districts or *mahallas*: from east to west the Serai, the Takya and the Topkhana. Notable families occupied the Serai; the Takya district was named after the homes of dervishes, which are called takyas; and the Topkhana district housed craftsmen and farmers.

During the early 20th century, there were three mosques, two schools and a Hammam (bath house) in the citadel. There were also two takyas. Takyas were meeting places for Sufis, devout Muslims, and dervishes, to practice religious recitals "Thikir" and hold dervish dances in a special hall called "Sama-Khana". There were two such takyas in the citadel, the oldest of which belonged to Sheikh Sharif and followed the "Qadiriya Tariqa" and held its activities every Monday and Friday. The other belonged to Haj Mulla Khidhir al-Telafari also followed

the "Qadiriya Tariqa". Both takyas have disappeared and can only be identified by their domed roofs from early 20th Century vertical photographs.

The citadel also housed a synagogue until 1957. The only religious structure that currently survives is the Mulla Afandi Mosque, which was rebuilt on the location of an earlier 19th-century mosque. Qassim Agha Abdullah built the hammam in 1775. It went out of service during the 1970s and was renovated

Door to the Hammam

Citadel Mosque

in 1979, although many original architectural details were lost.

The perimeter wall of the citadel is not a continuous fortification wall, but consists of the façades of approximately 100 houses that have been built against each other. Because they have been built on or near the steep slope of the citadel mound, buttresses to prevent their collapse strengthened many of these façades giving the city a fortress like appearance. There were approximately 30 palaces in the city at various times in history. It is believed that Darius III fled to one of these palaces briefly after his defeat by Alexander the Great on the plains of Gaugemela a scant hour or so away. The oldest surviving house that can be securely dated through an inscription was built in 1893. The oldest houses can be found on the southeastern side of

Palace in the Citadel

the mound, whereas houses on the northern perimeter date to the 1930s–1940s. Before the introduction of modern building techniques, most houses on the citadel were built around a courtyard. A raised arcade overlooking the courtyard, a flat roof and a bent-access entrance to prevent views of the courtyard and the interior of the house were characteristic elements of the houses in the citadel.

Hammam

To date the Erbil tel has never been fully explored. Layer upon layer of civilizations have combined to grant us a partial glimpse of antiquity but many of its secrets remain hidden and may forever be unknown. Perhaps future excavations may tunnel deeper beneath the city where some of the earths first inhabitants may well have walked. One thing is certain—lovers of history will not want to miss this most amazing city.

HIGHLIGHTS

Citadel Bath (*Hammam*)

Located in the center of the Citadel neighborhood next to the glittering and colorfully tiled mosque, it is located on the main road, which crosses the center of the Citadel from South to North and is near the Textile Museum. The Citadel Bath (Hammam) was probably built in 1775 though some scholars claim it to be hundreds of years older since it was built on top of another structure. Two main sections were traditionally used depending on the season — one for summer use and the other, for winter use. The structure includes two bathing halls topped by two large domes, which are tannish-cream colored from the outside. The northern side of the bath holds a unique, beautiful well that descends 45 m (148 ft.), to the base of the Citadel itself. In 1979-1980 the bath was renovated and the entire Citadel area has seen major restoration since 2005.

Qassim Agha Abdullah built the existing Turkish/Ottoman style public bath (*hammam*) in 1775 and it is typical of Middle Eastern public baths built around this time though curiously it

Extravangent Residence in the Citadel

has a blue stylized Star of David above the main entrance implying that Jewish inhabitants of the Citadel used the *hammam* as well. Women used the public bath until 11:00 AM and after that time the men used it. In addition to bathing and health reasons, *hammams* provided a place for gossip, business, and other daily affairs. The outer hall (*Barrani*) holds the larger of the two domes. The middle hall (*Wastani*) is the hall, which is meant to be slightly warmer for visitors. The inner hall (*Jawani*) is the very hot and steamy

area, much like a sauna. This inner hall, which contained six spots for private bathing, also retained a dome that had many small round glass openings (Oculus) to provide for natural light. These openings can still be seen today. Water was obtained from the ancient well in the center and dried sticks, vegetation, and garbage was collected daily and dried in order to heat the *hammam and* water cistern and under-floor (Hypocaust) of the inner hall. The water feeding the well for the *hammam* originated from an area which was part of a large-scale irrigation project of Assyrian King Sennaharib from the Bastora Valley, 20 km (12 mi) from Erbil. This well was the main water source for the inhabitants of the citadel. After the 1940s when oil became the preferred means of heating, the *hammam* started to lose its popularity. The Citadel *hammam* stopped being used in the 1970s and was left empty.

Palace interior

Citadel Mosque

Also known as the Grand Mosque, it is located in the Takya neighborhood of the Citadel next to the public bath (*hammam*). The mosque is in the center of the Citadel and the only religious structure still standing in the area. It is mentioned as early as 1220 AD in the book *The Compendium of Countries* and Ibn Mustawfi, the famous Kurdish historian and poet, referred to it as the "Fortress Mosque" in *The History of Erbil*, which was writ-

Citadel Mosque

ten around the same time. The Citadel Mosque was renovated several times over the centuries, particularly during the 18th century, since this is when the *hammam* was also renovated. The *mihrab* (prayer niche) includes an inscription referencing renovation from 1719-1720 AD under the supervision of Abu Bakr Ben Mulla Omar.

The mosque is also known as the Mulla Effendi Mosque, after the renown and respected imam (1863-1942 AD), who hailed from a long line of scholars who taught and preached at the Grand Mosque. He was regarded as being a trusted mediator among tribal disputes and was also respected by minorities in the area, particularly Christians in Ankawa. He was also highly regarded by Ottoman Sultan Hamid II as well as King Feisal. A.M. Hamilton and Gertrude Bell also wrote highly of him stating he was one of the most respected persons in the Kurdistan area during this time. Fun fact: Mulla Effendi was the first person to own a car in Erbil. He used his car to travel between his house in Badawa neighborhood and the Grand Mosque.

It is suggested that the mosque, though restored in the 19th century was perhaps once another mosque or even church since it was common practice after the Muslim conquest (640 AD) to hold main prayers in the center of towns or the citadel in this case. The mosque originally had a huge prayer hall with vaulted ceilings, surrounded by twenty-one domes resting on arches and columns. This was demolished in 1957 and rebuilt (unprofessionally unfortunately) in a more 'modern' style that is now a flat reinforced concrete roof.

The Textile Museum

PRESERVING NOMADIC CULTURAL HERITAGE OF KURDISTAN

From the Pen of
Dr. Anne-Marie Deisser

Anne-Marie Deisser joined the Textile Conservation Centre, University of Southampton, UK, in 2000 where she took her Master in Textile Conservation and did her PhD, on "conservation partnership" between local and institutional communities. She taught and worked as a conservator for the National Museums of Kenya, the National Museum of Ethiopia and the Institute of Ethiopian Studies. She was Chair of the Ethnography Section of the United Kingdom Institute for Conservation, ICON (2005- 2008).

Between 2009 and 2012 her work focused on the conservation of the tangible and intangible heritage of the Kurdish Nomadic tribes at the Textile Museum of Erbil. Since September 2012, she is Honorary Research Associate at the Institute of Archaeology (University College of London) and Research Associate at the Department of History and Archaeology of the University of Nairobi in Kenya. Her main field of interest is the research of ethical conservation practices in relation to social development and human rights. Anne-Marie is an active contributor to conservation debate and networks across related conservation disciplines such as archaeology, sociology and philosophy in heritage and nature conservation.

The Kurdish Textile Museum: Education and Conservation Practices

"Tracking the cultural treasures of Iraqi Kurdistan has become a heartbreaking task for archaeologists and conservators. Sunni, Sufi and Shia shrines, tombs, mosques, Ottoman period buildings, Christian Cathe-

Inside the Textile Museum

few. Much of the responsibility to preserve this legacy has been left to the Kurds themselves. Resources are scarce, but fortunately a few have risen to the task and are doing all they can to preserve this amazing culture dating from the beginning of civilization.

The Kurdish Textile Museum (KTM) is one of the more important examples in Kurdistan today of a focused effort to preserve the

drals and crosses, Synagogues, Yezidi Shrines, statues, books and oral traditions are part of the cultural legacy of Christianity, Islam and Judaism in the region. The list of destroyed, damaged or looted sites and artifacts is alarming due to recent war and turmoil. The Kurdistan Region of Iraq has been the center of the world for every great empire recorded in human history imposing an obligation on all peoples and governments to protect them.

However, International conventions meant to help safeguard and conserve cultural icons and structures during war or other calamities are weakly applied and international cultural heritage programs are

ancient wonders of the region and exhibit them for the world to behold. Mr. Lolan Mustapha founded the Kurdish Textile Museum in 2004 and it is the only museum of its kind in the region. The incredible collection of textiles, tribal carpets and antiquities has been the passion of generations of Lolan's family including his father and grandfather who spent decades and countless resources to find and give sanctuary to the crafts of Kurdistan. The trust has now passed to Lolan and his ancestors would be proud of his continued care and nurture of their vision. The objective of the KTM is to preserve both the tangible and intangible cultural heritage of Kurdish nomadic communities, develop research on this unique cultural tradition and teach others to continue the age-old endangered techniques employed for thousands of years in the region.

Until quite recently, the immediate natural environment has shaped the decorative arts of the nomadic Kurds of Iraq. The materials available to them as well as their distinctive lifestyle

Tribal Hat Collection

have in turn influenced their designs. The uniqueness of Kurdish decorative arts lies in the fact that their creation and production have survived as an unbroken thread for centuries and remain an integral part of their continuing traditions.

By supporting the preservation of the nomads' so-

of institutional and local communities thus creating a sustainable partnership between representatives of the nomadic tribes, the Kurdish Textile Museum, and national authorities. In addition the museum hosts social and cultural events, capacity building courses for Iraqi museum staff from different institutions

the mission of the International Council of Museums (ICOM): "to preserve, conserve, and share cultural heritage".

cial practices, knowledge and traditional arts the KTM helps local communities and individuals, wherever they are living, to re-learn forgotten skills enabling them to generate income while respecting their social integrity. The aim of conservation work at KTM is to build upon the experience

and knowledge-transfer of textile technologies to young Iraqi Kurds. Thus the museum adheres to

It has been one of the great pleasures of my life to assist this project over the years. It is my fervent hope that those who have the rare opportunity to see first hand the craftsmanship of this the "cradle of civilization" will return to their nations as ambassadors encouraging others to visit and support the Kurdish Textile Museum in its appointed task of conserving these rare treasures of humanity."

CHOMAN

GENERAL INFORMATION / HISTORY

Choman is a town and district of Erbil Province near the Iranian border and is one of the most breathtaking areas in Kurdistan. The area attracts many tourists due to the wide range of scenery; parks, rivers, green pastures and waterfalls are plentiful. The area includes an important agricultural and cattle breeding region located in the sub-district of the Halgurd-Sakran Park and Mountain chain. The town is located 45 km east of Soran (28 mi) or 30 minutes, 155 km (96 mi) from Erbil or two hours, and 258 km (160 mi) or three and a half hours from Sulaymani.

In 1970 it became its own district though thirteen years later, in 1983 Saddam Hussein destroyed it during the ongoing Iran-Iraq war. After the famous Kurdish uprising (*Rapareen*) in 1991, townspeople reconstructed their city. As a result of this dedication, its population now stands at more than 11,000.

While the area was once considered dangerous as it is near the Iran border and disputes between Iran/Iraq hindered the development of the region in the past, today it is a peaceful and accessible region and the beauty is unparalleled. For the first time investors are exploring development of the area for tourism. Adequate hotels are limited but this is soon to change. There is even serious discussion of developing the area into an International ski resort, as there are snow-covered peaks the year around in the nearby Zagros Mountains. It is **strongly** recommended that you have a local guide when you hike the

Choman

Choman and the surrounding mountains

area as several of the nearby mountains are heavily mined as a result of the Iraq-Iran War (1980-1988). Also anyone inadvertently wandering into Iran can be arrested, as was the case with a group of hikers in 1991.They were released after fourteen months imprisonment upon payment of a $465,000 fine. That said, many do hike in the area and it is perfectly safe to do so with proper guidance, which is readily available in the nearby towns and cities. It is truly a visually astonishing area and worth the effort.

As part of the development activities of the Kurdistan regional ministries, the Ministry of Health has allocated the amount of 701m (IQD) Dinars ($600,000 USD) for the construction of a general hospital in Choman. The hospital will be built on an area of 5,000 square meters (54,000 sq. ft.) using modern methods suited to the weather conditions of the region. It will be a class-A hospital with surgery, maternity and emergency sections/ wards. More than eighty percent of the work has already been carried out.

In 2007, a returnee from Sweden and then-KRG Minister of Sports and Youth, Taha Barwari opened a recreational center in Choman complete with a library, a gymnasium, a movie theater, and a radio station. The younger generation loved the project and has been instrumental in its success.

Additionally in May 2014, a local NGO *Nature Iraq* and its *Waterkeepers Iraq* program established the Choman-Rawanduz River Expedition near Choman. The expedition promoted and celebrated Iraq's largely unknown rivers and raised awareness about the environmental threats they face. The program included music, arts, nature walks and educational presentations. In addition there were demonstrations with experts on river safety and kayaking and water quality monitoring. This event helped spur more tourism to the region as well as educating people about nature. The goals of *Nature Iraq* were to demonstrate the eco-tourism potential of wild and scenic rivers in Iraq; bring attention to the threats facing the river basin; and encourage sustainable use of and protection for Iraqi rivers in general. More such events are planned in the future.

HIGHLIGHTS

Barza Cave and Waterfall

The Barza cave was used by prehistoric peoples as a residence and later provided refuge for Kurdish *peshmerga* (freedom fighters) during their fight against Saddam's military forces. Now, the cool cave provides shelter for tourists during warm summer months.

Bradost Area

The drive up to Bradost Mountains is absolutely stunning. One of the more popular destinations for hiking and sight-seeing, the area has a great deal to offer tourists of all varieties. At its highest peak, the mountain is 1,345 m (4,413 ft.).

The range of Bradost extends 40 km (25 mi) long, northwest from the winding Rawanduz River. The snow-fed Bradost river flows and is joined by other head-waters, which empties into Lake Urmia in Iranian Kurdistan. Bradost translates to "close friend" and locals have been visiting this "friend" for centuries.

Bradost is also the name of a Kurdish tribe, region, river, and political emirate in addition to the mountain itself. The tribe inhabits a large area within historic Kurdistan, namely between the Iraq and Iran border.

Bradost area

The long lost religious Assyrian capital city Muşaşir was located between ancient Assyria and Urartu. Many scholars now concur that Muşaşir is in the modern villages of Sidekan or Mdjeser in Sidekan in the Brados district. Discoveries first came to light in the 19th century. Remnants from a fortress/castle have been destroyed as well as foundational remains but in a nearby valley there are remains of a long

wall/fortification, which is sited as evidence of the ancient civilization.

Bradost Emirate was one of several semi-independent emirates across Kurdistan in the 10th-16th centuries. At the height of its power, the Bradost Emirate's territory extended from west of Lake Urmia (Iranian Kurdistan) to Erbil, Baghdad, and Diyarbakir in Turkey. After a famous Ottoman-Safavid (Persian) battle, the Chaldean Bradost Emirate swore allegiance to the victorious Ottomans. The last prince of Bradost was Abdullah Beg Benari.

Seemingly Endless Valleys

Raging Rivers in Bradost

In the 1980s and early 1990s the Bradost area was heavily mined making it dangerous for hiking without an experienced guide. However most areas have since been de-mined but it still always a good idea to use a local guide when hiking in this area.

The climb to the top is breathtaking and inspiring. For new or inexperienced hikers, there is one side that is not as steep, and it is easy to pace oneself. As you reach the summit one side has a sudden drop off which leads to a deep valley.

There are a wide variety of bird species in the Bradost area. The fauna also include many wild goats who spend their time on the mountainous areas, Golden Jackals, Grey Wolves, Indian Crested Porcupines, Syrian Brown Bears, Striped Hyenas, Wildcats, and the rivers — particularly the Rawanduz — contain several kinds of fish that are caught by locals and sold in the bazaars.

The Bradost area is also "famous" or one should say "infamous" for its reputation as a center of smuggling. In fact some of the locals refer to it as the "smugglers" region.

This is a perfect example of what makes Kurdistan one of the most amazing destinations in the world—combining ancient history and unparalleled beauty with the colorful legends of the land.

Bsta Waterfall

Just 3 Km (2 mi.) from Bsta village, in the North-East of Choman, lays the Bsta waterfall. The area is calm and refreshing; the water splashing off the falls gives a fresh and pleasant feel. It is a perfect place for picnics and sightseeing.

Cheekha Dar (Outer Row)

In the Zagros mountain range this peak is (according to the *CIA World Fact Book*) the highest in Iraq at 3611 meters (11847 ft.). It is located 6 kilometers (3.7 mi) on the Iran/Iraq border and is inaccessible to climbers without permissions from both governments. It was climbed in November 2004 by English explorer Ginge Fullen, who

Cheekadar

recorded a GPS reading of 3,628 meters (11,902 ft.) The first reported winter ascent was by Jonathan Beswick and Matthew DuPuy on March 18, 2011. There is a danger of land mines in the area on the approach between Hamilton Road and the village of Gundah Zhur and while red, triangular signs with skull and crossbones mark some fields, one should never attempt hiking in the area without a knowledgeable guide. It is possible to find Kurdish escorts through this area in the town of Choman. Without a proper guide it is easy to stray across the unmarked border to Iran, which can result in arrest and detainment.

Haji Omran

Haji Omran

Part of Choman district, Haji Omran is known for its hills, streams and meadows. Surrounded by mountains, including Sakran Mountain to the south, the region receives an abundance of rain and snow during winter and spring months. Lying at an altitude of 1700m (5,700 ft.), Haji Omran is one of the main border crossings between Iraq and Iran. A number of overland tourists enter Kurdistan from this border. Taxis can be rented in Iran that will take you to the border and while there is transport available once the border is crossed it is advisable to pre-arrange a pickup from a reputable travel agency. The nearest small city in Iran is Piranshahr where taxis can be rented.

Halgurd Sakran National Park

Halgurd Sakran National Park (HSPN)

Halgurd Sakran National Park (HSNP) is the first "official" National Park in the mountains of Kurdistan and in fact, the whole of Iraq. HSNP is situated in Erbil Province, 120km (75 mi) northeast of the city of Erbil and only a few minutes away from the town of Choman. HSNP will be the largest protected mountain area in Kurdistan, expected to cover more than 1100 km2 (425 sq. mi), with a height up to 3,609 m (11841 ft.) at Halgurd Peak, the second highest mountain in Iraq after Cheekha Dar, which is 3,611 m (11847 ft.). From Erbil the area is approximately 150 km (93 mi) and can be driven in 2.5 hrs. The passes are closed in the winter and while one can reach the lower levels by four-wheel drive a hike is necessary to reach higher levels and only experienced climbers with guides can attain the highest reaches.

The mountain is located among wonderful districts such as Galala, Haji Omran, Roost, and Sidakan. The peak of the

mountain is covered with snow throughout the whole year. There are many springs and lakes around the mountain that add to the breathtaking view of the area. Halgurd and Hasara Roost mountain chains are included in the Halgurd-Sakaran National Park. The national park extends from Sakran Mountain to Haji Omran and Sidakan district covering 1,100 square km (684 Sq. mi). Halgurd-Sakran National Park is visited by tourists from all over Iraq not only for the climbing adventure and hiking but also to discover famous herbs used in naturopathic medicines. Locals will be happy to share their knowledge with guests.

In April 2015, over a nine-day period, a group of trekkers from *Secret Compass* are scheduled to hike up Halgurd Mountain, which is Iraq's highest climbable mountain that is wholly located within Iraq. Among the many reasons for the hike apart from sheer enjoyment is to highlight the potential of the area to other travelers and help to develop a vital area of the local KRG economy. As there is currently no trail, traveling with a guide is an **absolute necessity**, especially since Iran is only 2.5 miles away. However, it should also be noted that many tourists and skilled hikers have hiked this mountain, and there should be no issue with local authorities as long as visitors are not climbing Cheekha Dar—which is partially in Iran.

From one of the past climbers, "The view from the top is worth the effort, a stunning panorama of mountains and ridges baked brown by the long hot summer even though temperatures at the top are near freezing. North across a deep valley is Iran where you can make out a series of Iranian border posts dotted along the ridge opposite, a useful warning that even in good weather you need to be careful to descend back the way you came and not stray into the hands of an Iranian border patrol, a point not lost on our guide."

Contact Phone:
+964 750 813 4616;
Mob.
00964 (0) 750 4474527
Abdulwahid Gwany
Email:
info@hs-nationalpark.org;
Email: gwany@hs-nationalpark.org
Website: http://www.hsnationalpark.org

Halgurd

Khoshkan Recreation Ground

From Choman: 20 km (12 mi) 15 minutes; Altitude: 2,665 m or 8,743 ft. This area is located in a village in the midst of an incredibly beautiful and unspoiled region. It is a very cold region due to the altitude, heavy snow and frequent rain but when the weather permits it is a wonderful place to hike and enjoy nature.

Roste Citadel

Roste Citadel is located in Roste village, 137 km (83 mi) north of Erbil city and east of Halgurd. Built at the top of the mountain, the Citadel is one of the most important archaeological sites in the area.

Roste Valley

Roste Valley is located at the foot of Halgurd Mountain, 137 km (83 mi) northeast of Erbil province, near Sirin village, on the highway between Soran and Choman. The valley has an abundance of fresh water, forests, and orchards, and a small river passes through the valley. Rich in folklore and tradition, the area is popular with tourists seeking rest and relaxation.

Sakran

Sakran Valley

From Erbil Sakran Valley is roughly 150 km (93 mi) or two and a half hours away. The valley is only 30 minutes or so east of Choman. On your way to Haji Omran, the protected area of Sakran Valley will appear on your right. Turn into the park after the sign for Sakran Valley where you can park.

Halgurd Lake

The landscape is beautiful and virtually untouched by human development. The road is rugged which limits the amount of tourism.

Even in spring four-wheel drive vehicles are required and often the travel can only be made on foot. However, there are also parts that are mined and local guides are required to safely explore the area. The KRG is planning to rid the entire area of this scourge and has been working hand in hand with International NGOs to accomplish this task in the shortest possible time.

The Sakran Mountain Range is part of the larger Zagros range. Sakran mountain and its sister, Halgurd are part of one of the most unspoiled areas in Kurdistan; the high elevations ensure that snow covers some parts of the summits of the highest peaks year-around. The

great diversity of natural habitats in the envisaged *Halgurd Sakran National Park* enables the many species of animals and plants that are rare, or near extinct elsewhere, to survive and re-generate in the environment in which they originated. Accordingly, there are over three-dozen species of birds found in and around Sakran Mountain and its valley.

Sheikh Balak Shrine

Near the city of Choman is the shrine dedicated to the 17th century Sheikh who was known for the introduction of the *Al Sehrudia* doctrine to Islam. There is little publicly accessible information as to what exactly this doctrine embodied which is common to many of the more obscure and esoteric sects of Islam that developed in the region of Kurdistan. However, the Sheikh's impact continues to this day through his thousands of followers who regularly visit the shrine.

Walze Waterfall

The Walze Waterfall is one of the most beautiful waterfalls in the country. It is a ten-minute drive southeast of Choman, which is roughly forty-five minutes northeast of Soran (45 km; 28 mi) and just over two hours northeast from Erbil (155 km; 96 mi). Many people come from all over the country to visit this gorgeous natural site that is known for its natural beauty and several different types of waterfalls. Lesser known than Geli Ali Beg or Bekhal waterfalls, this area is off the beaten path for most tourists, especially since it is not very close to Sulaymani or Erbil. However, the road to Walze waterfalls is paved and the trip is well worth it for nature lovers.

Walze is lush and green for much of the year and various orchards surround most of the homes in the village. Even the roofs, covered with soil, are planted with vegetables. While some tourists may not find comfort in the fact there are no facilities like garbage dumps or toilets, others may revel in the fact that it is virtually untouched. At present the area remains a largely undiscovered jewel and visitors will often comment on its pristine beauty.

Bradost Area

HIRAN

GENERAL INFORMATION / HISTORY

Hiran is a sub district of Shaqlawa, which is a district of Erbil Governorate. Only 23 km (14 mi) from Shaqlawa and 70 km (44 mi) from Erbil, or roughly halfway between Shaqlawa and Koya is the small village of Hiran. The village lies in the southeastern part of Shaqlawa district, not far from Safeen Mountain, and almost touches the Koya District. The Sulaymani Governorate lies to the East.

The infamous and genocidal Anfal Campaign of Saddam Hussein affected the area of Hiran on at least three occasions. The first time was on May 23, 1988; the second time was July 3, 1988; and the third time was August 25, 1988. On at least two of these occasions, the Iraqi Air Force bombed area villages.

The population distribution is unevenly distributed between sub-districts. Hiran sub district is the hilliest part of East Shaqlawa, and as a result, has a very low rural density (twenty-one persons per square kilometer). In 2011, Hiran's population was approximately 3,000, or 9 percent of the rural population in the Shaqlawa district. A large part of the region of Hiran is covered by rocky hills, which overall affect the size of the rural settlements and the population itself since the land capacity cannot support a large number of people.

In 2008 a large services project began in the Shaqlawa district of Erbil governorate. As a result, the roads between villages in Hiran became linked to each other. Two years later in 2010, the KRG constructed a large dam in the village of Aqhoban in the Hiran sub district. The Ministry of Agriculture and Water Resources has allocated funds for a dam to collect rainwater and

Hiran in winter

water from nearby springs to irrigate arable land and raise the level of groundwater, as well as to generate electricity.

HIGHLIGHTS

Roger Matthews, in his 2003 book *The Archeology of Mesopotamia: Theories and Approaches,* mentions Hiran as being a place where archeological digs and excavations are underway.

Famed for Pomegranites

Hiran has at least five freshwater springs and several groves and is generally known as a location for families to enjoy picnics and get-togethers among fresh, clean air amidst an abundance of trees and fruit. The village is shady and is considered by locals

Farmer of Hiran

as a place to "get away" from the bustle of the city. Visitors can stroll down the streets as merchants in traditional shops sell various souvenirs, food, and drinks. The area is renowned for its fruits—especially pomegranates.

Sheikh Hiran Shrine

The shrine itself is located on a hill in the center of the village of Hiran and is surrounded by tall oak trees, which gives the shrine a very spiritual and natural feel. The shrine is adjacent to a cemetery reserved for Sheikhs (Mullahs) of the Naqshabandi (written an-Naqshbandiyyah, Nakşibendi, Naksibendi, Naksbandi) Sufi order, one of the two largest in the Kurdistan Region.

There is also a rudimenta-ry monastery guesthouse used by Sufi dervishes and sect members who practice their unique Sufi religious rituals during holy and religious celebrations. These are conducted next to the deceased ancestors of Safi Hiran who are buried in the cemetery. Visitors make pilgrimages to the shrine asking for the spiritual intercession and blessing from the Sheikh in order for their wishes to come true.

Outside the entrance to the shrine, which is a cave-like room carved out from the stony hill in the village; there are at least six gravestones. Inside the single-room cave is the tomb of Safi Hiran, the most famous of the sheikhs. The tomb is covered in various green cloths and on top are prayers and holy books. The floor is covered in Mid-dle Eastern carpets.

The site is an important place to visit for those interested in the deep spiritual traditions of Kurdistan which has set the Kurds apart from much of the rest of the Middle East.

A large majority of Muslim and non-Muslim Kurds are followers of one of many mystic Sufi orders (or *tariqa).* The bonds of the Muslim Kurds to different Sufi orders have traditionally been stronger than to orthodox Muslim practices. Sufi rituals in Kurdistan, led by Sufi masters, or *shaykhs,* contain so many clearly non-Islamic rites and practices that an objective observer would not consider them Islamic in the orthodox sense.

The Naqshabandi sect is the only Sufi sect that traces its spiritual lineage to the Islamic prophet Muhammad, through Abu Bakr, the first Caliph and one of Muhammad's closest companions. The prominent Barzani and Talabani tribes are led by Naqshbandi Sheikhs. Following age-old tradition, the appellation "Sheikh" is often used as part of the name of high-ranking family members even if the bearer is not particularly religious in practice. The current President and Prime Minister of Kurdistan are both Barzanis with a heritage from the Naqshabandi order.

Valley and Mountains Surrounding Koya

KOYA

GENERAL INFORMATION / HISTORY

Koya, or Koye, or Koy-Sinjaq is 81 km (50 mi) from Erbil and 116 km (72 mi) to Sulaymani and 51 km (32 mi) from the town of Dukan, where Dukan Lake attractions and resorts are located. Pressed up on a jagged hill adjacent to a vast valley, surrounded by the Bawaji and Haibat mountains, the town is somewhat of a hidden gem within the Kurdistan Region.

Most of the town was the property of two families (Hawezis and the Ghafuris), but later the Iraqi government confiscated most of the land owned by the two families. Historically, there was a small community of Jews in Koya, and even today one may find locals who have Jewish relatives who converted to Islam (Benjews). Additionally there is a significant population of Assyrian Christians in the area, particularly in the nearby village of Armota, where some still speak a variant of the Aramaic language, *Koy Sanjaq Surat*.

Historians believe that Koya enjoyed great prestige under the Assyrian and Mede Empires. The city is also famous for its mosques, which were often centers for studies of sciences and arts. Many scholars, poets and artists were active in and around Koya. Today, its academic reputation continues through the Koya University, which is at the very far north end of

the city (built in 2003) and is an important hub of culture and learning in the region (http://www.koyauniversity.org/).

Famous People

Jalal Talabani former President of Iraq was born in the nearby village of Kelkan and went to school in Koya.

Dildar: Yûnis Reuf, better known as Dildar (1918–1948) was a poet and political activist. He is mostly known for writing the poem Ey Reqîb, which became the Kurdish national anthem in 1946 during the Mahabad Republic in Iranian Kurdistan.

Fuad Masoum: Muhammad Fuad Masum (b. 1938) is the seventh and current President of Iraq. He has held office since the spring election in 2014. Masum is the second non-Arab president of Iraq after Talabani, and is a confidant of Talabani as well.

Koya Quishla

Caravanserai

HIGHLIGHTS

Caravanserai

Located downtown in the city *souk* (bazaar) the 18th Century Caravanserai was used by travelers for centuries as a roadside inn on trading routes that traversed the Middle East. The building is in an advanced state of ruin and one needs a local or guide to point out the entrance but it is one of the most captivating sites in this fascinating city.

Chinarok Summer Resort

Chinarok resort is 1,260 m (4134 ft.) in altitude and is only 3 km (2 miles) northeast of Koya next to Haibat Sultan. This location is along the old road between Koya and Dukan.

The Journal of Kirkuk University–Scientific Studies (2009) published an article by a student Perykhan M.

Jaf entitled "Optical Illusion and the Magnetic Hills in Koya Region" which studied Chinarok's "magnetic hill." The illusion is that if one stops their car in this area placing it in the neutral position, the car will gradually roll *up* the hill. It is definitely a sight to be seen!

Chinarok is famous for its delightful cuisine as well as its beauty and interestingly enough, in a suburb southwest of London (Hounslow), there is a joint Kurdish-Arabic Restaurant, Chinarok Restaurant, which serves traditional Kurdish and Arabic food. When one tastes the delicacies offered in the local restaurants it is easy to see why the cuisine has spread to foreign lands.

Surrounded by rolling green hills, Chinarok is a wonderful area to enjoy nature and offers a wonderful view of the town of Koya below. Though the area is occupied by a number of il-

legal factories, the KRG is making it more difficult to work in environments that are otherwise used by the public in an effort to develop tourism in the region.

Central Citadel (Qshla Koya)

The citadel is located in the center of Koya. Researchers differ on the date of its construction as some place it during the Mamalik era while others claim the Ottomans built it in the second half of the 19th century during the rule of Ottoman Governor Midhat Pasha of Baghdad. Perhaps there is truth to both of these narratives, as is often the case in Kurdistan where buildings are built and rebuilt by succeeding rulers.

Although admittedly not as breathtaking as the Citadel in Erbil, this citadel also differs in that it was only meant to serve as a fortress, instead as an area of residency. Visitors can walk around the entirety of the citadel, either by circling around the heavily fortified walls above ground, offering a panorama over the town, mountains and valley or by walking around inside the fortress itself. There are no official visiting hours, but there is always a guard on hand who lives on the premise and is quite welcoming. If the gates are locked, try knocking. Directly outside the citadel is an ancient Muslim cemetery, which still attracts mourners. The cemetery also has a newer section.

Chwar Taqan (Four Water Jars)

Located just south of Koya toward the Little Zab River, Chwar Taqan was a resting

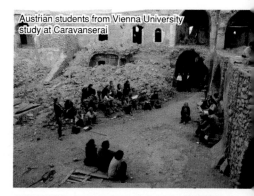
Austrian students from Vienna University study at Caravanserai

place and stopover for caravans (*Caravanserai*) traveling between Koya (Koy Sinjaq), Erbil, Kirkuk, and later, Sulaymani. During the British mandate/occupation during World War One, King (Sheikh) Mahmood Barzanji (1878-1956) resisted British rule from this area. The rebellion lasted until Mahmood was wounded in combat, which happened between Kirkuk and Sulaymani where the British captured him. Though he was sentenced to death he was instead exiled and imprisoned in a British fort in India, where he remained until 1922.

The District Commissioner of Koya, in Erbil Governorate, renovated the ruins of Chwar Taqan in 2002. They include four great water jars (chwar taqan), which were used by the caravan travelers and their mules.

Haibat Sultan

Pressed up on a jagged hill adjacent to a vast valley, surrounded by the Bawaji and Haibat mountains, the town is another hidden gem within the Kurdistan Region.

In 2013, the *Journal of Environment and Earth Science* published an academic article written by two professors at the University of Baghdad about the environment around Haibat Sultan and there has been a concerted effort to study this fascinating Kurdistan Region in earnest. Due to continual war and poor infrastructure, it was not feasible for such studies to be implemented under the rule of Saddam. However, with the downfall of the previous regime, scientific study of the Kurdistan Region has been able to increase manifold and will foreseeably continue to do so. The scientific journal Aro, from Koya University also produced an article in 2014 regarding geological issues in Haibat Sultan.

Located off of Danielle Mitterrand Boulevard, named after the famous French politician and former first lady who was known to be sympathetic to the plight of the Kurds, Haibat Sultan is a lovely place to sit and relax high up on the hill overlooking the small city of Koya.

Below Haibat Sultan Park is a popular destination for picnics, weddings, and sim-

ply enjoying a day out with your friends. This park is named after the nearby Shrine of Haibat Sultan, located in a mountain, which 1,260 m (4134 ft.) in altitude.

Haibat Sultan Park

From the park one looks directly down at Koya University. The park is a popular destination for picnics, weddings or for enjoying a day out with friends. This park is named after the nearby Shrine of Haibat Sultan and is located on a mountain 1,260 m (4134 ft.) high and only 3 km (2 mi) northeast of Koya.

Hamamok Recreation Grounds

Hamamok is a valley that serves as the main drinking water spring for Koya and the surrounding villages. In recent years the KRG built a dam here as well. Hamamok is only 2 km (1.2 mi) northwest from Koya and sits 650 m (2,133 ft.) above sea level.

Many different types of events and ceremonies are organized here on the grounds of the Hamamok Recreation Grounds.

There are many events organized in the park during official holidays and visitors often stroll around the spring or relax and picnic by the water.

Koya Bazaar (Qeysariya)

This bazaar is one of the oldest open markets in the region, with shops and stands selling a wide variety of local products. It is located in the center of the city. The market in Koya has largely been left in its natural state. For example, many doors and gateways date back to the 13th century. There are local artisans working in beautiful yet dilapidated buildings hand-making various items—many of which make wonderful souvenirs from this historic area.

Sari Kosar

Sari Kosar (Sari Kusar) is a tourist resort that offers visitors the opportunity to enjoy several freshwater springs and small waterfalls along with excellent fresh air in an open, green space on top of the famous Haibat Sultan Mountain. The resort lies only 4 km (2.5 mi) northeast of the ancient city of Koya, and 74 km (46 mi) from Erbil.

The project of the resort was completed in 2009 as the KRG added tourist attractions

to the Koya area. The resort or complex is built on an area of 10,000 dunams (2,471 acres) of land; the complex includes over twenty homes, two parks, gardens, a restaurant, and amusement park.

The resort is open to the public and rests on Haibat Sultan Mountain, a popular destination for many locals to picnic and enjoy scenic views of Koya. Many even hold weddings on top of Haibat Sultan and nearby Bawji Mountain. If a foreigner is lucky and happens onto one of these happy occasions, it is not unusual to be asked to join the festivities.

The resort overlooks the city and the surrounding area, and is a beautiful getaway next to natural beauty and stunning mountains.

Shrine Of Marbina Qadisha (Marbina Behnam)

Located northeast of the Armota village, 3 km (1.8 mi) from Koya is the large and imposing shrine of Marbina Qadisha, alternatively known as 'Marbina Behnam'. Some believe Mar Behnam (a revered King) and his sister Sara built this shrine. Monks from Mosul who were driven away apparently took refuge in the shrine during the Mongolian invasion of the city in the 13th century. It is a very popular pilgrimage site for local Christians.

Mar Behnam was born in the 4th century AD to Senarib, the Zoroastrian Assyrian King of Adiabene (Hadyab), which had its capital in modern day Erbil. During a hunting trip, he came across Mar Mattai and convinced of his theology, became a devout Christian and devotee of Mar Mattai. He brought his sister Sara, then suffering from leprosy who was reportedly miraculously healed and they were both baptized along with forty of Behnam's men. Upon learning of his children's conversion, king Senarib reportedly killed his children and their forty companions on a hill in Nimrud. However, the king soon after regretted his deed and was later reportedly baptized himself by Mar Mattai. He also built a monastery on the mount were Mar Mattai healed his daughter.

Jewish Quarter

Two centuries later, in the 500s it is recorded that a Persian Christian merchant built a shrine on the hill where Mar Behnam died, which became a very large monastery overseen by Jacobites (Syriac Orthodox) until 1839 when it became the possession of Syriac Catholics. Traditionally, priests administer the monastery from the small Christian town of Bakhdida (Qaraqosh), one of the largest Christian towns in Mosul (Nineveh governorate). Syriac Orthodox and Syriac Catholic churches honor both Mar (St.) Behnam and Sara every December 10 by. Mar Behnam is not only considered a saint but one of the early Christian martyrs by both the Assyrian and Chaldean Churches of the East.

Church records state that the monastery (and the Church) suffered greatly under the rule of Nader Shah (1743-1790), who was the Emperor of Persia at the time. Seeking alliances and assistance, monks established contacts with Rome in the 18th century, which brought about gradual conversion to the Syriac Catholic Church. It is also recorded that monks abandoned the monastery in 1819 though it is unclear why

although there is evidence it was the result of severe persecution. In the modern era, the monastery was renovated in 1986.

The shrine is a very popular pilgrimage site and is visited each year by thousands. Upon arriving, this vast flat area near the village appears like an amphitheater/church complete with renovated amphitheater style seating that includes the ancient church, a newer built chapel, and a statue of Sara. The church itself was originally built in the 4th century on a hill northwest of Koya.

The backside of the church has foursquare symbols of the Gospels:
• Symbol for Matthew's Gospel: Angel or Divine Being
• Symbol for Luke's Gospel: The ox
• Symbol for Mark's Gospel: The lion
• Symbol for John's Gospel: The eagle

The monastery contains many sculptures left from renovations that took place in 1164 and between 1250-1261. It is a fascinating place for all interested in the religious and revered sites for which Kurdistan is renowned.

Shrine of Marbina Qadisha

RAWANDUZ

GENERAL INFORMATION / HISTORY

Rawanduz In Winter

An hour and forty-five minutes (116 km; 72 mi) northeast of Erbil and an hour northeast of Shaqlawa (69 km; 43 mi) Rawanduz is perhaps one of the most famous general areas in the Kurdistan Region. Surrounded by majestic and ruggedly beautiful mountains and glistening waterfalls, Rawanduz holds the deepest gorge (Kharand Canyon or Gorge) in the entire Middle East; sometimes called the Kurdish Grand Canyon. Moreover, many of the Region's most popular tourist spots and resorts are near or around Rawanduz (Geli Ali Beg, Bekhal, Korek Mountain and Resort, and Pank Resort).

The area is also spelled as Rwanduz, Rawandiz, or other variants. Located in Soran district of Erbil Governorate the name derives from *Rawend diz* (Rawends Castle). Interestingly, Rawend was written as "Orontes" in ancient Greek and Roman sources, which is also the current name of a river in Syria lending credence to the notion of a widespread and ancient knowledge of the area and its history.

Rawanduz was known as the long-time capital of the Soran Emirate (1399 to 1835 AD). Like most other sizable towns in the Kurdistan Region, Rawanduz had a small Jewish population (until 1952) as well as several Christian villages, many of which are still in existence.

The town of Rawanduz sits on a mountain 1,005 m (3,297 ft.) high and thousands of visitors tour Rawanduz and its surrounding areas every year. It is a sleepy, calm town steeped in thousands of years of history. In 2013, an Italian NGO visited the Region with the expressed aim of creating a national park in and around Rawanduz. There are also several ongoing archeological excavations in this area as well.

Rawanduz Boasts the Deepest Gorge In The Middle East

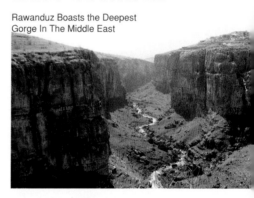

In the early 1920s the British occupied the environs of Rawanduz and it was during this time that the famous "Hamilton Road" was built (1928-1932) which started from Shaklawa near Erbil, snaking its way to Rawanduz and on to Haji Omran near the Iranian border. Hamilton stated that it was traditionally known as "a place of grim deeds and bloody retributions. It's greater and lesser rulers alike have nearly all met with violent deaths and even today this reputation is being well earned". However, today it is known as a peaceful and beautiful area for tourism and nature and the tribal and political issues are long forgotten. You

will not find a more colorful people in Kurdistan – proud and ever ready to rise to a challenge yet friendly and every ready to host a guest.

HIGHLIGHTS

Ali Begg Valley / Gali Ali Beg

An hour and forty-five minutes (116 km; 72 mi) northeast of Erbil and an hour northeast of Shaqlawa (69 km; 43 mi) this is the most popular waterfall in the Kurdistan Region, it is even featured on the 5,000 IQD note. It is west of Rawanduz between the towns of Khalifan and Soran and is fed by the Rawanduz River. It is a wonderful area for families and tourists to gather and enjoy the splendor of this tall and powerful waterfall in this majestic and entrancing valley.

The valley or canyon is 12 km (7.5 mi) long. The waterfall at Geli Ali Beg, 30 m (100 ft.), is in the middle of the canyon and flows nonstop year-around. After the falls, the water continues to flow along the valley slope to the North East, where it joins another watercourse and both go on together through a gap crossing the middle of the rocky valley. This valley is couched between Korek and Bradost mountains. There are many beautiful springs and smaller waterfalls leading to the Gali Ali Beg waterfall.

Visitors may also rent inflatable boats alongside the small pond created by the waterfall. There are many souvenir stands as well as picnic areas and during the summer months the area is absolutely packed and filled to the brim with tourists. There are even freshwater crabs hiding in the shade, perhaps food for the numerous birds that live along the mountains and canyon.

Adventurous tourists and visitors are able to climb over the tall waterfall and walk around on the mountain behind it, as there are walkways on either side of

Gali Ali Beg

the falls. Get wet if you wish —highly recommended in the summer! Though there is no public transportation available from Erbil, a shared taxi costs a mere 15,000 IQD or so ($10).

Barsrin Village

Located on the famed Hamilton Road the area is one of the most scenic in Kurdistan. A.M. Hamilton wrote of the area in his book "The Road through Kurdistan" as a place of great beauty. It is located approximately 30 kilometers (18 mi) or 30 minutes from Rawanduz. When traveling on the road to Sulaymani or Choman it is worth the time to stop as many do for picnics or merely to enjoy the incredible nature.

Barsrin Village

Bekhal Falls

duz or from Geli Ali Beg. Bekhal (Bexal) is a cluster of small waterfalls that originates from Kharand Mountain or Canyon.

The fall was once part of an irrigation system dating to the 700s BC. Fresh spring water flows into a beautiful rock formation and visitors are able to climb the rocks to the waterfalls leading to the spring. Towering over the waterfalls is a dam that was built by a South Korean company in recent years.

Bekhal Summer Resort

A ten-minute drive from Rawanduz (9 km; 5.6 mi), and 135 km (84 mi) or roughly two hours from Erbil, this beautiful and striking area in the Rawanduz area can be reached through either of two ways: from Rawan-

At first glance, the resort seems literally on top of the small rustic market below, which also functions as an area for visitors to eat at several different restaurants. Visitors step down a few steps into the market and it becomes immediately a few degrees cooler, which is great in the summer months. There are small shops selling clothes, food, toys, or other miscellaneous souvenirs as you walk through to the other side. One needs to be somewhat careful on the steps as the spring is literally underneath your feet and the walkway may be slippery. There are also stairs leading to the fresh water spring. As you sit down for tea, nargilah (a

water pipe), or a meal you can see the spring rushing all around you. The magnificently sculpted mountains and their ridges, multiple streams and beautiful canyons attract thousands of visitors every spring and summer. Many families come here on the weekends and some stop by on their way to/from somewhere else to relax for an hour or so. The workers in the shops are extremely friendly.

Cannon Of Wasta Rajab

Visitors can climb on the waterfall but should use extreme caution since the path is slippery and the water flows quite steadily. However, it is also worth the endeavor since it offers a beautiful view of the region's landscape. This is a very fun area and child friendly. During the summer months tens of thousands of Arabs from South Iraq visit the falls to escape the heat. They also marvel at the friendly atmosphere

and freedom Kurds enjoy in their delightful democratic society made all the more appealing for its sheer beauty.

Cannon of Wasta Rajab

On top of a hill in Soran is the cannon of Wasta Rajab, named for the Kurdish man sent to France by Prince Muhammed, of Soran (1813-1837) with the expressed purpose of learning the skill of weapon making (including cannons).

During the reign of Mir Muhammad (The Great Pasha) also known as the Blind Mir who ruled the Soran Emirate at the time, a weapons factory was established in the town of Rawanduz to manufacture weapons and ammunitions. It was under the supervision of Wasta Rajab. The cannon on display at the top of the hill is the largest one ever produced, at 1.5 m (5 ft.) created in 1823. Overall the factory produced 222 cannons and there were three different sizes made. Several of them are currently on display in the Baghdad museum. There is illegible engraving on the cannon, which is noticed upon close inspection—the meaning of which remains a mystery.

When he reached middle

age, Mir Muhammad gained control of the Soran Emirate and eliminated his real and or imagined enemies, taking control over much of what is today called the Kurdistan Region of Iraq. He was known to particularly target minorities, and was brutal against Christian, Yezidi, and Jewish communities. He is also credited with implementing some semblance of law and order and tried to use this "stability" as a political bargaining chip with the Ottoman Empire. Though his was one of the most powerful and successful of the Kurdish emirates his prowess threatened Istanbul, as it was the impetus for instability in the Kurdish areas of what is today modern Turkey. As a result there were many plots to eliminate him.

One of the key actors in the downfall of these Kurdish emirates (such as Mir Muhammad's) was the seemingly eternal internal tribal conflict. This allowed the emirates and tribes to be played against one another and was used by the Ottoman's to maintain or reassert control. Internecine struggles have prevented the Kurds on many occasions—even recently—from attaining their full potential and realization of the dream of statehood. Historically when the Kurds have united (as they did under the Median Empire) they have ruled vast areas of land. Today they are united once again and the region is prospering accordingly.

This site is a nice stopping point and side trip in that area. The new steps and surrounding area are well maintained. Today many people climb the few steps up the hill to be photographed with this most famous of cannons. From the peak the view is breathtaking and the spot is a must for any serious photographic expedition in Kurdistan. Also anyone interested in Kurdish history and folklore should visit this site and the surrounding region as it has long been the center of the ascension and decline of

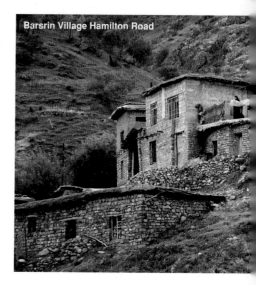

Barsrin Village Hamilton Road

great Kurdish leaders.

Gali Akoyan

From Erbil it is 116 km (72 mi) or almost two hours and is at an altitude of 980 m (3,215 ft.). Gali Akoyan is roughly 11 km (7 miles) east of Rawanduz and is a recreation ground dense with many varieties of trees: walnuts, pears, plums, as well as others.

Visitors can traverse several hiking trails, or enjoy a relaxing shady picnic while taking in the surrounding jagged and rugged mountains seemingly defending the stream. You can also obtain the many fruits and nuts available at very reasonable prices from locals.

Great Pasha Hill

The Great Pasha Hill or Fortress is located on the main road between Soran and Rawanduz, a 15-20 minute drive, and near the Rawanduz River. The Fortress, though mostly in ruins, was built from stone and

gypsum over a natural yet seemingly man-made hill during the rule of Prince Muhammad (Mahmood), otherwise known as the Prince of Soran (1813-1837). He was also known as the Great Pasha.

The fortress originally held four large circular towers but as of present hardly anything remains except the foundation and one wall. However the surrounding area is beautiful and many come to enjoy the scenery in the midst of a historic site.

Hamilton Road

The Hamilton Road was named for its chief architect, Archibald Milne Hamilton (1898–1972). Hamilton was a New Zealand-born civil engineer who was also the inventor of a bridge system without which this most amazing feat could not have been accomplished at the time. During the construction of the road, Hamilton became aware of the need for strong, adaptable bridges with components that could easily be transported and erected in remote and/or difficult terrain. Using a device called "Callender Cables", he spanned gorges that lesser men would have deemed impossible with the technology of the day. The system was called the Callender-Hamilton bridge system (Callender was the engineering company owned by Hamilton).

The strategic road he built was constructed between 1928 and 1932 and was at the time deemed an impossible task for many reasons. So impossible a task that some deduced Hamilton—who sometimes irritated his superiors—had been given the task for that very reason; it was impossible. But the word did not exist in Hamilton's vocabulary and he overcame every obstacle in his path and linked one ancient civilization to another opening the way for trade with Iran.

Hamilton Road

When complete the road ran from Shaqlawa outside of Erbil, through Rawanduz, to the Iranian border near Haji Omran and soon became known as the Hamilton Road. Although Hamilton hoped the road would unite the peoples of the region, it has been fought over many times due to its military strategic and economic importance. He described the building of the road in a 1937 book entitled *Road through Kurdistan.*

While the technical difficulties were enormous, Hamilton faced even greater obstacles—namely the violent tribes along the way that opposed the construction of a road they felt would end their way of life as they knew it with the influx of foreign traders. Hamilton was not only a genius from a technical standpoint but an incredible diplomat who won the hearts of the tribesmen from one end of the road to the other. At great risk, he would sometimes camp alone near antagonistic tribes to show he was a friend and not an enemy. He cajoled the headsmen and displayed incredible bravery, which won the respect of men who lived their entire lives facing adverse elements and warring neighbors. Hamilton over the years became one of them in many respects —"going native" as the British often referred to it. He also turned a ragtag band of imported Indian and local laborers into a crack engineering crew. Often the tribal leaders would sit on overlooking mountains watching this strange man dynamite a pathway across the face of a sheer mountain sure he would fail only to find at the end of the day he had come one step closer to his goal. For this they admired him and many in the end pitched in and together created the greatest engineering feat of the century.

For more information on this fascinating story see *Road Through Kurdistan: Travels in Northern Iraq* (2004), A.M. Hamilton.

Jundyan Resort

Jundyan Resort (Jundyan River)

From Rawanduz it is a short journey on the main road from Soran to Choman. Located at the base of Handren Mountain 115 km (72 mi) from Erbil and just south of the windy Rawanduz River. Jundyan is often romanticized as a "magical" spring since its water dries up for most of the year, only reappearing every spring.

Jundyan Resort is also known for its lush vegetation, as there are many trees that have been replanted over the past several years. The favorable climate during the height of the summer further attracts many tourists and there are facilities such as restaurants and shops selling beverages and snacks.

Many stop here and picnic or simply enjoy being out in nature. The valley is packed

with tourists during the spring and summer, as many go to nearby Bekhal waterfalls and/or Gali Ali Beg. During the spring the water roars along but during many other months it is as dry as the plains of Erbil itself.

Korek Mt. Resort

The more than $95 million dollar resort brings Switzerland to mind and this was the intent of the developer, Sheikh Sirwan Barzani. Korek Mountain itself is 2,120 meters (nearly 7000 ft.) at its peak, while the resort stands at around 1,800 meters (5900 ft.). A rough and rocky dirt road is one way up, but a new cable car (teleferic) offers a smoother ride. The road can only be used by permission and is normally reserved only for maintenance purposes or if heavy snows preclude the use of the teleferic. The glass cars travel 1,000 meters (3280 ft.) in a matter of minutes and as the trees and buildings beneath begin to blur, an enormous panorama unfolds, revealing a stunning view out across the fields and the rolling mountains.

While there is not snow year around the mountain gets as much as 2 meters (6.2 ft.) in the winter months and there are snow machines to fill in the gaps when the weather does not provide snow naturally. So far Korek offers two small ski slopes, one for novice skiers, one for people who can ski at an intermediate level and there are plans to build more advanced slopes for more seasoned skiers.

The now-famous cable car (teleferic) that takes visitors to the top of the mountain is reportedly one of the five longest in the world and was built by an Austrian company. Visitors can ski or participate in other winter sports, or stroll around the premise of the resort that sits atop the mountain. It is a modern complex comprised of over 75 luxury two-story chalets; restaurants and playgrounds for children. One can rent snowmobiles or take daring rides on hang gliders. A must see for any visitor to Kurdistan!

For more information on Rawanduz
Iraq and Rupert Hay's Two Years in Kurdistan (2008), Paul J. Rich

A Modern History of the Kurds: Third Edition (2004), David McDowall

Korek Resort

SHAQLAWA

GENERAL INFORMATION / HISTORY

Shaqlawa a small settlement of 25,000 people is a traditionally Assyrian and Chaldean Christian-majority mountain town that has recently become a popular day-trip destination for locals and tourists alike. Today it also has a large population of Muslims and the two faiths have lived in harmony for centuries. The town is nestled between two mountains, Safeen (2,000 m or 6562 ft.) and Sork, and is roughly 50 km (30 mi) northeast of Erbil and 65 km (40 mi) southeast of Soran. Presently, most of the inhabitants are Kurds, though there are also many Iraqi Christians from other parts of the country who have moved to escape Islamic extremists. From Erbil one can take the bus or private taxi for a nominal charge.

HIGHLIGHTS

During the summer, many tourists travel to Shaqlawa to escape the heat of Erbil, and for a change in scenery, which is replete with a panorama of mountains and small creeks where many picnic on weekends and holidays. It is also a popular activity to eat *mazgouf*, fish slow-grilled over charcoal, and also to shop at the bazaar where one can purchase famous Shaqlawa pomegranates and walnuts and other delicious and unique produce and famous desserts. There are also large vineyards dotting the landscape and the climate is excellent for growing wine grapes. The locals produce a syrupy wine that is not usually appealing to foreigners but there has been discussion about developing the industry and certainly the climate would be conducive. It is very similar to the climes of the wine growing regions of Northern California. There are many hotels and restaurants throughout

Valley below Safeen Mountain

the town as well as a scenic hiking trail.

Tourists increase after 3:00 PM on the weekends and by dusk the area is almost entirely full. Many tourists choose to mere-

ly walk through the safe and peaceful roads shopping, people-watching and eating.

Shera Swar

Shera Swar Recreation Ground

Less than ten minuets (7 km; 4 mi) southwest of Shaqlawa this open, expanse is now an area primarily used for recreational purposes such as picnics and celebrations. Shera Swar is located on the main road between the Erbil suburb of Salah Al-Din and Shaqlawa, 42 km (26 mi) north of Erbil, roughly a forty-five minute to hour drive.

Shrine Of Raban Boya

The name refers to Shera Swar who was a fighter who participated in the battle of Jerusalem during the Crusades. He was a soldier under Salah Al-Din Ayoubi (Saladin) during the Muslim victory. Salah Al-Din conferred on the soldier the title "Shera Swar," (Intrepid Knight). After the battles in Jerusalem, Shera Swar returned to Kurdistan, settling in this area.

There is also a nearby cave named Shera Swar on Safin Mt. next to Shaqlawa and close to the recreation ground. In 2009 two previously unknown species of cave-dwelling geckos were discovered in the cave.

Shrine of Raban Boya (Sheikh Wso Rahman)

Above the tourist town of Shaqlawa nestled in a mountain overlooking the Valley of Safeen Mountain is the ancient Christian monastery of Rabban Boya (Buya, or Beya). There is also a church named after Rabban Boya.

Rabban Boya is a monastery, which is found in a small cave roughly halfway up the mountain. Visitors have to climb up a gravel path as well as some steps right near the monastery in order to reach the cave. It dates back to the fourth century and is still used as a pilgrimage site by Christians and a smaller number of Muslims as well, who refer to the place as Sheik Wso Rahman. The hike itself is short and should take less than an hour. In the nicer months, it is a very popular hike and the trail is packed with young and old, especially on the weekends and holidays.

A small shrine filled with years of accumulated candle wax remains hidden in

Shaqlawa in winter

a crevice of the cave. Inside the shrine, a large stone is revered as a "Wishing Rock." Many locals swear by the power of this stone and it is one of the major reasons for the crowds apart from the stunning view. It is said that if a woman slides down this rock on her belly, head first, she will soon

Pilgrims Pray For A Miracle

after become pregnant. Although it is primarily considered a Christian Shrine many Muslims also visit it and have faith in its healing powers. This is also a testimony to the fact that Shaqlawa, which today is roughly split between Muslims and Christians at present, have lived in harmony for centuries.

There are a couple of other shrines tucked away into the hills further away but not as frequently visited. The people who come on pilgrimage mostly ask for children though others visit for a plethora of other reasons as well. Historically there were Chaldean Christian Monks living in the Cave of Rabban Boya but it has long since been quiet. Off days are most enjoyable to hike the trail because it is less crowded and visitors can leisurely visit the monastery or other caves. Surrounded on three sides by the mountain walls, it offers a great place to sit and relax, picnic, and marvel at the fact that this area has been similarly used since the 4th century.

SORAN
(Erbil Governorate)

GENERAL INFORMATION / HISTORY

Soran is both a town and a district. It is 65 km (40 mi) northeast of Shaqlawa, and 110 km (64 mi) from Erbil. The outskirts of Soran are considered particularly attractive due to the rivers that cross the area especially the Rawanduz River, which flows around the town. Many people picnic

by these rivers especially on Friday and Saturday. There are several major mountains in this area, namely Hendrin, Zozik, Hassen Bak, Bradost, and Korek.

Kurdish settlement in the region pre-dates the establishment of the Sassanid Empire. Persian Emperor Ardashir I mentioned this area during his battle against the Medean King Madig.

The major Kurdish dialects; Sorani and Bahdini are spoken in the Soran area and due to its proximity with Iran; Persian is widely spoken as well. This is also due to the fact that many inhabitants of the town are returnees from Iran, and a large number of them were born and raised in Iran. The returnees fled to Iran between 1974 and 1989. Over the last 15 to 20 years the population of Soran district grew to around 125,000. Most of these returnees settled in and around Soran, unable to return to their villages that had been destroyed by Saddam's army during the Anfal campaigns of the late 1980's.

HIGHLIGHTS

Diyana

Next to Soran is the Christian village of Diyana. Assyrian Christians initially founded the city and the name is rooted in the old Kurdish word for Christian. However, it has tradition-

Soran

Kani Maran

lage. In 2009 there were reports that Kani Maran partially collapsed, but as of 2014 it has been revitalized and open to tourists. Kani Maran was the location of a now famous meeting between Mullah Mustafa Barzani and an Iraqi leader, Fuad Aref. On March 4th, 1963, Barzani handed Aref a list of claims in which the Kurds negotiated for self-rule over Sulaymani, Kirkuk, Erbil, Mosul and Diyala Governorates and also sought to share oil income among Arabs and Kurds. There is also a mention of the village of Kani Maran in Rupert Hay's famous travels to Iraq and Kurdistan *Iraq and Rupert Hay's Two Years in Kurdistan* (2008).

Soran University

In an attempt to bolster its image, the Kurdistan Region established Soran University, which has attracted many students and educators from across the Kurdistan Region and has established close relationships with universities in the United Kingdom in particular.

Soran University: Kawa St., Soran, Iraq
http://www.soran.edu.iq/
+964 66 350 6666

ally been ruled by Kurdish Aghas. Diyana is located on the famous Hamilton Road, which connects Erbil to Iran through Haji Omran. Assyrians Christians of Hawdiyaan and Diyana villages speak Syriac along with Kurdish and Arabic and have their own Syriac language schools.

Gulan Park

The park is three km from the center of town and is family friendly, offering various rides for children and families. The park is visited by many tourists and is also popular for its beautiful scenic views.

Kani Maran

Kani Maran is located west of Soran. Kani Maran is derived from the scarce waters in the area "barely enough to quench the thirst of snakes" and thus translated to "snake springs." As of 2013 there were over 250 families living in Kani Maran vil-

BARZAN
(City and Region)

GENERAL INFORMATION / HISTORY

Barzan is 152 km (94 mi) or two hours north of Erbil. Barzan is (46 km) (29 mi) or 45 minutes west of Mergasor (Mergasur), 64 km (40 mi) or roughly one hour east of Amediye. The town of Barzan is located along the Great

Zab in Erbil Governorate. It is well known as the birthplace of Sheikh Ahmed Barzani and Kurdish leader Mustafa Barzani.

Although the Barzani family reportedly originated from the nearby Amediye region, Barzan is considered the ancestral home of the Barzani tribe. The current President of the Kurdistan Regional Government Masoud Barzani is also considered the leader of the tribe and is an avid conservationist and hunting in the area is strictly prohibited. Although there is no current "legal" status signifying Barzan as a nature reserve

Road to Barzan

it is, in reality, the first such preserve established in The Kurdistan Region of Iraq.

Grave of Mullah Mustapha Barzani and son Idris.

HIGHLIGHTS

The region is renowned for its sheer beauty and bountiful wildlife boasting many genus not found elsewhere in Kurdistan although at one time in the past there were plentiful species throughout the region. Unbridled hunting has depleted and in some cases completely exterminated much of the wildlife

of Kurdistan. Uncontrolled deforestation and war has ravaged the natural habitat of many animals and left the countryside barren in many other places. However in Barzan one can find the delightful results of President Barzani's efforts of conservation with many areas reclaiming their previous stature among the world's magnificent places of breathtaking beauty and abundance of wildlife. Hiking in these mountains is a favorite pastime of locals who travel from all parts of

Breathtaking scenery

Wild Animal Refuge and Nature Reserve

the region and indeed from other parts of Iraq and even the rest of the Middle East to enjoy trekking in the region. It is advised that one have a local guide when hiking, as there has been mining of the region in the past although most areas have been cleared.

Ketin Horse Club – See article on the "Horses of Kurdistan"

The Medes from whom the Kurds are descended were renowned for their horsemanship. According to Merhdad Izady, former Professor of Near Eastern History at Harvard University, in *The Kurds: A Concise Handbook*, the Kurds were the first to engage in animal husbandry including the domestication of horses. One of the oldest archaeological evidence of horses in the Middle East were found in the region dating back 4,500 years to this—the cradle of civilization. Many maintain the indigenous stock, which is very similar to the so called "Arabian" horse of renown actu-

ally originated and spread from Kurdistan throughout the world during wars and via trade. The horses of Kurdistan were popular as a source to improve other breeds, as they were swift, had great endurance, and

Descendant of
Mullah Mustapha's Horse

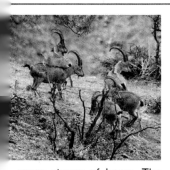

were strong of bone. The Kurds have long lamented that through the many centuries of war and upheaval horses of any breed became a rare sight in Kurdistan. See the fascinating article by the founder of the *Ketin Horse Club* (Karwan Barzani) who along with another prominent Barzani (Sheikh Sirwan Barzani) is seeking to restore the presence and prominence of equestrianism in Kurdistan.

If you are in Barzan drop by and enjoy what is—if nothing else—one of the most beautiful regions and nature preserves in the world.

Bestoon Prehistoric Cave

BESTOON CAVE

GENERAL INFORMATION / HISTORY

Discovered' in 1951, Bestoon is a thin rectangular shaped cavern north of Soran in the Barzan region. It dates to the prehistoric, Stone Age, and Neanderthal eras. Evidence of Neanderthals were found here along with countless shards of ancient pottery—much of which still lies openly in the cavern floor. There has, as of yet, been little official excavation and research, either locally or by internationally supported efforts and the cave though far more dramatic in appearance than the better-known Shanidar Cave, is seldom visited by International tourists.

From Erbil Bestoon is northeast by roughly 100 km (62 mi). Located on Bradost Mountain north of the Rawanduz River. This stunning cavern extends nearly 500 m (1,640 ft.) underground though according to local legend, the cavern is endless!

To access this site, one must drive either on the road through Spilik Mountain towards Khallan village

Stalagmites and Stalactites

and Banwe Valley or from Gali Ali Bag by the westbound road between Hawdean village and Sardaw village as you ascend in altitude toward Bradost Mountain.

HIGHLIGHTS

Bestoon is most famous for its exquisite and numerous examples of stalactites and stalagmites. Along with these ancient stones, there are "newer ones" made from frozen ice, though this is more so the case in colder months. Inside the cave visitors can stand up straight with great ease since the ceiling is cathedral like in many places.

In the past there was frequent looting of the cave with people from larger cities carrying away the stalactites and stalagmites to serve as décor in their houses. As a result one of the prominent members of the Barzan tribe took control of the cave and it is now guarded around the clock. Permission to enter must be obtained at the steps leading to the cave. There are plans

for a nearby guesthouse/cafe and improvements that will make it easier for the site to be visited, while preserving its integrity.

If you do visit be sure to bring a warm jacket regardless of the time of year, as it is quite chilly in the lower reaches of the cave. Powerful flashlights are required to descend as one quickly finds they are plunged into complete darkness when only a few meters inside the cave. Do not pick up shards of pottery for souvenirs, as this is illegal as is the export of all antiquities from Kurdistan.

Dwelling for prehistoric man

Jelly River

JELLY RIVER
(Jelly Wells)

GENERAL INFORMATION / HISTORY

Between Shaqlawa and Koya rests a very famous spot where many locals believe they can be healed from their various diseases by the natural waters that exist in this area. 95 km (60 mi) or an hour northeast of Erbil and 22 km (14 mi) northwest of Koya, the surrounding area has an altitude of 600 m (1,968 ft.). The water flows through the Smaquli valley, a beautiful region rich with many orchards and varieties of trees. Next to a trail off the Jelly River, is an adjacent natural hot mineral pond that attracts those seeking to be cured from their ailments. Shallow and clear blue, people have been flocking to this area for centuries hoping to rid themselves of pain and infirmaties.

There are currently three different roads from Erbil that reach Jelly River:

1) Erbil to Gomaspan junction to Smaquli valley-Jelly wells (62 km; 39 mi)
2) Erbil–Koya–Jelly wells (87 km; 54 mi)
3) Erbil–Heran–Nazaneen–Jelly wells (88 km; 55 mi)

HIGHLIGHTS

There are two pools: one is smaller (2 sq. m. – 21 sq. ft.) and has not been made into an attraction. It is surrounded by grass and largely inaccessible. The other is much larger (6 sq. meters- 64 sq. ft.) and surrounded by concrete steps and a paved walkway leading down to the circular pool. It is reported that both maintain temperature of 38 Celsius (100 Fahrenheit).

In his book, *Two years in Kurdistan: Experiences of a Political Officer, 1918-1920* Rupert Hay describes the area, "Here, too, were extensive fruit gardens with plantations... the pomegranates of Nazanin are supposed to be the best in Kurdistan. We now descended to the sulfurous stream of Jali, which has its source in a long and intricate cave in the hills above. By the side of it was a warm spring full of fishes; its water left a blue-grey deposit and had a strong chemical smell. The Kurds bathe here to cure skin complaints."

MERGASOR
(City and District)

GENERAL INFORMATION / HISTORY

Mergasor is 64 km (40 mi) or roughly one hour east of Amediye; and lies 32 minutes northwest of Soran, or 35 km (22 mi). Mergasor district encompasses Barzan, as well as an additional 252 villages and several small towns. While over 170 villages were rebuilt after the Anfal campaigns, 80 villages are still currently uninhabited.

Fakhir Mergasori was a famous Kurdish leader who was well known to have participated in the Kurdish struggle. He was born in 1933 in Mergesor. In the late1950's he became politically active and in the 1960s he became a central committee member of the Kurdistan Democratic Party (KDP), led by Mustafa Barzani. He was well liked and brave. In 1970 he was given charge of the KDP in Sulaymani Governorate but political rivals killed him in 1975. To honor his memory there are several schools named after him throughout the Kurdistan Region. Additionally, there is a non-profit foundation named after him based in Sweden, which seeks to support positive and modern development in education in the Kurdistan Region and provides financial support to pupils, staff and schools.

Before 1917, there was a sizable Assyrian Christian presence in the area as well as two Chaldean Catholic churches. There were also a small number of Jews in the area, and despite the fact they had generally good relations with tribal leaders, they left Iraq for Israel from 1950-1952 after threats from Baghdad.

HIGHLIGHTS

There are many natural areas here. The zone surrounding Mergasor is famous for its forests as well as its many crops, orchards, vineyards and fruit.

Though the region may focus a lot on political tourism and Anfal-related themes; the natural surroundings are unparalleled almost anywhere in the rest of the Kurdistan Region and equal to most in the world. It is a "must-see" for anyone remotely interested in ancient and modern Kurdistan as well as its wildlife and nature.

Ble

As one passes through Shanindar, you will come to the sleepy town of Ble, part of the Ble-Barzan area. In between these two locations, there is a long stretch of green space that has been made into public parks where people can take nature walks, picnic and enjoy the beautiful scenery.

Maidanok (Darsatan-i-Maydanok or Meydanok)

Maidanok forest is between Mergasor and Soran. The Maidanok forest is a very large forest with many spe-

cies of trees. The nature here is unaffected by pollution and the modern age and cutting trees for firewood and hunting are prohibited. Locals have reported sighting of brown bears and other mammals such as deer.

Martyrs Cemetery

Outside the city limits, on a hill is where the Barzani Martyrs Cemetery rests. In the 1980s Saddam Hussein killed over 8,000 Barzanis — simply because of their name. It was for this crime that Saddam was ultimately charged with genocide. He was hanged for crimes against humanity before he could stand trial in Kurdistan for the very different crime of genocide. To prove genocide is far more difficult than war crimes or crimes against humanity as it must be shown that the perpetrator sought to "deliberately and systemat-

ically exterminate an entire national, racial, political or cultural group." This was most assuredly the case in Barzan and there was ample evidence to convict him. The Kurds protested vehemently that Saddam was not kept alive long enough

Maidanok

to stand trial in Kurdistan and feel to this day that justice was never truly served and the crimes fully aired. One of the relevant documents captured during the First Gulf War when Saddam's secret police fled before the Coalition Forces contained a message from Saddam to his henchman in Kurdistan who deservedly earned the title "Chemical" Ali Hassan al Majid. It was an order for Al Majid to enter Barzan and "Kill every man, woman, child, plant, beast and living thing." Al Majid sought to do exactly that, murdering every male between the ages of seven and seventy, gassing villages, poisoning wells, and defoliating the countryside. Al Majid was later hanged for the crime.

The memories of Saddam's victims are memorialized in the beautiful yet simple cemetery. The main attraction in Barzan itself is the gravesite of the father of modern Kurdish revolutionary ideology: Mullah Mustafa Barzani. Revered as a great leader and warrior fighting against oppression, Barzani was known to be a modest and humble man, and died in Washington, DC in 1979. Visiting his grave his modesty is apparent, for the site is simple and austere. Buried next to his son, Idris, visitors are encouraged to visit year round, though the two main occasions people come to pay respect are his birthday and anniversary of his passing: March 14 and March 1, respectively. Visitors are generally offered complimentary tea and if you arrive before lunch, there is a good chance you'll be invited in to the dining room, across from the graves of Barzani and his other relatives. Currently there is a planned museum that is being constructed across a sprawling campus adjacent to the graves site though the date of completion is unknown. This graveyard is visited by hundreds of thousands of people annually from different parts of Iraq as well from foreign countries. Many officials and

delegations visit the site and pay homage to the great leader of Kurdistan.

Mergasor - Rezan Summer Resort

The resort area, located within the town of Rezan, lies 22 km (14 mi) southeast of Barzan. It offers a wonderful climate and fresh springs for people to visit during the hot summer months and visitors can picnic alongside the river and take in the breathtaking scenery.

Shanidar Cave

SHANIDAR CAVE

GENERAL INFORMATION / HISTORY

Approaching the area from Erbil, the closest significant-sized town to Shanindar Cave is Barzan, 152 km (94 mi) or two hours north. Driving to Barzan, visitors drive along the Greater Zab River, and pass by the village of Zawi Chemi Shanidar, on the banks of the Greater Zab, due east of the famous cave by 4 km (2.5 mi). This area is now a nature reserve famous as a beautiful area in its own right, but also known to have been a region inhabited by Neanderthals. Mergasor (Mergasur) is another close town to Shanindar, 30 minutes northwest of Soran, or 35 km (22 mi). The cave sits on Bradost Mountain and is easily accessible to visitors. There are steps that make the hike easier so many can visit one of the largest and most important caves in all of Iraq and in fact due to its historical significance – one of the most important in the world. At its tallest height it is 18 m (59 ft.) with a width of 27 m (89 ft.); its depth is 40 m (131 ft.).

In 1957, Columbia University archaeologist Ralph Solecki and his team first excavated the area after he had visited the cave a number of times beginning in 1951. He wrote several articles and books on his previously unprecedented findings. Prior to Solecki's involvement, local Kurdish Sherwani tribesmen used the cave seasonally for various purposes and the *Peshmerga* used it as a refuge during times of conflict. None had any clue as to its enormous historical

significance until Solecki "discovered" it. Scholars date its settlement to between 40,000-60,000 BC. It includes remains from the Stone Age, Paleolithic, and Neolithic eras.

Neanderthal Remains

The cave ultimately revealed two pre-historic cemeteries together containing ten individuals. Among the most famous past inhabitants of the cave were remains of a Neanderthal called Shanidar 1, who was obviously nurtured through and survived several injuries. Excavators gave him the nickname "Nandy" and he quickly became the most famous Neanderthal ever to walk the earth. He was estimated to be nearly 40 years old when he died which today would equate to 80 some odd years. This was quite a feat in the time in which he lived where one could easily meet an end at the claws of a wild beast while hunting not to mention by any number of other natural and unnatural causes. The other most renowned occupant of the cave, Shanidar 4, was found, buried beside flowers and the evidence was strong that he

The skeleton of Shanidar IX was found buried with many different species of wild flowers and herbs. There were at least six different species of flowers, mainly those having small brightly colored flowers.

was interred with ritual and care. This discovery changed the way the world viewed Neanderthals and inspired a book by Solecki titled, "Shanidar: The First Flower People."

These were not the only examples indicating ritual burial and nurture—merely the best preserved. Soil samples taken near burials of several Shanidar skeletons also contained a great deal of pollen from several flowers, including ephedra (also

Ralph Solecki

known as Joint Pine or Woody Horsetail), a herbal remedy and Yarrow, Cornflower, Bachelor's Button, St. Barnaby's Thistle, Ragwort or Groundsel, Grape Hyacinth, and Hollyhock—plants known for their diuretic, stimulant, astringent and anti-inflammatory properties. It became quickly apparent that previous ideas about Neanderthals as a sub-human race were wrong and that in fact they were a people who tended their sick and engaged in ritual burials replete with flowers to commemorate the loss of one who was cared for. There is still much dispute concerning these findings and skeptics have tried unsuccessfully to explain the overwhelming evidence as mere "animal pollution". The discovery is perhaps the most important to date concerning this oft mysterious people and has provoked thought and speculation not previously considered.

Most of these Neanderthal inhabitants were found by Solecki and the remains of Shanidar 3 are found in the Smithsonian Institution, in Washington, DC, shown inside a highly secure glass enclosure that Rick

Achillea Millefolium (common name "Yarrow")	Papaver Rhoeas (common name "Poppy")
Cnicus Benedictus (common name "Blessed Thistle")	Matricaria Chamomilla (common name "Camomile")
Althea Ficifolia (common names "Alcea Rosea/ Hollyhock")	Lolium Temulentum (common names "(Poison) Darnel" / "Cockle")

Potts, director of the museum's Human Origins Program, describes as a "fossil treasure case." Shanidar 3, Potts adds, "Is the Hope Diamond of the Human Origins collection, and we treat it accordingly." Moreover he states, "There is quite a severe and deep cut to a rib on his left side which would have been deep enough to collapse his lung, so Shanidar 3 is the oldest known individual who could have been "murdered."

Shanidar Cave was also reportedly the basis for the Clan's cave in the movie, *The Clan of the Cave Bear* by Jean Auel.

HIGHLIGHTS

There are 300 steps leading up to the cave and a memorial to Solecki, which was constructed in 2014. Numerous improvements were recently made to the cave site, which has made visits easier and more informative.

The nature of the Cave is important. It is in the shape of a triangle of 25 m (82 ft.) wide and 8m (26.ft.) high. This formation helped the Cave to be lit by sunlight across the day, which in turn made life possible for man, especially during the fierce winters and freezing seasons of the Stone Ages.

Quote from Ralph Solecki / Wall Street Journal - July 11, 2013
"Discovering my first Neanderthal skeleton in Iraq's Shanidar Cave in the spring of 1957 took my breath away. Archaeology is a time-consuming, labor-intensive science, so when you find remains in a former residential space dating back 40,000 years, you start to imagine what life must have been like then and how anyone could have survived for long."

TAQ TAQ

GENERAL INFORMATION / HISTORY

Taq Taq

Taq Taq is 500 meters (1640 ft.) above sea level and is known for its amazing landscapes and lush gardens, natural surroundings adjacent to the river. It is an hour and a half southeast of Erbil (98 km; 68 mi), on the Little (Lesser) Zab River in Koya district. The main focal point is the modern bridge that is utilized by commercial and private traffic. The small town is five km (3 mi) downstream from the Taq Taq Dam, which was begun in 2007. The purpose of the dam is intended for better irrigation, flood control, and for a hydropower station.

In 2011 the KRG released information from their Board of Investment publication that the Taq Taq Dam/reservoir will serve as a regulating reservoir from the hydropower station from the Dukan Dam in Sulaymani Governorate. The power station will produce 620 Megawatts of power.

Taq Taq is also well known for its oil wealth, and indeed it is the largest oilfield in the Kurdistan Region. There was a large find

during the reign of Saddam but he had the wells capped to keep the Kurds from profiting from it. After the 1991 uprising when the area fell into the hands of the nascent KRG, the wells were restored. After the 2003 Gulf War, the area was developed extensively by Genel Energy, which is an Anglo – Turkish company.

The Taq Taq field produced a gross average of 103,000 bpd in 2014, compared to 77,000 bpd in 2013. Pipeline exports to international markets via Turkey commenced in May 2014 and steadily increased over the year. Exports (via pipeline and truck) and domestic sales were split roughly equally over the year.

HIGHLIGHTS

Much like at Haibat Sultan, there is a great deal of scientific study being undertaken in and around Taq Taq. Conservation has not been a high priority in the past. However, the oilfield and surrounding area will see much more attention paid to it by the KRG in the coming years with a view to preserving its natural beauty.

There are picnic benches alongside the river and many people also take walks alongside the river. If you fancy a scenic day-out in Kurdistan, Taq Taq is a must-visit for you.

DAIREI CITADEL

GENERAL INFORMATION / HISTORY

The construction dates to The Soran Emirate's Prince Muhammad's reign (1813-1837) AD. The citadel is situated on a tall and imposing hill in the western part of the foot of (Permam) mountain chain 38 km (24 mi) from Erbil, only 2 km (1.2 mi) from Darabizmar (Sarukani village) road. A rigid wall meant for defensive positions and other military purposes surrounds it. Some of the original walls remain and are between 1-6 m (3-20 ft.) high.

HIGHLIGHTS

The citadel consists of five separate rooms, a large hall and a big yard in addition to a currently non-functioning well. Presently, shepherds use the surrounding area to herd their sheep and goats.

Dairei Citadel

This is a little known but interesting site and area.

DWIN CASTLE /CITADEL

GENERAL INFORMATION / HISTORY

Dwin Castle is thirty minutes west of Shaqlawa (25 km; 16 mi). While Saladin (a Muslim of Kurdish decent) was born south of Dwin in Tikrit, Dwin is the generally accepted ancestral home of "Saladin the Conqueror." He became Sultan of Egypt and Syria and one of the most powerful Islamic leaders ever, eventually subjugating much of the Holy Land (including Jerusalem). At the height of his power, Saladin's territory stretched from Egypt throughout Mesopotamia and into the Arabian Peninsula. He was later defeated at the Battle of Arsuf by Richard I of England (Richard the "Lionheart") in 1199.

One side of the road holds the remains of the castle itself and on the other side is an ancient graveyard. Both the castle and surrounding area are called Dwin. It is believed Saladin's parents and grandfather originated from Dwin and both are reportedly buried here.

There are plans to create a more tourist-accessible area such as cleaning the site and adding signs de-

Dwin Castle

Dwin Castle

began. Some of the graves have clear inscriptions, while others are blank or are illegible to the naked eye. Though Saladin was Muslim, these graves date to different eras. The graves toward the entrance, for example, are Zoroastrian. These graves include suns, swords, daggers, and other symbols associated with Zoroastrianism. Graves next to a stone wall date to the era of Saladin himself, and many locals believe one belongs to his grandfather. There is a third grouping of graves that is reportedly dedicated to Saladin's knights, though this is not confirmed.

tailing the history and general background. As it is there are few who are aware of the significance of the site even when visiting it unless a knowledgeable guide accompanies them. There is a fairly significant group of "Saladinophiles" who have made a point to visit all of the castles of Saladin. While the castle of Dwin is not nearly as dramatic as those in neighboring countries such as Syria, the survey would not be complete without a visit to Dwin.

HIGHLIGHTS

This is an important site for Kurdish history as well as ancient Mesopotamian history in general and a fascinating morning or afternoon excursion from Erbil. Much of the castle including its foundation and many of its walls are visible, and the guard posts are still somewhat in tact as the castle is constructed of stone. It is believed that the castle was built to watch over the ancient Dwin village of which there are still many remains, located near the Rubat Kargh River.

The castle, though somewhat collapsed, commands a spectacular 360-degree view and it is believed that it was from here that the incredible saga of Saladin

Dwin Cemetery

In November 2014, a joint Hungarian-Kurdish team explored and began to excavate Dwin Castle. They conducted a survey and began preparing a 3D image of the castle, which will be a five-year undertaking. The initial results will most likely be published in early 2015.

Saladin in Battle

GAUGAMELA

GENERAL INFORMATION / HISTORY

Gaugamela ("The Camel's House") was a village near the banks of the river Bumodus. The site of the battle is thought to be Tel Gomel (Hebrew - "Camels Mount"). The actual site of Gaugamela and its exact location is a matter of some dispute but it is generally held to be at the base of a hill near a small village approximately 50 kilometers (30 miles) east of Erbil off a main road to Duhok and not far from the archeological site of Jirwana. The site has never been excavated to confirm the location.

The Battle of Gaugamela, also called the Battle of Arbela, (Oct. 1, 331 BC) was a conflict between the forces of Alexander the Great of Macedonia and Darius III of Persia that decided the fate of the Persian Empire.

Gaugamela was both an unsurpassed victory for perhaps the most accomplished general in history but at the same time represented a personal defeat for Alexander. Following the assassination of Phillip II, Alexander's father, in 336 BC, Alexander and

Battle of Gaugemela – Flemish Tapestry 18th Century

his army left their home of Macedonia for the last time and set out on a goal of conquering all of Persia. The three main ambitions Alexander had set for his life were:

Alexander

1) To best his father's accomplishments, which he did in his defeat of, Darius III – an ever-elusive dream of his father as well,

2) To capture Darius in order to learn from this man who was master of the greatest Empire on earth and if unable to do so, to personally kill him. Alexander was deprived of this goal as Darius fled the battlefield of Gaugamela only to be assassinated later by his own captains.

3) Finally, it was the wish of Alexander to reach what he thought was the end of the earth at what is now called Kanyakumari (Cape Comorin at the southern tip of India). He was also deprived of this goal as his army rebelled against him before reaching the destination and he was forced to return back to Persia (Babylon) where he died a wounded man and broken alcoholic.

Colonel Schute lectures a tour at Gaugemela

HIGHLIGHTS

When visiting the hill above the village one will no doubt be followed by excited children who are more fascinated by their infrequent visitors than by the ancient history of their surroundings. When reaching the top of the hill you will be treated to a panoramic view of a lush valley with a river to the west where Alexander crossed to face the great king Darius. It is a quiet place and many have remarked that they can almost see the armies facing each other on the plain below. Perhaps the greatest highlight of one of the most important historical sites in the world is yet to come. It has, as of yet, never been excavated and one can only imagine the treasures that lie beneath this ancient battlefield where men vied for the title "Lord of the Earth."

There are preliminary discussions by the owners of *Kurdistan Iraq Tours* and other interested parties to construct a *Tourist Information Center* on the site. No plans have been finalized but it is felt the site is not only one of the most important historical locations in Kurdistan, but one of the most neglected and it is anticipated this will be remedied in the not too distant future.

See the following article by West Point historian and retired Colonel Harry Schute for a detailed account of what has been hailed by many as one of the most important battles of all time.

THE BATTLE OF GAUGAMELA

From The Pen of Colonel (ret) Harry Schute

Colonel Harry Schute (retired) has a great deal of experience in the Kurdistan Region. He came to Kurdistan in April 2003 as the

commander of a US Army Reserve Civil Affairs battalion and within two months was the senior US Army commander responsible for the three governorates of the Kurdistan Region. He later served with the Army as the Chief of Staff for the Coalition Provisional Authority (CPA) Northern Region Office in Erbil.

In these capacities, he travelled to all parts of Kurdistan getting to know people at all levels of society, from the most senior leaders, to the man in the street. Mr. Schute has a degree in history from the US Military Academy at West Point. Below he recounts the famous Battle of Gaugemela…

"Imagine, if you can, overlooking an expansive plain with mountainous foothills in the distance to your left, and rolling hilly terrain off in the distance to your right. You can see more than 30,000 men armed with long spears and giant shields; they are joined by another nearly 10,000 cavalrymen. And off to your front is a huge expansive army of probably more than

Alexander The Great

100,000. It is the home of the field where the Battle of Gaugamela was fought on October 1st, 331 BCE a mere 40 miles or so northwest of Erbil, the capitol of Kurdistan.

It was here that Alexander the Great of Macedon brought his army of some 40,000 infantry and cavalry to face Darius III, the King of the Persian Achaemenid Empire; who was commanding an army according to modern sources of as many as 100,000 infantry and cavalry (ancient sources claim as many as one million in his army), with 200 scythed chariots and 15 war elephants. At the end of that day, the Persian Army would be crushed and the Persian Empire would essentially cease to exist leaving Alexander as ruler of most of the known Western world. This battle ranks among the top 10 to 20 most decisive and important battles in all of military history.

Unfortunately, nothing exists today to indicate that a battle was ever fought

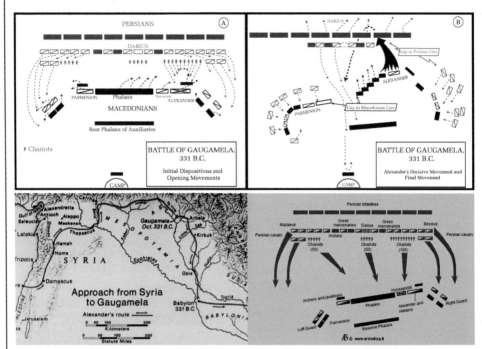

PERSIANS Ⓐ

DARIUS

PARMENION   Phalanx
MACEDONIANS   ALEXANDER

Rear Phalanx of Auxiliaries

♦ Chariots

BATTLE OF GAUGAMELA, 331 B.C.

Initial Dispositions and Opening Movements

CAMP

DARIUS   Ⓑ

Gap in Persian Line

ALEXANDER

PARMENION   Gap in Macedonian Line

BATTLE OF GAUGAMELA, 331 B.C.

Alexander's Decisive Movement and Final Movement

CAMP

Approach from Syria to Gaugamela

Alexander's route

Gaugamela Oct. 331 B.C.

SYRIA

Babylon 331 B.C.

Persian Infantries

Mazaeus   Greek mercenaries   Darius   Greek mercenaries   Bessus

Persian cavalry   Persian cavalry

Archers

Chariots (50)   Chariots (50)   Chariots (100)

Archers and javelins   Hypaspists

Phalanx   Alexander and Hetairoi   Right Guard

Left Guard   Parmenion   Reserve Phalanx

Ⓑ © www.arsbellica.it

on the ground near Tel Gomel, which is believed to be close to the central focus points of the conflict. All one can see today is a gently rolling fertile plain, with grazing sheep and goats, cultivated fields and scattered villages. Of course, in October, the ground would be generally dry from the summer dry season. I will try to paint you a picture of what happened on that fateful day two millennia ago. But first let's set the stage for this critical battle.

Alexander, the King of Macedon and leader of the Hellenic League, launched his assault on the Persian Empire in 334 BC. This attack was executed partly to fulfill the dream of his late father Phillip II, which was to avenge the attacks the Persians had made on the Greek city-states 150 years earlier. Alexander crossed the Hellespont to begin his campaign and almost immediately met the Persian vanguard at Granicus in modern Turkey.

Over the next year, Alexander campaigned across Asia Minor winning successive victories against the Persians. This first stage of the campaign culminated in 333 BC with the Battle of Issus near modern Iskenderun. At this battle, Alexander met Darius on the battlefield for the first time. The battle was significant in that Darius

132

could not effectively deploy his much larger army due to terrain restrictions, and in the end, he fled from the battlefield. This would be significant later.

Over the next year, Alexander campaigned in the Levant. After his successful siege of Tyre and capture of Gaza in 332 BC, he controlled the entire eastern Mediterranean. He continued to move further south and took the surrender of Persian controlled Egypt, where he was crowned Pharaoh. In the succeeding months, Darius tried to negotiate a settlement, but to no avail. Alexander told Darius he was coming.

Alexander began to move his army toward the Euphrates and Tigris planning to take a northern route towards Babylon, the first major Persian city he would encounter. This route would keep him on terrain with better climatic conditions and more suited for forage, as he would skirt the southern edge of the Armenian hills. Upon

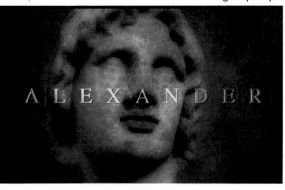

crossing the Tigris, Alexander encountered Darius' advance guard, capturing some of them and gaining some valuable intelligence regarding the deployments of Darius' vast army. He discovered that Darius had apparently learned from his mistakes at Issus and had staged his army on a wide plain to allow a complete deployment of his numerically superior army. He had also prepared the ground, leveling it in places so as to better allow the deployment of his chariots. His soldiers had also laid booby traps on the ground so as to restrict the movements of Alexander's forces.

With this intelligence Alexander was better able to deploy his men. Since he knew Darius greatly outnumbered him, he had to be concerned that Darius would be able to turn one of his flanks. Accordingly, he deployed his long main group of phalanxes (closely packed infantry) with the flanks protected by angling the end units, arranged to the rear. He also deployed a second reserve phalanx to the rear of the first to prepare for a potential breakthrough. Alexander positioned himself to the right of his formation as usual with his Companion Cavalry.

Darius' vast army was deployed in a long line with all of the component parts of the still large Persian Empire represented: Persians, Babylonians, Medians, Scythians, Syrians, Parthians and others. His chariots were forward in the middle. Darius also positioned himself in the middle, with his cavalry on the flanks.

The battle commenced with Alexander ordering his main phalanxes forward.

A thrust to capture Darius

As Alexander moved to the right, elements of his cavalry turned to the left and probed the Persian line looking for gaps or weakness. Initially, the Persians responded to these probes, prompting Alexander to continue moving further to the right. Finally, however, Alexander sensed that the gap he had been looking for was created. When he saw this opening, he turned the element with him 90 degrees and attacked into a seam in the Persian line. Alexander's thrust created the shock effect that cavalry often could achieve on the battlefield as the mounted assault slammed into the Persian line, opened and enlarged a hole. Alexander did what he had done time and again on the battlefield. Leading from the front he pressed forward, exploiting success and further breaking open the Persian line.

In the meantime, the Persian assault on the Greek left was having some success. The Greek commander on the left, Parmenion – an able commander who had served Alexander's father – was pressed by the Persian assault and his line was bending. At the same time, elements of the Persian cavalry from the right center, exploited a gap in the Greek line, and broke through to the rear. However, instead of turning and attacking Parmenion from the rear, or directly assaulting the second rank phalanx, they continued on to the Greek camp looking for plunder. The second rank phalanx turned and struck back at this element attacking their camp, ultimately driving them off and destroying the rest.

Simultaneously, Alexander began riding with his Companion Cavalry and Companion Infantry toward the right apparently attempting to turn the left flank of the Persian line. Elements of the Persian Cavalry moved to their left paralleling Alexander's move.

In response to the movement of the Greek Army, Darius ordered his infantry forward from the center and right. He also directed the scythed chariots to attack. It was expected they would be a shock force to punch holes in the Greek line. However their attack was ineffective as Greek javelin and other missile throwers disabled many of the chariot drivers, and at the locations where the chariots did reach the main line, the Greek infantry was prepared and simply opened holes in the line and literally absorbed the attack, again disabling the drivers and horses.

As Alexander pressed forward his assault on the Persian left center, he noticed Darius mounted in his luxurious regal chariot. When Alexander observed Darius, he pressed his attack directly toward Darius,

Arrowheads possibly from Gaugamela

as he wanted to face him directly on the battlefield. As Darius noticed Alexander approaching, he turned his chariot and fled as he had before. As Darius' men observed their king and commander fleeing the field, they responded in kind, breaking and running. It was at that time that the battle became very bloody as the Greek's routed and slaughtered the fleeing Persians.

As Alexander attempted to pursue Darius, Parmenion's son found Alexander on the field and delivered a message that the Greek left was in danger and sought Alexander's immediate support. Alexander immediately broke off his pursuit of Darius, turned and rode to the relief of Parmenion. As Alexander arrived, the Persian right began to collapse in any regard, as word of the collapse on their left began to reach them.

The rout was complete. At the end of the days fight, tens of thousands of dead and injured Persians laid on the field. The ancient historians tell us the Greek casualties were in the several hundreds – perhaps as many as 1,000. Darius had again fled the field and was scrambling back to Arbella (Erbil or Hawler as it is known today) to attempt to secure his personal baggage, which he ultimately abandoned.

Darius' defeat was decisive and Alexander's victory was complete. Within a short time, Darius' own men would murder him, leaving his body for Alexander to later recover. Alexander would be accepted into Babylon as a conquering commander. The Persian Army ceased to exist, and the rest of Persian lands lay ready for Alexander to pillage as he saw fit. As a consequence of this battle, the once mighty Persian Empire was destroyed and Hellenic influence would ultimately extend to the western expanses of Indian lands.

This is the reason why Gaugamela – fought on an open plain of Kurdistan – is one of the most important battles of history. There is no evidence on the field today of the expansive fight, but if you look across the expanse and close your eyes; listen hard enough, perhaps you can hear in the distance the clash of arms and armor and the shouts of men in mortal combat. This is the Gaugamela of Kurdistan!

Sources:

Warry, John. Alexander 334-323 BC: Conquest of the Persian Empire. Osprey Publishing, 1991
Heckel, Waldemar. The Wars of Alexander the Great: 336-323 BC. Osprey Publishing, 2002

Plain of Gaugamela

KHANZAD (BANAMAN) CITADEL

GENERAL INFORMATION / HISTORY

This Citadel is 3 km (1.8 mi) east of the small town of Harir and 22 km (14 mi) north of Erbil. To the south of the citadel is a spiraling road down toward the highway between Shaqlawa and Erbil.

The Citadel was the home of Khanzad Soran and her brother Prince Suleiman in the 15th century. Khanzad was a ruler of the Soran Emirate, a vassal state of the Ottoman Empire and one of, if not the only female ruler in their history (1816-1825). Also called Banaman Citadel/Castle most of the older structure can be dated to the mid-late 19th century.

The Soran Empire was a semi-independent vassal state of the Ottoman and Persian Empires that last-

Artist's concept of Khanzad Soran

ed through the mid-late1800s and spread from modern day Dohuk Governorate past Rawanduz and south of Erbil. Its Kurdish-speaking rulers originated from several different ethnic origins, including Circassians. At some point they were assimilated into Kurdish culture. The emirate is recorded to have gained some semblance of full independence shortly after the Ottomans captured it from Safavid (Persian) control in the 1530s. The Ottomans eventually reincorporated Soran into their own empire in the mid-late 1800s.

At one time there were a small number of Jews in the area and there is still a sizable Christian population in the area known in Syriac as *Ba* or *Beith Soren* (*land of Soren*), which may be linked to the Aryan Soran clan.

HIGHLIGHTS

Some parts of the original citadel remain intact, though the majority is new. There is a stone staircase as you walk up to the imposing but attractive structure. The Citadel has two floors, and features a turret on each of the four corners as well as famous saw-toothed style battlements on the main building, making it look more like castle.

It is a fascinating site for many reasons not the least of which is evidence that women once ruled the region—unusual in the Middle East historically. It is of note that women still play a significant role in the governance of Kurdistan with over 30% percent of the parliamentary seats reserved for women. See the following article by Ms. Pakshan Zangana, Director of the High Council for Women's Affairs on the role of women in Kurdistan.

Citadel of Khanzad

KURDISH WOMEN: NOBLE AMBITIONS AND A BRIGHT FUTURE

From the Pen of Pakhshan Abdullah Zangana

Secretary General of the High Council for Women's Affairs in the Kurdistan Regional Government – Iraq

I see a ray of hope shining incandescently from the eyes of the young girls and women of Kurdistan with ambition and hope for a better future than that of their mothers and grandmothers. I remember twenty years ago, when I, along with a group of other girls my age, were part of the Peshmerga forces in the mountains of Kurdistan fighting for the freedom of our land. We who struggled in those days are now mothers and grandmothers whose persistence laid the foundation of the modern day Kurdistan Region. Indeed we had the same hopes, the same ambitions, and the same glowing eyes that I see today.

The hopes and aspirations that Kurdish women carry and are consistently working for are not mere fantasies but based on objective facts and a historical journey consistently supported by the political will of our leaders.

Today, Kurdish women have ambitions that reach to the sky and in spite of difficulties are catching up with other women of their age in more developed societies. It is not only our right, but also more precisely, our duty to carry such ambitions. From the earliest times Kurdish society has recognized and valued the contribution and participation of women in various fields; not only on a community level but also on official and governmental levels as well. While taking into account the current realities of our society, as well as the role and the status of women historically, we look to the support of the public, and the support of friends and our community realizing that a comprehensive approach is required for the development of democracy, and to achieve, through laws and strategic plans, the principles of Human Rights, including increased human rights for women.

The nature of transition in our society poses a clash of two sets of values, which influences our chances of

Dr. Layton meeting in Parliament with Evar Ibrahim, head of Women Rights Committee in Kurdistan Parliament.

success. In the past some were steeped in fixed values of cultural heritage based on discriminatory relations between women and men. Some did not support constructive programs and the development of women on both materialistic and humanitarian levels. While the new set of values in Kurdistan has visions and ambitious aspirations of the future, which are not yet complete, the future is reflected clearly in the insistence of young women to

Talar Faiq, Director of EIH with the women in her staff

achieve further progress and development in all aspects of life. These possibilities have become especially attainable in the past twenty years and we are looking forward to a promising future and the emergence of the role of Kurdish women in all aspects of society.

A thousand greetings to the young people of Kurdistan, their noble aspirations and their consistent eagerness to gain more knowledge and experience, and their brave insistence that constantly adds new degrees in the ladder of ambition, which is continually enriched by the successful experiences of the advanced societies of the world.

Ms. Bayan Rahman - High Representative of the Kurdistan Regional Government (KRG) to Washington DC.

Women training in the security forces and Kurdish military

138

GROW YOUR WORLD,
EXPAND YOUR HORIZONS
AND DEVELOP YOUR CAPABILITIES

Enjoy a fast Internet connection on your smartphone; video calls and
data download with Extra G service from Korek.

To activate any of the bundles:
• Dial *250# and follow the instructions
• Visit "Selfcare" on the following link:
http://selfcare.korektel.com

Dare to Dream

f 🅑 🅑 411 ☎

korektel.com

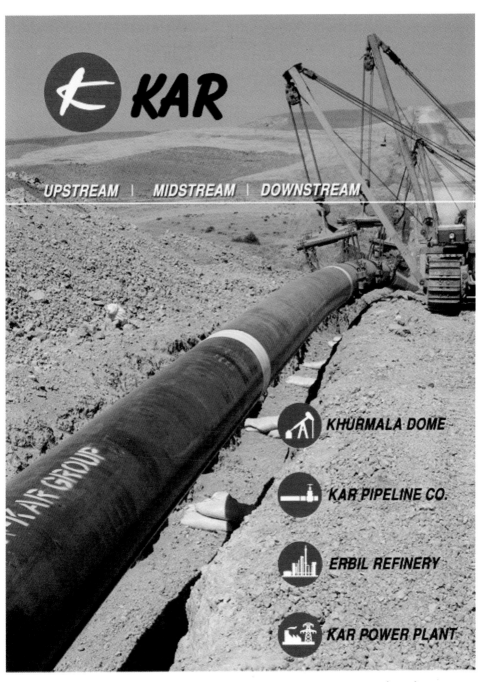

KAR

UPSTREAM | MIDSTREAM | DOWNSTREAM

KHURMALA DOME

KAR PIPELINE CO.

ERBIL REFINERY

KAR POWER PLANT

www.kar-k.com

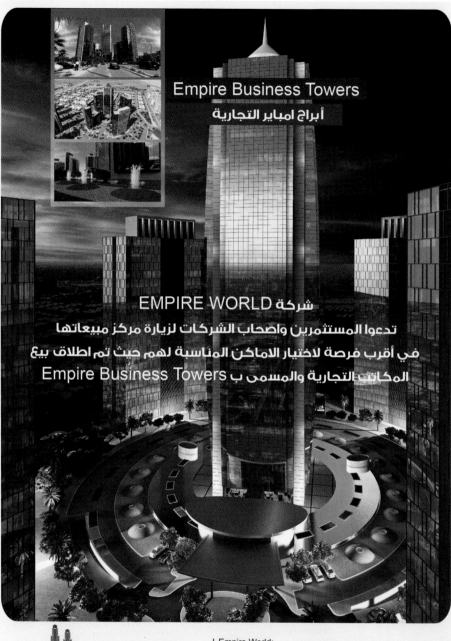

Empire Business Towers
أبراج امباير التجارية

شركة EMPIRE WORLD

تدعوا المستثمرين واصحاب الشركات لزيارة مركز مبيعاتها

في أقرب فرصة لاختيار الاماكن المناسبة لهم حيث تم اطلاق بيع

المكاتب التجارية والمسمى بـ Empire Business Towers

Empire World:
Empire Business Complex C4, Erbil, Iraq
Tel: +964 (0) 66 257 6006 - +964 (0) 66 257 6007
info@empireiraq.com - www.empireiraq.com

Erbil International Equestrian Racing Club

Masif Road, Erbil, Iraq

the KOREK Mountain Resort

Bekhal,Erbil, Iraq
www.thekorekmountain.com   Phone Number: 009647502458888

فرۆشتن Sales

خزمەتگوزاری Services

پارچەی یەدەگ Spare Parts

COROLLA

جیهان مۆتۆرز بۆ بازرگانی ئۆتۆمبیل
جیهان موتورز لــتجــارة المركبــات
CIHAN MOTORS FOR AUTO TRADING

🌐 www.cihanmotors.com 📘 facebook.com/cihanmotors

دهۆك :
ریگای هەولێر، پلازای گروپی جیهان
فرۆشتن : ١٢١٢ ٢٧٣ ٠٧٥٠
خزمەتگوزاری : ٢٨١٠ ١٨٨ ٠٧٥٠
پارچەی یەدەک : ٢٨١٦ ١٨٨ ٠٧٥٠

سلێمانی :
چوار ریانی مەلیك محمود پلازای گروپی جیهان
فرۆشتن : ١٢١٢ ٢٦٣ ٠٧٥٠
خزمەتگوزاری : ٥٠٤٩ ٠١١ ٠٧٤٨
پارچەی یەدەک : ٩١٨٢ ٠١٥ ٠٧٤٨

هەولێر :
ریگای کەرکوك، پلازای گروپی جیهان
فرۆشتن : ١٢١٢ ٥٨٧ ٠٧٥٠
خزمەتگوزاری : ٤٣٠٧ ٧٦٠ ٠٧٥٠
پارچەی یەدەک : ٦٧٠٠ ٣٣٩ ٠٧٥٠

divan

erbil

Do You Know Divan ?

The Affordable Luxury in Erbil

For reservations please call 066 210 5000

Gulan Street, Erbil,
Kurdistan Region of Iraq
P: +964 66 210 5000
F: +964 66 210 5001
E: info.divanerbil@divan.com
www.divan.com
/DivanErbil /DivanHotelErbil

L V X℠

Preferred
HOTELS & RESORTS

ALBiT
CONSTRUCTION AND TRANSPORTATION

Gullan Street English Village Plot NO. 243 Erbil-Kurdistan IRAQ
Phone: +964 750 445 1091
Email: info@albitcompany.com • www.albitcompany.com

EXPAND YOUR BOUNDARIES WITH MASTERCARD

سنورەکانت فراوان بکە لە گەڵ ماستەرکارت

وسع آفاقك مع ماستركارد

 /RegionTradeBank   RegionTradeBank

Gulan Street, 40m Road, Opposite of Turkish Consulate, Erbil, Kurdistan Region, Iraq.
E-mail: erbil@rtbank.net
Web: www.rtbank.net
Tel: +964 66 353 9777

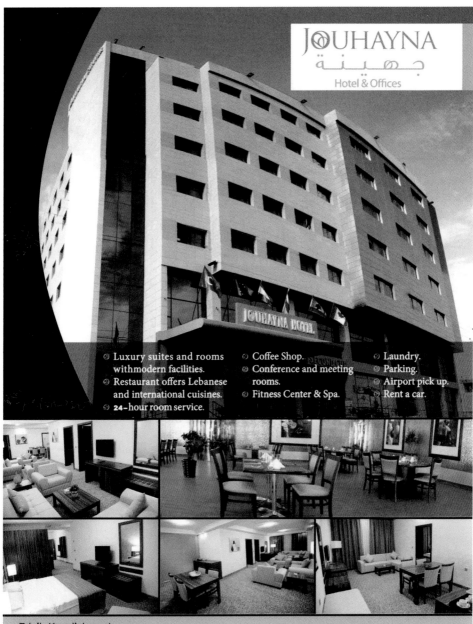

JOUHAYNA
جــوهــيــنــة
Hotel & Offices

- ◎ Luxury suites and rooms with modern facilities.
- ◎ Restaurant offers Lebanese and international cuisines.
- ◎ 24-hour room service.
- ◎ Coffee Shop.
- ◎ Conference and meeting rooms.
- ◎ Fitness Center & Spa.
- ◎ Laundry.
- ◎ Parking.
- ◎ Airport pick up.
- ◎ Rent a car.

Erbil, Kurdistan, Iraq
100 M. Street, Int'l Airport Road
Tel: +964 750 7120777
info@jouhaynahotel.com
www.jouhaynahotel.com

TANGRAM نانكرام
HOTEL ERBIL

THE SMART HOTEL IN ERBIL

Tangram Hotel is the new smart hotel in Erbil that understands your needs while travelling. Our 118 rooms have comfortable beds and spacious working desks to make both relaxing and working as enjoyable as can be. Free WiFi access allows you to stay connected with colleagues as well as with family and friends.

For successful business meetings or even corporate events, our conference rooms are equipped with the latest audiovisual equipment. After taking care of business, you can workout in our state-of-the-art gym and have an exquisite meal in our variety of restaurants and lounges. Whether you are travelling for pleasure or business, you can enjoy both at the Tangram Hotel in Erbil.

For booking & information
+964 (0) 750 889 5554
+964 (0) 66 229 6900
Kirkuk road, Erbil, Kurdistan Iraq
E-mail: info.erbil@tangramhotels.com
www.erbil.tangramhotels.com

Tangram is a member of the

 Anantara

THE DOYLE COLLECTION

FIRST

INDIVIDUAL COLLECTION

Kempinski

THE LEELA

MARCO POLO HOTELS

MOKARA HOTELS & SPAS

Omni HOTELS & RESORTS

PAN PACIFIC HOTELS AND RESORTS

PARKROYAL HOTELS & RESORTS

 RIXOS HOTELS

 RYDGES HOTELS+RESORTS

 SHAZA HOTELS

TANGRAM

TIVOLI HOTELS & RESORTS

HOTEL

DARIN PLAZA

ERBIL

Welcome to Darin Plaza Hotel, Erbil's newest luxury address. Featuring 80 state of the art rooms, including one, two bedrooms and residence suites. Adding comfort to convenience, the hotel features Darin Restaurant, Darin Tranquil Spa, Swimming Pool, Sauna, and Gym. There is also and the meeting spaces designed for formal and informal gatherings to meet the needs of business as well as leisure events.

Darin lobby café is the perfect spot to cut a deal, hold a meeting, or just relax and enjoy the ambiance over a fine house-made pastry or fresh squeezed glass of juice.

Iraq, Erbil, Kurdistan Region, 60 Meter St. Opposite to Jalil Al-Khayat Mosque.

| 00964 (0)750 210 0001 | 00964 (0)750 210 0003 |
| 00964 (0)750 210 0002 | 00964 (0)750 210 0004 |

www.darinplaza.net • darinplazahotel@hotmail.com • info@darinplaza.net

DARIN HOTEL

This Four Star hotel has 49 comfortably equipped rooms and suites. All rooms are modern and have air condition, mini bar, bathroom, Bathtub, hair dryer, Safe boxes, TV, 24 Hour room service, phone and free internet access. Apart from accommodation, there is, also, Darin Restaurant which servers the most delicious western and eastern dishes.

Being healthy means practicing your sports regularly, so Darin Hotel provide you with gymnasium hall, Sauna and indoor swimming pool.

Being located in 100 Meter St., near Family Fun Darin Hotel gives you the perfect place for your stay whether it is for an entertainment or a business trip.

Iraq, Kurdistan Region, Erbil, 100 Meter St. Near Family Fun.

| www.darinhotel.com | 00964 (0)750 319 7111 |
| info@darinhotel.com | 00964 (0)771 161 2111 |

AL HAYAT Soft Drinks and Mineral Water Co.
IRAQ-Erbil-Makhmoor St.

A NEW STAR IN THE SKY

+964 750 418 4444
+964 750 420 4444
www.zagrosjet.com

Gatherton is an **events, marketing and market development company** with offices in Dubai and the Kurdistan Region of Iraq.

GATHERTON
EVENTS | MARKETING

+964 (0)770 044 2871
info@gatherton.com
www.gatherton.com

With over 7 years experience in Kurdistan we will ensure that your company and its products & services are presented to this **vibrant and emerging market, professionally and effectively.**

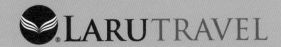

LARUTRAVEL

Creating Memories all around the world

Our goal is to provide you with world class services at affordable prices.

For more information

...and a lot more

Erbil : Iraq
Divan Hotel Ground Floor next to Setur Duty Free - Gulan St.
Tel. :+ 964 750 446 8960 /+964750 455 44 11

Jordan : Amman
Abdeen Complex - Next to New English School Building # 35 , 2nd floor , office # 203 Amer Bin Malek St. Khalda, Mob : + 962 79 555 04 08

habrurı
GRILL

Serving Great Chinese Food For Great People

Off Two-side street, Near Al Qasra, Ankawa Mob: 0750 685 8000

emp

Human   Real   Event   Consultancy
Resources   Estate   Management

INNOVATIVE SOLUTIONS FOR A GROWING MARKET

Headquarters: 088 English Village
Compound, Gulan Street, Erbil, Iraq

Sulaumaniyah Branch: Hiwa Building
1st Floor Ashty Str. Sulaymaniyah , Iraq

Mobile: +9647501449000
        +9647701449000
E-mail: info@erbilmanpower.com
Website : www.erbilmanpower.com

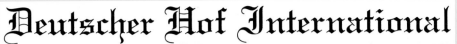

Deutscher Hof International

Willkommen
Bienvenido
Welcome
Bienvenue
Benvenuto

German Restaurant & Beer Garden

Iraq KRG Erbil/Ainkawa
00964(0)750 316 2396
www.deutscher-hof-international.com • deutscher-hof-international@web.de

Abu Afif Sweets

Erbil 60meter street,
Bekhtyari main road
+964 750 555 000 1/2
Info@abuafif-sweets.com
f Abu Afif Sweets

Slymaniah near Park Azadi
+964 748 155 7000
Info@abuafif-sweets.com
www.abuafif-sweets.com
abu_afif_sweets

ERBIL Int. Hotel

+964 (0) 66 223 4460
+964 (0) 750 464 07 84
+964 (0) 770 654 8008

www.erbilinthotel.com

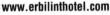

Khanzad

+964 (0) 662 245 273
+964 (0) 750 322 0599
+964 (0) 770 000 2692

www.khanzadresort.com

SHAQLAWA INT HOTEL

+964 (0) 665 22 1919   +964 (0) 750 443 1002-03
www.shaqlawainthotel.com

EXCLUSIVE WINE & BEER
+964 750 454 4743 • sales@the-counter.info

KURDISTAN IRAQ TOURS
A Division of The Other Iraq Tours LLC

ALWAYS FIRST!

TRAVEL WITH THE MOST EXPERIENCED PROFESSIONALS IN THE REGION!

For information on booking a tour to Kurdistan contact:
Email: info@kurdistaniraqtours.com Tel: +964 (0) 750 339 9999

www.kurdistaniraqtours.com

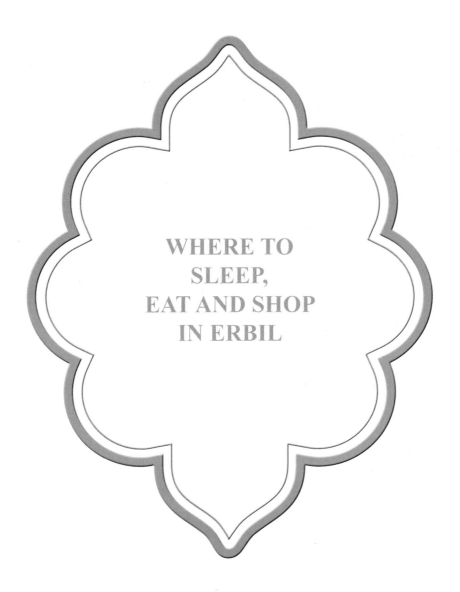

WHERE TO SLEEP, EAT AND SHOP IN ERBIL

HOTELS IN ERBIL

SHARAF KHAN HOTEL AND RESTAURANT	0750 731 2423
OSCAR	0750 235 1818
NOBLE	0750 431 2244
TANGRAM	06 62 29 6900
CRISTAL	06 6211 3000
JOUHAYNA	0750 712 0777
BELLA ROMA	0750 411 7755
CAPITOL	0750 373 6600
CANYON	0750 372 5119
CLASSY	0750 854 6663
AL JAWAHIRI	0750 824 9702
CHWAR CHRA	06 62 23 1508
HELIN DE VILLE SHAQLAWA	0750 221 1000
INTERNATIONAL	0750 443 1002
KHANZAD	06 62 24 5273
ERBIL INTERNATIONAL	06 62 23 4465
LOMANA HOTEL	0750 4561718
ANKAWA PALACE	0750 4791780
MY HOTEL	0750 4790022
BARZ ROZ HOTEL	0750 4454308

divan

The Luxury Hotel in Erbil

JOUHAYNA
جهينة

Hotel & Offices

Erbil, Kurdistan, Iraq
100 M. Street, Int'l Airport Road
Tel: +964 750 7120777
info@jouhaynahotel.com
www.jouhaynahotel.com

DARIN PLAZA
HOTEL

Iraq, Erbil, Kurdistan Region,
60 Meter St. Opposite to
Jalil Al-Khayat Mosque.
00964 (0)750 210 0001
00964 (0)750 210 0002
00964 (0)750 210 0003
00964 (0)750 210 0004

www.darinplaza.net • darinplazahotel@hotmail.com • info@darinplaza.net

Iraq, Kurdistan Region,
Erbil, 100 Meter St. Near Family Fun.
00964 (0)750 319 7111
00964 (0)771 161 2111

DARIN HOTEL

www.darinhotel.com • info@darinhotel.com

ERBIL
Int. Hotel

+964 (0) 66 223 4460
+964 (0) 750 464 0784
+964 (0) 770 654 8008
www.erbilinthotel.com

Khanzad

+964 (0) 662 245 273
+964 (0) 750 322 0599
+964 (0) 770 000 2692
www.khanzadresort.com

SHAQLAWA INT HOTEL

+964 (0) 665 22 1919
+964 (0) 750 443 1002
+964 (0) 750 443 1003
www.shaqlawainthotel.com

SHAQLAWA INT HOTEL

TANGRAM تانگرام
HOTEL ERBIL

THE SMART HOTEL IN ERBIL

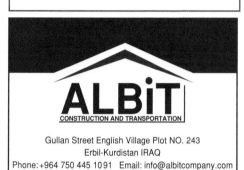

Gullan Street English Village Plot NO. 243
Erbil-Kurdistan IRAQ
Phone:+964 750 445 1091   Email: info@albitcompany.com
www.albitcompany.com

ROYAL PALACE	0750 423 7326
MONACO PALACE HOTEL	0750 484 0415
BEJAN PALACE	0750 499 9121
JABAR PALACE HOTEL	0750 444 2440
NEXT PLAZA HOTEL	0750 488 5664
HAWLER INTERNATIONAL	0750 467 1875
MALI TO	0750 429 0303
SHAYAN HOTEL	0750 446 7118
ERBIL TOWER HOTEL	0750 751 8888
ROTANA	0750 449 4965
LAMASSU HOTEL	0750 447 7448
LARSA HOTEL	0750 462 0988
DIVAN	0750 134 4070
DARIN PLAZA	0750 210 0002
VAN ROYAL HOTEL	06 62 23 5840

RESTAURANTS

SHORISH RESTAURANT	0750 448 2204
HAPPY TIME	0750 454 5371
MARINA	0750 445 2732
KOSHKY RASHID	0750 445 3962
CHRAKHAN RESTAURANT	0750 445 1975
SARI RASH RESTAURANT	0750 467 8361
TODAY RESTAURANT	0750 453 0000

KABAB FARUQ	0750 446 8142
DAWA RESTAURANT 2	0750 451 0012
DEUTSCHER HOF	0750 488 3981
ASHTAR SWEETS	0750 446 2418
KFC	0750 561 8484
SECOND CUP	0750 345 1203
KAFEDO	0750 466 9996
ONYX	0750 505 2222
MAMOUNIA SKY BAR	0750 752 5555
BURGER QUEEN	0750 752 5555
CARVEL	0750 075 0750
CINNABON	0750 075 0750
HABRURI	0750 685 8000
O'CAFÉ	0750 395 6485
PREGO	0750 272 7271
GREEK GRILL	0750 854 6663
AL AFANDI	0750 373 6600
SAJ AL REEF	0750 313 0008
CASPER & GAMBINI	0750 270 0700
DC STEAK HOUSE	0750 138 8377
SCOOP	0750 113 8238
NARANJ	0750 454 6399
CASTELLO	0750 231 2727
SAMAD RESTAURANT	0750 408 9888

به ساردی بینۆشه

habruri
GRILL

Off Two-side street,
Near Al Qasra, Ankawa
Mob: 0750 685 8000

Deutscher Hof International

German Restaurant & Beer Garden

Iraq KRG Erbil/Ainkawa
00964(0)750 316 2396
www.deutscher-hof-international.com
deutscher-hof-international@web.de

emp
+9647501449000
+9647701449000
info@erbilmanpower.com
www.erbilmanpower.com

Abu Afif Sweets

Erbil 60meter street,
Bekhtyari main road
+964 750 555 000 1/2
Info@abuafif-sweets.com

www.abuafif-sweets.com

Slymaniah near Park Azadi
+964 748 155 7000
Info@abuafif-sweets.com

Abu Afif Sweets
abu_afif_sweets

TARIN RESTAURANT	0750 483 3005
TCHE TCHE	0750 445 2600
PARADISE	0750 463 8385
HARDEES	0750 861 1582
CUSHION LOUNGE	0750 699 2288
QALADZE	0750 453 5430
B 2 B	0750 814 1444
1001 NIGHT	0750 445 2578
ABU SHAHAB	0750 447 5562
LAFA	0750 450 9996

SHOPPING MALLS IN ERBIL

FAMILY MALL

MAJIDI MALL

ROYAL MALL

VANA MALL

TABLO MALL

SOFY MALL

MAXI MALL

HAWLER MALL

MEGA MALL

NISHTIMAN SHOPPING CENTER

MapCom Company

- Land Survey
- GIS Solutions
- Environmental Studies
- IT & Telecommunications

Iraq, Erbil, 100m Ring Road, Facing Italian City

www.mapcom.org , info@mapcom.org

GATHERTON
EVENTS | MARKETING

+964 (0)770 044 2871
info@gatherton.com
www.gatherton.com

the counter
TRADING COMPANY

EXCLUSIVE WINE & BEER
+964 750 454 4743 • sales@the-counter.info

LARUTRAVEL
Creating Memories
all around the world
Our goal is to provide you with world
class services at affordable prices.
For more information

Erbil : Iraq
Divan Hotel Ground Floor next to Setur Duty Free - Gulan St.
Tel. :+ 964 750 446 8960 /+964750 455 44 11
Jordan : Amman
Abdeen Complex - Next to New English School Building # 35 , 2nd floor ,
office # 203 Amer Bin Malek St. Khalda, Mob : + 962 79 555 04 08

SULAYMANI GOVERNORATE

SULAYMANI

CIHAN GROUP   DARINGROUP   KAR   KURDISTAN IRAQ TOURS   KOREK   RAMADA SULAYMANIYAH   VSC

Sulaymani Skyline

GENERAL INFORMATION / HISTORY

Sulaymani (Sleimani, Slemani, Sulaymaniyah or Suli/Suly for short) is the second largest city in the Kurdistan Region, and the capital of Sulaymani Governorate. It is two hours and forty-five minutes east of Erbil (202 km; 126 mi), and nearly two hours northeast of Kirkuk (127 km; 79 mi). Known as "Kurdistan's second city," it has a population of roughly one million and is widely accepted as the cultural capital of Kurdistan. It is also the most liberal and Western city in Iraq as a whole.

Prince Ibrahim Pasha Baban founded modern Sulaymani 14 November 1784 and named it after his father Sulayman Pasha. Sulaymani is surrounded on all sides by mountains: Azmer, Goyija, and Qaiwan to the northeast; Baranan in the south, and the Tasluja Hills envelop the city to its west.

In ancient history the area that makes up modern Sulaymani Governorate was known as Zamwa or Zamua and was often the site of many conflicts between the Persian Sa-

favid Empire and the Ottoman Empire. In more modern times the city has been one of the main centers of Kurdish nationalism. It was here that Sheikh Mahmoud Barzanji began his rebellion against the British in 1919 and declared the "Kingdom of Kurdistan" two years later.

The city has traditionally been demographically diverse and though most are Kurds there are many Arabs and Christians living

Iraq's most modern city

in the city. At one time there were also many Jews in the city and a neighborhood called "Jewlakan," though it largely fell into disrepair after 1952 when the remainder of Iraq's Jews were evacuated to Israel. There are a few Assyrian, Chaldean, and Syriac churches

in the city as well as a Shi'a mosque, or *husseiniyeh*.

GETTING AROUND

Taxis in town cost between IQD 2,000 and IQD 5,000. There are also many busses and shared taxis/minibuses that travel frequently to many locations.

MAIN POINTS OF INTEREST

BAZAARS

Handicraft Gallery

This gallery was established in 1971 and lies in the center of the city, by the Sulaymani Museum. Interactive, this gallery offers courses on local traditions of ceramics, minerals, silk-screening, carpet weaving, leather works, carpentry, sewing, flower works, and covering works. The overall objective is to preserve and foster local cultural arts and heritage.

Municipal Bazaar

This bazaar is the largest traditional market in the Kurdistan Region, and is larger than the Qaysari Bazaar in Erbil stretching 1.5

Gold Bazaar

km (1 mi) along Malawi and Goran Streets to Ibrahim Pasha St. The bazaar includes traditional shops and stalls as well as street vendors. It is a wonderful place to enjoy the traditions of a Middle Eastern Bazaar where one will find anything from hand crafted gold jewelry to indigenous sweets such as the famed "manna" as well as clothes, carpets and even artwork created in this city renowned for its artists and poets.

Hall of Mirrors

Sardam Gallery

The art gallery is inside the Sardam Publishing House and highlights rotating exhibits by local Kurdish artists. It is a wonderful and somewhat hidden secret in the city and a great place to meet local artists, many of whom speak English.

By the artist's of Sulaymani

MUSEUMS

Amna Suraka Museum

The museum is also known as the "Red Intelligence Museum" and is located in the former Ba'ath intelligence headquarters of Sulaymani prison and intelligence services. It focuses on the former regime's brutality and oppression of Kurds. Visitors can be self-guided but usually are led by a guide through the prison and its many interrogation rooms. Sometimes one of the former inmates serves as the escort and will relate from a personal perspective the horrors the Kurdish people experienced at the hands of Saddam's secret police—the *Mukhabarart*. Thousands were imprisoned and tortured here and many simply vanished.

Outside and amid the pockmarked and bullet-ridden buildings there are several mostly Soviet-era armored fighting vehicles anbandoned by Saddam's army in 1991. *Peshmerga* liberated the prison and in 2003 Hero Ibrahim Ahmed, wife of Kurdish leader and former Iraqi President Jalal Talabani and Kurdish leader, initiated plans to turn the building into the country's first war-crimes museum, which has since become a reality.

The first indoor stop in the tour is the "Hall of Mirrors," a long and narrow hallway lined by 182,000 shards of mirrored glass, which represents the number of people killed or "disappeared" by Saddam during al-Anfal. Additionally the ceiling seems filled with stars with around 4,500 lights—one for every Kurdish village destroyed under Saddam's regime. The basement shows a quite graphic photo gallery depicting the aftermath of the chemical attack on Halabja, which took place on March 16, 1988. The museum guides conduct free tours of the complex and though not all may speak English well or at all, most of the museum needs little explanation. The

Ancient Assyrian Statue

museum isopen 8:00am to 4:00pm daily and is located near Azadi Park.

Ethnographic Museum

This museum focuses on Kurdish folklore. It is in the

process of being moved to a new more adequate location. It is currently located on Khak St. and Azadi Park by the north end of Shorish neighborhood.

Sulaymani Museum

In the center of town by Sekhami Bakhud and Salim Streets is a rare cultural gem. This museum is the second largest in Iraq after the National Museum in Baghdad and houses many Kurdish and ancient Persian artifacts dating back to 1792–1750 BC.

Thousands of ancient artifacts bring visitors to view history dating to Paleolithic times through modern history. One of the most peculiar

Replica of Zarzi Cave Sulaymani Museum

Museum of Antiquities

lies and young people. To the northwest of the park is an amusement park that is lively during the spring and summer in particular.

Bakhi Gisthit Public Park

This park is in the center of Sulaymani and built in 1937 is thought of as the oldest park in the city. The park features statues of famous Kurdish poets and artists. There is also a small playground.

and fascinating artifacts includes a ceramic coffin containing the remains of a 6,000-year-old woman found near Duhok. Another gem is a Greek statue of Hercules from 334 BC. There is also an almost exact replica of Zarzi Cave where some believe the genesis of animal husbandry found its place. The Director of the Museum is often traveling throughout Iraq to obtain new additions to this exquisite collection but when in residence is more than happy to guide foreign visits through the pride of Kurdistan's museums.

Sharaf Khan Bitlisi

PARKS AND NATURE

Azadi Park

Translating as "Freedom" Park it is off of Khak Street and Azadi Park St. The original site was a military base during the former Ba'ath regime. After the 1991 uprising, it was converted to a park and features beautiful gardens, restaurants, a small lake, sports areas, and playgrounds.

Azadi Park is popular for jogging, picnicking or simply people watching. However the most popular time to visit is Friday night, when the park is packed with fami-

Goyzha and Azmar Mountains

Two often snow-covered beautiful and clean mountains overlook the city, making for a wonderful place to picnic, or photograph some of the most dramatic scenery in Kurdistan. On the one side you can view the entire valley wherein nests this great city renowned for its sophisticated culture. Looking out over the other side of Azmer one can see all the way to Iran on a clear day. In the winter, people visit the area to enjoy the snow and in summer, to enjoy the cool temperatures and the natural beauty. It is not uncommon to need a light jacket in the

"City of Parks and Poets"

maniyah and a fifteen-minute drive to Sulaymani International Airport. The area is not new in and of itself, but has developed as a suburban area adjacent to Sulaymani and offers all the essentials of living in the city yet is quieter and more removed from the hustle and bustle of city life.

The area is known for the resort area Sarchinar Park, covered with flowers and surrounded by trees. Recently a number of tourism facilities have been established here; namely hotels, restaurants, swimming pools, and playgrounds. In addition to the well-known Sarchinar Park, there are others such as Nawroz Park and Chaqchaq Park. There is also a very small zoo. Another famous feature is the Tanjero River with its small waterfalls. It is a narrow long river that

evenings even during the hottest of summers in the valley below. Goyzha (Goyja) is famous for the amusement park Chavy Land, which is filled with families and children especially in warmer months.

On top of Azmar is the famous PUK headquarters and commercial tourist attractions, but to get the most enjoyment one needs to drive up and around the mountain. To the eastern part over the village of Bragh you can begin to see the western part of Iran and to the far west the famous Qandil Mountain, one of the main headquarters of the Kurdistan Workers Party organization (PKK) which has long been at odds with the government of Turkey over the rights of the Kurdish people in that country.

Sarchinar Resort (Sarchnar)

This resort is just 8 km (5 mi) or a fifteen-minute drive northwest of Sulaymani. The resort is across the Sulaymani-Kirkuk Rd. from the prestigious American University of Iraq-Sulay-

Grand Mosque

eventually flows into the Derbendikhan Lake near Sarchinar Resort on the outskirts of Sulaymani.

RELIGION

Great Mosque

The Great Mosque of Sulaymani was completed in 1785 by Ibrahim Pasha Baban and contains three small cemeteries as well as the shrine of Haji Kaka Ahmed and his more famous grandson, King Mahmoud. Dominating the center of the city, every day hundreds of people attend the mosque for prayer and to pay homage at these shrines. Friday it is packed, as this is the Muslim holy day. It is near the confluence of Mawlani St. and Kawa, Sabunkaran, Goran, Piramerd Streets.

NIGHTLIFE

The major hotels have bars and often live entertainment. Coffee shops abound throughout the city—both local and International—and are favorite gathering places for locals and expats alike. There is a never-ending supply of restaurants serving both local and International cuisine. Food is usually at the center of any evening out in Sulaymani.

UNIVERSITIES

American University of Iraq–Sulaymaniyah (AUI-S)

It was established in 2007. It is considered one of the most prestigious universities in all of Iraq and instructions are only in English. It is located next to the airport, on the west side of the neighborhood and resort of town of Sarchinar. In June 2010 AUIS was awarded an unconditional five-year accreditation from the American Academy of Liberal Education.

Komar University of Science and Technology (KUST)

The main campus is located in the city of Sulaymani, KUST Building, Near Hiwa Hospital and Malik Mahmoud Circle Street.

American University

Among other courses of studies it is well known for the Center of Intensive English Program and the discipline titled *Ethics: A System Of Moral Principles Knowledge.*

The mission of the Komar University of Science and Technology-Sulaymani (KUST) is to provide an international-standard teaching and learning environment that promotes intellectual, social and personal development of students; to assist them in developing the ability to think critically, creatively and reflectively; and to prepare them for productive careers in Applied Sciences, Business, Engineering, and Engineering Technology.

Sulaymaniyah Polytechnic University

Located in south-central Sulaymani, it was established in 2012, and instruction is in Kurdish, English and Arabic.

University of Human Development

Located outside of the city to its southeast, it offers degrees in four fields: Administration and Economics, Science and Technology, Language, and Law and Politics.

The University of Sulaymaniyah

It was opened in 1968 and offers instruction in Kurdish, Arabic, and English. The university offers degrees in Engineering, Agriculture, Arts, Science, and Medicine and is the largest university in the Kurdistan Region. A new branch was established in 1991. It is in the center of town.

HOSPITALS AND CLINICS

Sulaymani has many clinics throughout the city. Like Erbil it has been steadily modernizing and has many qualified physicians and medical practitioners available.

Faruk Medical Center (FMC)

Located in the southeast part of the city; Malik Mahmoud Ring Road and is one of the most respected hospitals in Kurdistan and in Iraq.

Hiwa (Hope) Cancer Hospital

Located in between FMC and Zerinok on Malik Mahmud Ring Road.

Rapari Hospital

It is next to the airport on Sulaymani-Kirkuk Road.

Sarchinar Hospital

Located (northwest Sulaymani in Sarchinar town.

Shar Hospital

Located northeast, on Malik Mahmud Ring Rd, near Chevy Land Tourist City).

Sulaymani Maternity Hospital/Plastic Reconstructive and Burn Surgery Hospital

Located in the center of town (Qanat and Kawa Sts.)

Sulaymani Teaching Hospital

Located next to University of Sulaymaniyah.

Zerinok

Located south central, at the beginning of Sulaymani-Arbat Highway.

SULAYMANI (SLEMANI) INTERNATIONAL AIRPORT

On July 20, 2005, Sulaymani International Airport opened its doors with regular flights across Europe and the Middle East. It is the Kurdistan Region's second airport, after Erbil International Airport. There is soon to be a third international airport in Duhok.

The airport code is ISU, though also known as ORSU. Located on the southwest part of the city, very close to the American University of Iraq-Sulaymani, the airport's first stone was laid November 29, 2003. The main runway is 3,500 m (11,483 ft.) with a width of 45 m (148 ft.). The airport facilitates both cargo and passenger planes though presently it does not serve charter flights unlike Erbil International airport. ISU

maintains three terminals: Departures, Arrivals, and VIP and serves over a dozen different carriers.

http://www.sul-airport.com/
Further Information
Tel:+964.053.317.0017;
+964.053.317.3322
Email: info@sulairport.net
http://www.sul-airport.com/
http://www.sul-airport.com/

Tour Group in the Citadel

Harry Schute lectures at Gaugemela

First American tour group in Ministry of Tourism

Austrlian students at Koya Caravanserai

Tour guide with tour in Choman Region

Dr. Layton Lectures first American tour group

KURDISTAN IRAQ TOURS
A Division of The Other Iraq Tours LLC

ALWAYS FIRST!

FIRST TOUR COMPANY IN KURDISTAN

Kurdistan Iraq Tours was the first inwardly focused tour company established in the Kurdistan Region of Iraq. The company was officially formed seven years ago and hosted the first official post war tour from abroad originating from the USA.

FIRST IN EXPERIENCE

Kurdistan Iraq Tours founders have been working in the region for nearly 22 years hosting visitors from around the world including VIPs, historical tours, student tours and even the occasional fly fisherman. The directors have nearly 35 years combined experience in Kurdistan with long standing relations from the highest levels of government to the average citizen.

FIRST IN SERVICE

Kurdistan Iraq Tours guides are professionally trained with expansive knowledge of every historical site in the region. We are proud of our attention to detail and specialize in custom designed tours to fit every interest and purse from luxury to economy.

FIRST COMPREHENSIVE TOUR GUIDE

Kurdistan Iraq Tours has produced the first comprehensive Guide to the Kurdistan Region of Iraq. While there are other companion guides and simple overviews this Guide provides the traveler with information on every aspect of Kurdistani society.

TRAVEL WITH THE MOST EXPERIENCED PROFESSIONALS IN THE REGION!

For information on booking a tour to Kurdistan contact:
Email: info@kurdistaniraqtours.com Tel: +964 (0) 750 339 9999

www.kurdistaniraqtours.com

Dare to Dream

It's true that dreaming is important in life. But most importantly you should believe in your dreams and dare to achieve them. Korek believes in you & your potential and encourages you to pursue your dreams.

f t You Tube 411 📞   korektel.com

**GROW YOUR WORLD,
EXPAND YOUR HORIZONS
AND DEVELOP YOUR CAPABILITIES**

Enjoy a fast Internet connection on your smartphone; video calls and data download with Extra
G service from Korek.

To activate any of the bundles:
• Dial *250# and follow the instructions
• Visit "Selfcare" on the following link:
http://selfcare.korektel.com

Dare to Dream

 411 📞   korektel.com

Erbil International Equestrian Racing Club
Masif Road, Erbil, Iraq

the **KOREK** Mountain Resort

Bekhal, Erbil. Iraq
www.thekorektmountain.com • Phone Number : 009647502458888

Family Mall
Shopping & Entertainment Center
Erbil

Family Mall - 100m street – Erbil – Kurdistan Region – IRAQ
www.familymallarbil.com

E-mail: info@familymallarbil.com
Phone Number: 009647505618484

Family Mall
Shopping & Entertainment Center
Sulaymaniyah

OPENNING SOON

Family Mall- 60m street-Sulaymaniyah-Kurdistan Region- IRAQ

Family Mall
Shopping & Entertainment Center
Dohuk

OPENNING SOON

Family Mall- Zaxo Road-Duhok-Kurdistan Region- IRAQ

HOTEL GRAND
SWISS
★ ★ ★ ★ ★

Shaqlawa Road Pirmam (Selahaddin) Erbil, Iraq
Phone Number : 00964 750 440 0044 - 00964 750 440 0045   info@hotelgrandswiss.com

Credit & Debit Cards
البطاقات الائتمانية

ميّز نفسك
بمستوى راق من الخدمات
Be Distinct with a
Finer Level of Services

CIHAN BANK
مصرف جيهان

Main Branch
Cihan Group Plaza Building – Kerkuk Road – Erbil - Iraq , Tel: +964 66 226 2816, Mobile: +964 750 703 59 00 / +964 770 977 19 58
Fax: +964 66 226 28 17 , P.O. Box: (0116-17), Email: info@cihanbank.com, Swift Code: CIHBIQBAXXX | Bank Site: www.cihanbank.com

Bajger Branch	Suleymania Branch	Najaf Branch	Basra Branch	Zakho Branch
Erbil – Near Sirwan Market	Chwarbakh – Kaso Building	Al Rawan Street near to	Al Jazaer Street near to	Ibrahim Khalil Road
Mob.: 00964 750 745 00 95	Tel: 00964 53 326 10 24	the airport intersection, Najaf – Iraq	the Al-Ishar Street, Basra – Iraq	Mob.: 00964 626 738875
Email: br.bajger@cihanbank.com	Email: br.suly@cihanbank.com	Email: br.najaf@cihanbank.com	Email: br.basra@cihanbank.com	Email: br.zakho@cihanbank.com

Baghdad Branch	Kerkuk Branch	Jamila Branch	Mosul Branch	Duhok Branch
End of Al Nidal Street,	Al Madina Street next to	Jamila Market near to the	Al Dirkazliya opposite Alnabi	Korek Street Near Meer Hotel
Near National Theater	Turkmeneli TV Channel, Kerkuk – Iraq	Husseinia Al-Ansar, Baghdad – Iraq	Younes Market, Musoul – Iraq	Duhok - Iraq
Mob.: 00964 770 4640520	Mob.: +964 770 1322692	Mob.: +964 770 4771199	Mob.: +964 770 3800019	Mob.: +964 750 7153227
Email: br.baghdad@cihanbank.com	Email: br.kerkuk@cihanbank.com	Email: br.jamila@cihanbank.com	Email: br.mosul@cihanbank.com	Email: br.duhok@cihanbank.com

CİHAN TEA®
PREMIUM QUALITY TEA

چای جیهان

بەرهەمی بەناوبانگترین باخچەکانی سیلانە

پلازای گروپی جیهان - ڕێگای کەرکوک - هەولێر
Cihan Group Plaza - Kerkuk Road -Erbil
Tel: 066 253 0043 - 0750 445 2434

: www.cihanuniversity.edu.iq
: info@cihanuniversity.edu.iq
: www.facebook.com/cihanuniversity
Mobile (Korek): 009694(0)750 7381000
Mobile (Asia Cell): 009694(0)770 9764040

Experience world's best flavours at Our Panorama Restaurar

Address: Sulaymaniyah, Salim Street, beside public library
Tel:+964 (0) 533 209 515   +964 (0) 533 209 516
Email : reservation@ramadasulaymaniyah-salimstreet.com
     marketing@ramadasulaymaniyah-salimstreet.com

Come experience the
secrets of relaxation.
RELAX, RENEW, REVITALIZE

RAMADA®

SULAYMANIYAH

★★★★★

 RAMADA.Sulaymaniyah   Ramada_sul   @RamadaHotel_SUL

THE FUTURE
IN ACTION

Falcon Security

Falcon Construction

Falcon Agriculture

Falcon Oil & Gas

Falcon Batch Plant

Falcon Travel Agency

Falcon Real Estate

Falcon Logistics

FALCON GROUP
www.falconiraq.com

As a multi-service conglomerate, Falcon Group's mandate is to successfully manage a wide spectrum of dynamic business ventures. Whether in the real estate, security, construction, oil & gas, travel or agriculture sectors, Falcon Group is committed to world-class product and service delivery here in Kurdistan.

Empire World   Empire Business Complex C4   Tel: +964 (0) 66 258 6008 / 6009
Erbil, Iraq   info@falconiraq.com

FULL SERVICE

Full Service is a facility/property management company created to provide world class services to leading residential and commercial projects like Empire World in Erbil, Iraq. In a short time Full Service has become the contractor of choice to major oil and gas companies working in Kurdistan.

Our Services

- Facility / Property Management
- Services for residential and commercial projects
- Maintenance · Cleaning · Catering · Procurement
- Logistic services · Electricity provision · Camp management
- Landscaping · Manpower

Empire World
Empire Business Complex C4
Erbil, Iraq

+964 (0) 66 258 6008/6009
www.fullserviceiraq.com

- Luxury suites and rooms with modern facilities.
- International cuisine.
- 24 hours room service.
- Coffee Shop.
- Conference and meeting venues.
- Fitness Center & Spa.
- Laundry.
- Parking.
- Airport pick up.
- Rent a car.

Erbil, Kurdistan, Iraq, 100 M Street, Int'l Airport Road
Mobile: +964 750 7120777 info@jouhaynahotel.com www.jouhaynahotel.com

JOUHAYNA
جهينة
Hotel & Offices

TANGRAM تانگرام
HOTEL ERBIL

THE SMART HOTEL IN ERBIL

For booking & information
+964 (0) 750 889 5554
+964 (0) 66 229 6900

Kirkuk road, Erbil, Kurdistan Iraq
info.erbil@tangramhotels.com
www.erbil.tangramhotels.com

DARIN PLAZA
HOTEL

Welcome to Darin Plaza Hotel, Erbil's newest luxury address.

Iraq, Erbil, Kurdistan Region, 60 Meter St. Opposite to Jalil Al-Khayat Mosque.

00964 (0)750 210 0001   00964 (0)750 210 0003
00964 (0)750 210 0002   00964 (0)750 210 0004
www.darinplaza.net • darinplazahotel@hotmail.com • info@darinplaza.net

DARIN HOTEL

Being located in 100 Meter St., near Family Fun Darin Hotel gives you the perfect place for your stay whether it is for an entertainment or a business trip.

Iraq, Kurdistan Region, Erbil, 100 Meter St. Near Family Fun.
www.darinhotel.com   00964 (0)750 319 7111
info@darinhotel.com   00964 (0)771 161 2111

AL HAYAT Soft Drinks and Mineral Water Co.
IRAQ-Erbil-Makhmoor St.

divan
erbil

The 5 Star Hotel in Erbil

For reservations please call 066 210 5000

L V X™

Preferred
HOTELS & RESORTS

Gulan Street, Erbil, Kurdistan Region of Iraq
P: +964 66 210 5000, F: +964 66 210 5001
E: info.divanerbil@divan.com, www.divan.com
/DivanErbil /DivanHotelErbil

Fastlink

BE THE FASTEST

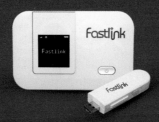

4G LTE Be The Fastest

066121
www.fast-link.com
www.facebook.com/Fastlink4G

Gullan Street English Village Plot NO. 243 Erbil-Kurdistan IRAQ
Phone: +964 750 445 1091
Email: info@albitcompany.com • www.albitcompany.com

ALBiT
CONSTRUCTION AND TRANSPORTATION

RT Bank
مصرف الإقليم التجاري | بانكى لەقليمى بازرگانى

MasterCard

EXPAND YOUR BOUNDARIES WITH MASTERCARD

سنورەکانت فراوان بکە لە گەڵ ماستەرکارت

وسع آفاقك مع ماستركارد

 /RegionTradeBank   RegionTradeBank

Gulan Street, 40m Road, Opposite of Turkish Consulate, Erbil, Kurdistan Region, Iraq.
E-mail: erbil@rtbank.net   Web: www.rtbank.net   Tel: +964 66 353 9777

A NEW STAR IN THE SKY

+964 750 418 4444 | +964 750 420 4444 | www.zagrosjet.com

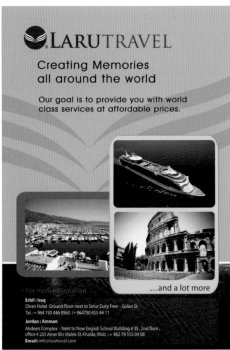

LARU TRAVEL

Creating Memories
all around the world

Our goal is to provide you with world
class services at affordable prices.

...and a lot more

For more information

Erbil : Iraq
Divan Hotel Ground Floor next to Setur Duty Free - Gulan St.
Tel. : + 964 750 446 8960 / + 964750 455 44 11

Jordan : Amman
Abdeen Complex - Next to New English School Building # 35 , 2nd floor ,
office # 203 Amer Bin Malek St. Khalda, Mob : + 962 79 555 04 08
Email: info@larutravel.com

GATHERTON
EVENTS | MARKETING

+964 (0)770 044 2871
info@gatherton.com
www.gatherton.com

emp

Human Resources — Comprehensive HR services including recruitment, payroll, and policy writing

Real Estate — All-inclusive real-estate & facility management services

Event Management — Assisting companies and organizations at every stage of the process, from event planning to implementation

Consultancy — Provide access to local market information

Mobile: +9647501449000
Website : www.erbilmanpower.com

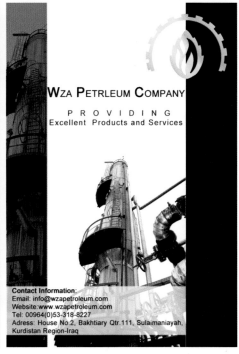

WZA PETRLEUM COMPANY

PROVIDING
Excellent Products and Services

Contact Information:
Email: info@wzapetroleum.com
Website:www.wzapetroleum.com
Tel: 00964(0)53-318-8227
Adress: House No.2, Bakhtiary Qtr.111, Sulaimaniayah,
Kurdistan Region-Iraq

KAR

UPSTREAM | MIDSTREAM | DOWNSTREAM

ERBIL REFINERY

KAR POWER PLANT

www.kar-k.com

KHURMALA DOME

KAR PIPELINE CO.

habruri GRILL

Serving Great Chinese Food For Great People

Off Two-side street, Near Al Qasra, Ankawa
Mob: 0750 685 8000

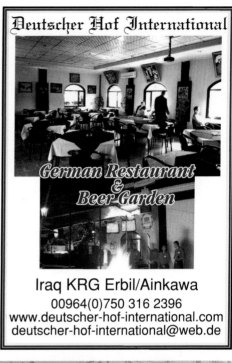

Deutscher Hof International

German Restaurant & Beer-Garden

Iraq KRG Erbil/Ainkawa
00964(0)750 316 2396
www.deutscher-hof-international.com
deutscher-hof-international@web.de

Mystic Art & Design Studio

Ressam Basmacılar Cad. No.22 Kapalıçarşı /
Fatih / İstanbul / TURKEY
gurselbulut@yahoo.com

Geverké Restaurant

Barzan Main St., Duhok, Kurdistan
Tel:+964 750 4268 400 • +964 750 4358 400

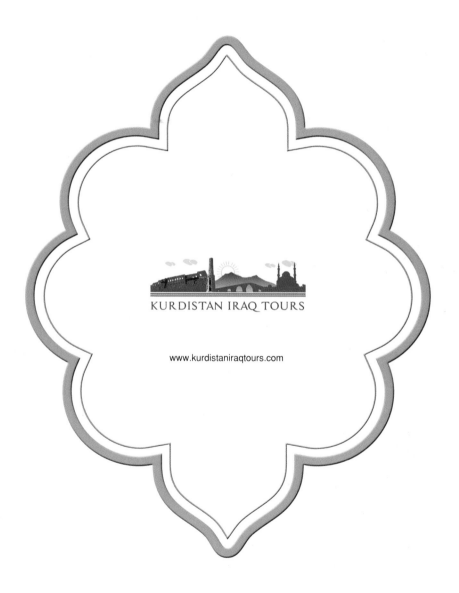

KURDISTAN IRAQ TOURS

www.kurdistaniraqtours.com

HALABJA
(Halabja Governorate)

GENERAL INFORMATION

Until very recently Halabja was considered a part of Sulaymani Governorate but has since been granted status as a Governorate in its own right. Halabja is largely comprised of small towns and villages. The primary city is Halabja City, which lies 74 km (46 mi) (one hour) southeast of Sulaimaniyah and 83 km (52 mi) or one hour and fifteen minutes from Derbendikhan. It is a mere 13 to 16 km (8 to 10 miles) from the Iranian border.

The city lies at the base of what is often referred to as the greater Hewraman region stretching across the Iran-Iraq border. The Kurds in the city of Halabja generally speak only the Sorani dialect of Kurdish, but some residents of the surrounding villages speak the Hewrami dialect.

The town's main bazar surrounds the central grand mosque. There are a few simple restaurants and teashops, but little else. There are frequent buses and some shared taxis from the nearby city of Sulaymani. It is entirely possible to leave Suly in the morning, see the sites of Halabja and make it back to Suly before nightfall, which most visitors prefer, as there are scant adequate hotel facilities locally although this is changing soon.

Halabja is the birthplace of many great Kurdish poets including Ahmed Mukhtar Jaff, Mawlawi, Abdullah Goran, Tahir Bag Jaff, Qanie, and others.

In 2008, plans were announced to construct an international airport for the city.

Memorial Statue

HISTORY

Halabja is a very ancient town, dating back to the Lullubi era. The Lullubi were a loose confederation of tribes residing in the region in the third century BC. Little is known about them apart from accounts of battles they fought against the Akkadians. It is believed that the ancient city of "Khar-Khar" c. 2000 BC is today's Halabja. In the year 641 AD, the Islamic Army captured the town from the Sassanid Empire and it became a part of the Muslim Empire.

During the Abbasid Caliphate, between 959-1015 AD, the Princedom of Hassnawya reigned followed by the reign of the Princedom of Annazi between 1016-1117 AD. The Dukes of Halabja reconstructed the town in 1650 near the present Takya mosque. In 1889, it became a district during the Ottoman Empire. The first school was built in 1919. According to British statistics, the town had a population of 6509 in 1920 and it administrated Penjwin, Khurmal, Warmawa and Derbendikhan. In the 1920s, the city played a great role in assisting the Sheikh Mahmoud Hafid's revolts and defending the town against the Admonz's British warplanes that invaded the town.

At the beginning of the 20th century, there were many British soldiers

Halabja Memorial

stationed in Halabja. During World War I, Adela Khanum saved the lives of several British soldiers, resulting in the British hon-

Reenactment of the Genocide

oring her with the title Khan Bahadur, *Princess of the Brave*. She was also responsible for the building of a new prison, setting up a court of justice, of which she was the first president and one of the few women in the Middle East to hold such a prestigious position.

The Iraqi Regime bombarded the town on 26th of April 1974 resulting in 100 casualties in addition to destruction of houses leaving many people homeless. On May 13th, 1987 Halabja inhabitants initiated an uprising against the Ba'ath regime. In return, the regime bombarded the town to suppress the uprising but the Kurds were successful in gaining temporary freedom from the Baath regime.

On March 16th, 1988, after the uprising and freedom of Halabja from Ba'ath regime, Iraqi planes dropped gas canisters and bombs containing chemical weapons. As an immediate result of the chemical attack at least 5,000 innocent people died and another 7,000 to 10,000 more were severely injured, most of them civilians. The attack is believed to have included the nerve agents Tabun, Sarin, and VX, as well as mustard gas. Iraqi forces using bulldozers and explosives then systematically razed the town, still littered with unburied dead. Many of the town's residents still suffer from cancers caused by Saddam's gas attacks. Survivors assisted by *Peshmerga* and Iranians hastily buried most of the dead in makeshift mass graves. After Halabja was retaken from Iranian and Kurdish rebel forces, Iraqi troops in HAZMAT suits came to Halabja to study the effectiveness of their weapons and attacks. The city was partially rebuilt by the returning Kurds later, even as chemical weapons still contaminated the food and water supplies, soil, and animal populations. The Japanese government later financed a $70 million project to provide access to safe drinking water in response to this humanitarian issue.

It was the first of many chemical attacks against the Kurds and there is an annual national remembrance day of the atrocity in which nearly all Kurds stop for five minutes of silence. Saddam was to have stood trial in Kurdistan for Genocide but was executed for murders he committed in the Shia-majority south before he could be brought to trial. Many believe some Western countries did not want the trial to occur, as there were some Western corporations who supplied Saddam with chemicals used in these weapons.

According to well documented accounts the know-how and material for developing chemical weapons were assuredly obtained by Saddam's regime from foreign sources. According to the documents acquired after the Gulf War most precursors for chemical weapons production came from Singapore (4,515 tons), the Netherlands (4,261 tons), Egypt (2,400 tons), India (2,343 tons), and West Germany (1,027 tons). One Indian company, Exomet Plastics, sent 2,292 tons of precursor chemicals to Iraq. Singa-

A Prayer for the Martyred in Stone

pore-based firm Kim Al-Khaleej, affiliated to the United Arab Emirates, supplied more than 4,500 tons of VX, Sarin and mustard gas precursors and production equipment to Iraq.

From the 2002 *International Crisis Group* (ICG) "Arming Saddam: The Yugoslav Connection" concludes it was "tacit approval" by many world governments that led to the Iraqi regime being armed with weapons of mass destruction, despite sanctions, because of the ongoing Iranian conflict. Among the chemical precursors provided to Iraq from American companies such as Alcolac International and Phillips was thiodiglycol, a substance needed to manufacture mustard gas, according to leaked portions of Iraq's "full, final and

Memorial Cemetery

complete" disclosure of the sources for its weapons programs. The provision of chemical precursors from United States companies to Iraq was enabled by a Ronald Reagan Administration policy that removed Iraq from the State Department's list of State Sponsors of Terrorism. Alcolac was named as a defendant in the Aziz v. Alcolac case in the United States District Court (district of Maryland May 12, 2011) which was dismissed on a technicality. Both companies have since undergone reorganization. Phillips, once a subsidiary of Phillips Petroleum is now part of ConocoPhillips, an American oil and discount fossil fuel company. Alcolac International has since dissolved and reformed as Alcolac Inc."

On December 23, 2005, a Dutch court sentenced Frans van Anraat, a businessman who bought chemicals on the world market and sold them to Saddam's regime, to 15 years in prison. The court ruled that Saddam committed genocide against the people of Halabja; this was the first time the Halabja attack was described as an act of genocide in a court ruling. In March 2008, the Government of Iraq announced plans to take legal action against the suppliers

"Never Again"

of chemicals used in the attack but little more has come of the threat.

Saddam's cousin Ali Hassan al-Majid who commanded Iraqi forces in northern Iraq during that period, which earned him a nickname of 'Chemical Ali' was condemned to death by hanging by an Iraqi court in January 2010, after being found guilty of orchestrating the Halabja massacre. Eighteen tons of documents were uncovered during the 1991 Gulf War detailing the atrocities

of Saddam—one of the more damning was an order written to Ali Hassan al-Majid by Saddam which stated he was to "Kill every man, woman, child, beast, plant and living thing" in the region of Barzan. Ali certainly did his best to comply.

The Kurds to this day complain that they were deprived of the right to try Saddam for his crimes committed in the Kurdish region, and denied the right to close the book on the tragedy by bringing the perpetrator to justice.

HIGHLIGHTS

Despite its dreary history Halabja is a bustling place with a market area and attractive parks on the outskirts of the city. People are very friendly and many people from the world over come to discover Halabja's natural beauty and various types of fruit and vegetation. The local people are pleased and welcoming to foreigners.

Gulan Park

This is an attractive green picnic area 5 km east of Halabja city. The park is known for its fresh water springs, orchards and high trees. There is also a play area for children.

Over 5000 lost loved ones

Halabja Sports Center and Stadium

The newly built Halabja sports center offers a wide range of sporting activities and a world class Stadium. Visitors are welcome to come along and enjoy sports with the locals.

Hawig Park

It is an attractive green picnic area set 5Km east of Halabja city. It is characterized by a fresh water spring, orchard, high trees, fabulous scenery, excellent weather, and playground for children.

Martyrs' Monument and Cemetery

Located at the far end of Halabja is a large park with good views over the town and the surrounding hills.

National Halabja Monument

The Halabja Monument commemorates one of the worst atrocities of the Saddam Hussein era, a gas attack in March 1988 resulting in 5000 deaths. The monument is maintained mostly by survivors and family of the victims, and is used to display doc-uments, pictures and films. The initiative for this monument came from former Iraqi President Jalal Talabani and was supervised by former KRG Prime Minister Dr. Barham Salih to see its opening on 15 September 2003. The vision of the Halabja Monument is to eliminate weapons of mass destruction. Their mission is to work for peace, for the rehabilitation of the survivors and defend the rights of the families of the victims.

Address: Yadgaree Street 964, Halabjah, Iraq
halabja.eu/halabjamonument@yahoo.com

Pasha Mosque

The construction of this mosque dates back to the seventeenth century built by Grand Mohammed Pasha who was the grand father of Othman Pasha Jaff. The mosque also serves as a mausoleum to Pasha Jaff and his wife. In the old times, the mosque served as a center for Islamic sciences and graduated the famous Islamic scholar Mula Abdullah Qutb.

KHURMAL

GENERAL INFORMATION / HISTORY

This small historic town of roughly 11,000 is almost a stone's throw away west from Ahmad Awa (11 km - 7 mi) or 15 minutes. On 16 March 1988, the Iraqi Air Force infamously launched a chemical strike against Halabja but also attacked numerous other cities such as Khurmal, which is lesser known.

Khurmal additionally made the international news as it was claimed that Iraq (under Saddam Hussein) had a chemical weapons factory there. *Al Qaeda in Iraq* working with Kurdish extremists in the area also had its headquarters there at one time. This is the organization that has morphed into ISIS, which is now the main terrorist organization in Iraq. They have however long ago been driven from the region and Khurmal is now a peaceful region open to visits by the international community.

HIGHLIGHTS

The old mosque and minaret are two of the main focal points of the town and purportedly built by Abdullah ibn Omar ibn Al-Khattab — the second Caliph of the Islamic world but there is some dispute as to their origins. The other famous landmark in the town is the increasingly well-known outdoor mineral pond and springs, locally called Garaw where many people come for treatment of skin ailments. There is also a public park with a small stream that is on the northwest part of the city.

In 2003, a US Army soldier teamed up with an American charity, *Spirit of America*, and brought musical instruments to Khurmal. For roughly fifteen years before the 2003 war, Khurmal and the surrounding villages were controlled by an Islamic extremist organization and forbidden to play or listen to music. Ironically enough, these areas were known throughout Kurdistan for their cultural history, including music. *Spirit of America* raised nearly $50,000 USD, including $6,000 USD for instruments that went to Khurmal — 10 pianos, 10 violins, and a portable amplifier. One can sometimes hear the result of this gift in the local teahouses and from the houses of the musically inclined.

In 2013 a group of experts came from Iceland to Khurmal to investigate possible tourism at the mineral pond and designs have been drawn up for this project. The water temperature at Khurmal is 30 degrees Celsius (80 Fahrenheit) rich in silicon dioxide, sulphate, fluorine and chloride and it is considered a "healing" pool making Khurmal a prime area for tourism development.

Many tourists come to Khurmal to escape the fast paced living in the cities, to enjoy the fresh mountain air, and to dip into the mineral pool and springs.

City center art

in the district were forcibly removed from their homes by Saddam Hussein and taken to concentration camps (Daratu, Jdida, Khabat and Kawergosk) in Erbil Governorate, and (Hajiawa, Piramagrun, Bazyan and Baynjan) in Sulaymani Governorate. This forced removal was followed by completely destroying their homes, and villages. During the 23rd anniversary of this event (2012), the KRG UK Representation Office held a seminar to commemorate this horrific act and discussed the need for international recognition of the Kurdish Genocide.

PIJDAR

GENERAL INFORMATION / HISTORY

Pijdar, Pizhdar, or Pshdar is a district northeast from Dukan Lake that abuts the Iran border. Indeed, the Kele border crossing has become a more important point of entry/exit for tourists and commercial purposes alike, as trade with Iran approached $4 billion in 2013. Pijdar is 140 km (87 mi) and two and a half hours north of Sulaymani and 72 km (45 mi) and one hour and a half northeast of the town of Dukan, which is on the southern end of the Dukan Lake. Pijdar is known to be in an area that is part of a fault line, and receives many earthquakes (averaging one major quake every fifty years) though rarely are they more than seven on the Richter scale.

The area is mildly populated, particularly because many villagers fled during the Iran-Iraq War as well as during al-Anfal. In June 1989, more than 100,000 people

Pijdar is also known as the ancestral home of the Mirawdali tribe. This expansive tribe has an estimated 5,000 families, mainly located in Pijdar area on the border with Iran. Some Mirawdali live in the Iranian Kurdish city of Sardasht. The influence of the tribe within Kurdish politics and culture is widely known — their history is said to date back to pre-Islamic Zoroastrian times. Due to the humanitarian and political circumstances in the region many Mirawdali have since settled in Europe, the United States, and Canada.

Pijdar

Rania

expertise and as such, the surrounding areas of Rania are extremely fruitful.

Rania is located very close to Qandil Mountain, famous for being one of the main headquarters of the Kurdistan Workers Party (PKK). Land here is noted for being very fertile as well. The mountains including Kewarash Mountain in the north (1,200 m (3,937 ft.) and Hajila and Makok to the southwest surrounding the city. Between Rania and Chwarqurna, there is a small mountain called Kilkey Kollîn. Between Ranya and Qaladiza, there is another small mountain called Derbend, beside the lake. Rania District itself is surrounded by Kosrat Mountain and Derbend-ikhan Lake in the South, and by Asos and Kolara Mountains in the west.

HIGHLIGHTS

Different from the rest of Sulaymani, there is an extremely high occurrence of periods with extreme drought. Though the area is beautiful year round, September has the most sunshine and brilliant colors. There are many trails and mountains to hike and many natural springs to enjoy while picnicking. Local guides are recommended for those who wish to hike the area.

RANIA

GENERAL INFORMATION / HISTORY

Rania (Ranya) is 118 km (73 mi) east of Erbil (an hour and a half), 72 km (45 mi) southeast of Soran (one hour and fifteen minutes), and 130 km (81 mi) northwest of Sulaymani (two hours). Rania is surrounded by three mountain ranges, and is known as a town and district containing several intriguing sites that include a traditional bazaar in the center of town, and several natural springs in the Dola Raqa valley. Rania and Rania District have more than 100,000 residents. This is beside the four towns and 126 villages that are connected to Rania district. Rania is known for its produce and agricultural

Rania

Rania is known to Kurds as the place where the 1991 uprising, or *Rapareen* began against Saddam Hussein and in fact many people refer to the town as *Darwâza-I Râparin or* "The Gate of the Uprising." This uprising was spontaneous: on March 5 the town suddenly erupted with pent up rage and within ten days, almost every single Kurdish party and their *peshmerga* started a war against the brutal oppression and genocidal policies of the Ba'ath regime. As a result of the Kurds' success, the Iraqi army was forced out of most of the Kurdish regions of the country, thus bringing into power the democratically elected Kurdistan Regional Government (KRG).

There is no consensus on how the town and district got its name. Some believe the name is derived from an ancient king whose name was Rahansha. Others believe it is related to the word *Ran*, (flock of sheep) since the land was fertile and suitable for raising sheep. In an article in *Kurdistani Nwe* newspaper the author claimed the name is rooted from *Orania*, Greek for sky. Regardless, the town was under the

Darbend-i Rania

control of the Kurdish Baban Empire in the middle of the 17th century and this empire received a degree of autonomy under the Ottomans.

Darbend-i Rania Bridge Ze-i Bechuk (Small River)

HIGHLIGHTS

Every March 5 is a particularly exciting and unique time to be in Rania. Celebrations include photographic exhibitions, athletic activities, musical concerts, picnics and delicious food. The University of Rapareen is named after the pivotal uprising in modern Kurdish history. The university is public, and was established in 2011. Overall in Rania District there are three colleges and three other academic institutes.

In the eastern part of the city there is a square called *Qalat,* or citadel. The *Qalat* is thought to be the oldest square of the city. In 1930, the famous Kurdish writer, Ali Said Gawrani, wrote

"Rania has an ancient hill, which is thought that, it is established by the Persian Army, and now it has houses upon each other just like the Castle of Hawler [Erbil]."

Beside the *Qalat*, the city of Rania is home to another famous hill, *Shimshara*, which was excavated as early as 1957-1959 by a joint Danish-Iraqi archaeological team. This hill is counted as one of the oldest hills in the history of Homo Sapiens. More than 250 ancient remains have been found from that hill including a temple or shrine. In addition, a group of Danish and Dutch archaeologists have recently visited the Kurdistan Region to dig in Rania, excavating some of the earliest farming cultures.

Culturally, there is a youth center; several drama groups, musical groups, and six noted private libraries as well as the Public Library of Rania. There are many different kinds of women's organizations as well. As of 2013, there were three magazines, two newspapers, five TV channels, six radio channels, an educational organization, and forty-two social and civil organizations. There are a number of celebrated sporting competitions, literary and artistic festivals held annually. The first known newspaper published in Rania appeared in 1942 under the name of *Blêse* (flame).

Benari Hâjila

This is a tourist area located by the Hajilah mountain chain, between Rania and Chwar Qurna village. People visit this place frequently in order to enjoy its fresh water and clean air.

Betwâta (Sar-Ashkawtân)

Located just 20 km (12 mi) from Rania's town center, Betwâta is an attractive area due to its remarkable geographical location; the area has many springs, waterfalls, gardens, and several large privately owned farms.

Darbend-i Rania

Rania Strait is 6 km (4 mi) east of Rania. There is a new bridge that crosses the Ze-i Bechuk (Small River), which provides spectacular views of the water and surrounding landscapes.

Dâristan-i Rania

Rania Forest is 1 km east of the town center. The total area of the forest is around 600 acres, and lies on the main Rania-Qaladiza road. There is a long mountain chain along the road, called Kewa Rash (Black Mountain). The forest is visited by many due to its greenery.

Doll-i Akoyan and Shawra

Valley of Akoyan and Shawra is 19 km (12 mi) west of Rania. This area is quite mountainous and has several trails where individuals can take in the lush greenery and scenic views.

Gird-i Dimme

The Hill of Dimme is located near the Qalat in the town. In 1957, the Danish archaeological team excavated the site and discovered many historical documents and a temple dating possibly to the Assyrian Empire.

Mezar-i Gor-u-Gulzer

The Shrine of Gor and Gulzer is an ancient cemetery that lies 15 km (9 mi) west of Rania, near the Kishan village (in the valley of Akoyan). The Shrine contains the graves of the lovers Gor and his mistress Gulzer, which lay beside one another. This folkloric tale goes back at least 400 years.

Qure Goyee

This water spring located 5 km east of Rania and lies on the main Rania-Qaladiza road. Many locals believe the spring has medicinal purposes that treat several skin ailments.

Shamshara

The village is located 7 km (4 mi), southeast of Rania. Shamshara's history goes back 4000 years when it was the capital of the region Rania and Pijdar, during the reign of the Assyrians. In 1957 a Danish archeological team excavated the area.

Darbend-i Rania

Takht-i Khorshid-I Khawer Zamin

The Residence of Khorshid is a tourist area near Betwâta village, 20 km (12 mi) west of Rania. The construction of this monument dates roughly 2000 years.

Biyara

TAWELA

GENERAL INFORMATION / HISTORY

Tawela (Tawella, Tawila) is a small village less than a mile from the border with Iran in the famous Hawraman region, approximately 35 minutes east of Halabja (33 km; 21 mi) or an hour and a half southeast of Sulaymani (95 km; 59 mi). Some have dubbed it "the last village in Iraq" since it is almost the furthest east one can go in the country of Iraq.

Much of the village was destroyed during the Iraq-Iran War (1980-1988), but a significant amount of its herringbone stonework remains intact, and reconstruction of the village is continuing. Prior to the war there were 800 families, and as of 2008, 750 have since moved back.

From 1994 through 2003, Islamic extremist groups restricted movement in and out of the village and these groups further did not allow media, and food distribution was either cut or restricted. As a result, UN agencies and NGOs were forced to stop their previous activities in this region. After *peshmerga* and U.S. forces defeated these Islamist groups in 2004, local women's organizations were once again able to help local villagers with medical and psychological support and additionally helped promote health-related education in Tawela including training medical assistants, female doctors, and social workers.

HIGHLIGHTS

The village is at the foot of craggy mountains. A focal point is an aquamarine colored mosque that towers over every other building in the village. Tawela is also known for their walnuts and many of the villagers are walnut farmers.

A main reason why locals and foreigners often travel to Tawela is because this is one of the last areas where unique Kurdish *kalash* (klash) shoes are made. These traditional handmade men's shoes are made using a crochet technique. The tops are painted white and the bottom soles are cloth painted blue. In Tawela it takes ten people to make each pair. Beautifully done, at first they are not entirely comfortable, but after you've worn them several times they begin to get worn in and comfortable. They are worn with the rest of the Kurdish traditional male attire, but sometimes, young men will wear them with jeans or western style clothing. It is advisable not to wear them in the rain, as the paint will likely run.

Aweisar

Aweisar is an area in the well-known Hawraman district, 3 km (1.8 mi) east of the village of Tawela, virtually on the Iraq/Iran border.

Like Tawela itself, Aweisar area is renown for its walnut trees, fruit orchards and fresh water springs. Aweisar is a popular tourist destination where people sit by the stream outside of the village shaded by the forested area and picnic and enjoy the cooler climate. There is a public park as well that is quite beautiful in the fall and spring months in particular.

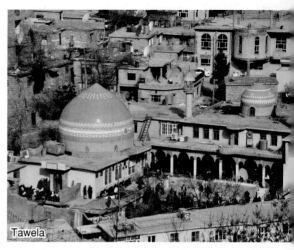

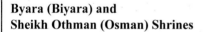
Tawela

Byara (Biyara) and Sheikh Othman (Osman) Shrines

The village is less than one mile from Tawela, and is often referred to as the "heart of

Hawraman" It is beautifully lush and green and mostly surrounded by mountains on all sides that stretch from Sulaymani Governorate through Kermanshah province in Iran.

Sheikh Osman Siraj Eldin Naqshibandi is sometimes incorrectly said to be buried in Tawela. In actuality, the Sheikh (sometimes referred to as Othman instead of Osman) is buried in Byara (Biyare), which is the neighboring village of Tawela. Both are on the road to Halabja. To complicate matters even more, in both villages there are *khanaqas* (dervish lodge) and shrines with the graves of various members of the sheikhs' family.

Sheikh Osman Sirajuddin founded one of the most influential Naqshbandi and Qadiri Sufi orders (khanaqa/tarikya) of the 20th century. His full name was Muhammad Othman Siraj al-Din ibn *Sheikh* Muhammad Ala al-Din al-Huseini. His family line extended back to other important sheikhs, and the Naqshbandi order itself has been present in Kurdistan since at least the 1600s ("The Naqshbandi order in Seventeenth-century Kurdistan," Martin van Bruinessen, published in *Mullas, Sufis and Heretics:*

Unique Kurdish *kalash* (klash) shoes

The Role of Religion in Kurdish society. Collected articles. Istanbul: The Isis Press, 2000)

As a child he was known for his exemplary behavior and was seemingly always inclined to Islam in its purist form and loved Quran recitation. In the early 1950s he took upon many responsibilities leading prayer and was also knowledgeable in herbal medicine and treated many people for their ailments. After leaving Byara in the late 1950s he moved to Iran and established a school. It was said he had more than one million followers at the height of his influence. He was known for his compassion and service to all Muslims and as many as three hundred people would visit him daily. He assisted the poor and destitute and regarded himself as a servant of the poor.

In 2002 or 2003 when Ansar al-Islam, an al-Qa'ida offshoot controlled Halabja and its environs, they destroyed some of the graves in the mausoleum of the Byara *khanaqa*, dug up the remains and carried them off. Surprisingly, they did not destroy the most important graves and the Imam of the now rebuilt mosque was able to save the bones and replaced them in the tomb. Today, there are regular services and Sufi performances in the *khanaqas* in both Byara and Tawela since joint *Peshmerga* and U.S. forces defeated Ansar al-Islam. The site accommodates several shrines of spiritual sheikhs, such as the shrine of Sheikh Ala'addin Naqshabandi. Thousands of followers visit the village each year to pay homage to the Sheikh.

Not only do many visitors travel to these shrines to pay respects to the Sheik's families but many also come to pray for better health, children, spouses, and so on.

Special thanks to Dr. Martin van Bruinessen and Dr. Jan Bojer Vindheim for their input and clarification on the various Sheikhs and their actual locations

Inside Sheikh Osman Shrine

AHMAD AWA RESORT

GENERAL INFORMATION / HISTORY

Ahmad Awa

From Sulaymani, the best way to get to Ahmad Awa is to drive southeast for 80 km (50 miles), which is an hour and fifteen minutes drive. From Halabja to Ahmad Awa it is only 30 km (19 mi) northeast, which is approximately a 30 minutes drive.

This beautiful and unique resort is close to the town of Khurmal, in the mountainous Hawraman region of Kurdistan, which stretches into Iranian Kurdistan. The resort is tucked away in a lush green valley, and crossed by the Zalm River, which flows down the middle of the mountain.

Many Kurds, Arab-Iraqis, and increasingly foreign tourists travel here year round, though particularly in the spring and summer since it is cooler during these months. It's remote location makes Ahmed Awa significantly less popular than more centrally located resorts like Gali Beg, for example. This remoteness is also relevant because shortly after the waterfall the mountain becomes steep and there are no roads, and the area is known to be a smuggling route — and mined. While it is safe for foreigners to visit this area, it is not advisable to venture off onto any "unbeaten paths" and never without a local guide. Guides are readily available.

HIGHLIGHTS

The waterfall is the most well known sight and contributes to the already gorgeous surrounding areas. Visitors can walk almost up to the base of the waterfall via the tall abutting rocks jutting out from the middle of the water. There is a ledge off to the side and for those who want to stretch their legs a little more, there are very nice, new, and wide steps leading to the top of the waterfall. Some bravely dive into nearby pools, which though scary seemingly appear deep

enough! Try it at your own risk.

The most notable and attractive locations are currently without any hotels or motels and it is also advised that care should be taken as there is a dearth of signs pointing people toward the waterfall and resort in general. A proper taxi or guide is advised. There are also not many restaurants or proper restrooms in the area, though this improves every year. In 2012 the Kurdistan Tourism Board (KTB) reported that over 25,000 tourists visited Ahmad Awa during one holiday that year and 40 percent of these tourists were Iraqis living in other parts of the country.

Despite the lack of services one may find in resorts elsewhere, many families picnic in the area overlooking the waterfall, and there are several teashops as well as other shops selling snacks and assorted goods.

Other streams originating at higher elevations feed the large spring and waterfall. This created the Zalm River, which in turns flows into the Tanjero River, which then in turn flows into the Derbendikhan reservoir several miles away. There is an abundance of vineyards, pomegranates, walnut trees, wheat and barley growing by local farmers who live in the smattering of neighboring villages and who utilize the streams for water and other domestic usages.

There have been sighting of wild mountain goats and Egyptian Vultures in addition to hosting around 70 different bird species. Some claim there are a couple of Persian Leopards in the area, and surprisingly a variation of the Azerbaijan Newt! This area is an unprotected resort and human interference has hurt the ecological surroundings but there are conservation efforts being contemplated to protect this amazing and largely unspolied area.

DERBENDIKHAN

GENERAL INFORMATION / HISTORY

Derbendikhan, Darbandikhan, or Derbendîxan, is a town in Sulaymani Governorate. The city is close to Derbendikhan Lake and on the border with Diyala Province, 83 km (52 mi)

Derbendikhan

Ancient Bas Relief

twenty-six species of fish and a hundred and twenty five species of plants. The lake is home to the (nearly threatened) Eurasian Otter, Golden Jackals, and Eurasian Lynxs. Incredibly, and only on rare occasions one may be able to find endangered species like Egyptian Vultures or even Persian Leopards!

Darbandi Bilolh Sculpture

Darbandi Bilolh (Bilolah, Bilula or Darbadi Bilula) is a bas-relief carved onto the cliff of Derbendi Bilula Mountain, in the Hori and Shekhan areas of Sulaymani, near the Iranian border and is located northeast of Bilolh village.

The most captivating feature of the area is a carving made c. 2,100 BC. It features a victorious man with two captives before him; one is kneeling and the other one is under his victors' foot. To the right of the relief are ancient Akkadian cuneiform inscriptions written over four columns. The Akkadian Empire was an ancient Semitic empire that spread from Mesopotamia through the Levant to part of Iran.

from Halabja (an hour and fifteen minutes), 65 km (40 mi) from Sulaimani (one hour), and 75 km (47 mi) (one hour) from Kalar.

HIGHLIGHTS

Derbendikhan is surrounded by a great deal of wildlife and natural settings including several mountains known to locals such as Baranan, Bashari, Zmnako and Zawaly. Many people take walks or picnic next to the nearby lake or rivers. Derbendikhan's main feature is the large freshwater reservoir generated by the Derbendikhan Dam. Two historical rivers feed the dam, the Tanjero in the north and the Sirwan (Diyala) in the east. The area is additionally unique ecologically as numerous distinct species vital to the ecosystem can be found in the immediate environs. There are over fifty distinct species of birds while the Lake boasts

Derbendikhan Dam

This is a multi-purpose embankment dam on the Diyala River in northern Sulaymani Governorate, Iraq constructed between 1956 and 1961. The purpose of the dam is largely irrigation, flood control, hydroelectric power production and recreation. Due to poor construction and neglect, the dam and its 249 MW power station have undergone several repairs over the years. In

City center art

Derbendikhan Lake

2007, the World Bank began a US$40 million project to repair the Derbendikhan and Dukan Dams.

Derbendikhan Lake

The surrounding environment is biologically diverse for wildlife and listed as an "Important Bird Area" by *BirdLife International*. Many people derive various uses from this lake. It is used as a major source for drinking

and irrigation water and an area for crucial fisheries.

Today Derbendikhan is primarily a tourist/picnic destination, and is surrounded by a great deal of wildlife and gorgeous natural settings including several mountains such as Baranan, Bashari, Zmnako and Zawaly.

Sartaki Bamo

East of the town of Derbendikhan by 15 km (9 mi), or 78 km (49 mi) from Sulaymani is a naturally beautiful area where tourists visit mostly during the spring and summer months. In fact the word "Sartak" loosely translates to "fabulous natural area" and is located on the base of Bamo (Bimu) Mountain. Because of its high altitude, the summer months are known to be cooler in the Sartak Valley, which makes it a great

place for tourists during this time. On the top of Bamo Mountain are remains of an ancient town, Yazdan Kurd, likely a Yezidi/Zoroastrian-inhabited area.

In the last several years there has been an increased interest in the ecology and geology of this area and many scholarly papers have been published as well as presented at conferences about new findings in the Kurdistan Region and particularly the Sulaymani environs. However, in order for this area to be more thoroughly investigated, it must be completely cleared of mines, likely dating to the Iraq-Iran war (1980-1988). In 2012 a young man was found killed by a landmine on Bamo Mountain and no one should hike in the area without an experienced guide.

Tuni Baba

A long and winding path carved into the rock by wind and sea long ago, this natural wonder is worth a visit. It is just south of the town of Derbendikhan. It is said that ancient nomadic civilizations used this path on their migrations. This small and lengthy valley contains water resources. In the area you can also spot ruins of ancient civilizations.

Dukan Valley

DUKAN

GENERAL INFORMATION / HISTORY

55 km (35 mi) or 45 minutes northwest of the city of Sulaymani, Dukan (Dokan) is one of the better-known tourist destinations in the Kurdistan Region. It is 70 km (44 mi) or one-hour southeast of Rania.

Lake Dukan is the largest lake in the Kurdistan Region. The Dukan Dam and reservoir was built between 1954 and 1959 as a multi-purpose dam to provide water storage, irrigation and hydroelectricity. Prior to the flooding of Lake Dukan, the area was replete with archaeological sites. Inhabitants of some 50 villages in the flooded area (1,000–1,200 families) were resettled to the west of the lake.

Lake Dukan

HIGHLIGHTS

The main attraction is the man-made reservoir-dam (the largest in the Kurdistan Region), which includes a hydroelectric power station. Dukan Dam is located on the Lesser Zab River, a tributary of the Tigris River. The area boasts hundreds of species of birds, several hundred plant species, dozens of reptiles and mammals such as the (near threatened) Eurasian Otter and Striped Hyaena. There have also been reports of wolf attacks on local animal herds.

The Dukan area is famous as a resort area. Currently, the resort contains, the Ashur Hotel and for those seeking a different kind of vacation, 'cabins' are also available, though visitors should bring their own food (or car). The cabins are hotel suites and not rustic in the least. They are quite pleasant and comfortable, and the staff speaks English well.

The Lake also offers its own Rowing Club which is the official Iraqi rowing team seeking to qualify for the Olympics. The club aims to help the development of rowing in Iraq and the Middle East. The Iraqi National Team sent a double to the 2008 Beijing Olympics. Lake Dukan Rowing Club seeks to provide a training venue to Iraqi athletes. In promoting the sport of rowing, the club also hopes to play some small part in peace building through athletics in Iraq and the Middle East.

The resort boasts several new projects, newly built hotels, cabins, restaurants, and other tourist facilities either in the upper side of Dukan by the lake or downward by Qashqoli River.

Hazar Merd Cave

The lake is ideal for swimming, boating, and fishing. There is a plan being undertaken by major Middle East corporations to further develop the resort, which would include more hotels, restaurants, residential areas, cinemas and even casinos.

Hazar Merd Cave (Cave of aThousand Men)

Hazar Merd is a group of Paleolithic cave sites excavated by Dorothy Garrod in 1928. The caves are located south-southwest of Sulaymani. Garrod's investigations in two caves in the Hazar Merd group provided evidence of Middle and Epi-Paleolithic (stone age) occupation. The Dark cave or Ashkawty Tarik in Kurdish has a commanding view of the local valley and is close to a small spring and a village with the same name and has a single lofty chamber 11 by 12 m wide (36-39 ft.) containing many hearths, burnt flints and bones.

The remains of bones are from wild goat, red deer, gazelle, field mice, mole rats, hare, bats and several birds of woodland and scrub habitat. This evidence, and that from the presence of snails indicates a mixed environment of woodland, grassland and scrub, much as exists today.

Hazar Merd Cave

Jasana Cave

This cave is about 50 Km (30 mi) west of Sulaymani city on the Sulaymani – Dukan highway. It is located at the foot of the mountain near behind Kani Khan village. On 3/2/1923 the British army bombarded Sulaymani city by aircraft during their conflict with King Mahmood who was forced to leave Sulaymani and move to Sardash area making "Jasana Cave" his headquarters and safe haven. This cave is also famous as the site of the first edition of *Bangi Haq* newspaper meaning (Call for Truth, or Call for Justice) printed on a press secreted to the location.

Jasana Cave

Badawa/Dukan

Qashqoli Resort

On November 30, 2011, a small NGO, *Development Now* partnered with *Nature Iraq* and others, and implemented an environmental project at the Qashqoli River. The staff of these NGOs and volunteers partnered with local school children and cleaned two sites on the Qashqoli River. Due to a great deal of infrastructure and tourism related construction, such as tourist cabins and residential areas and resulting sewage runoff, there has been a high negative impact on the environment. The NGOs assisted in cleaning the area and initiated a more comprehensive urban development plan as well as water management plans and even hope to improve the efficiency of the dam itself in the future.

Qopi Qaradagh

Qaradagh is known for its adjacent high mountainous sites (Qopi), each of which are three kilometers (1.8 miles) away from the other. The highest peak is 1822 m (5,978 ft.). There there are several water springs that attract people who come to enjoy the natural beauty. Tourists can take rest at the resort cabins. The area has many important historical sites such as one of the sires related to the King of Lullubi

Qashqoli Resort

Pasha Gawra

above Dukan. It was built between 1813 and 1837 A.D. during the era of Mir Mohammed, who was also called "Pashai Gawra". Mir Mohammed was the prince of the "Soran" principality at the time. Some of the Castle's foundations and parts of the wall are still standing today.

Mir Muhammad (sometimes popularly known as Pasha Kor, Mir Kor, (Kor is sometimes rendered as Kore), essentially 'Blind King' (kor means blind in Kurdish) was the ruler of the Soran Emirate which stretched all the way to Dukan—making this fortress somewhat of a last outpost. Soran was one of the more powerful emirates and the capital of Rawanduz was at the time one of the most powerful as far as Kurdish nobility goes. Mir Muhammad, like his predecessors, had rivalries with many of his neighbors but entertained grander notions of being declared 'King' of a Kurdish state.

The collapse of the Badinan reign due to Ottoman pressure occurred in 1837. The assault of the Ottoman Sultan Abdul Majeed I against the Kingdom of Botan resulted in the killing of the Kurdish ruler Pashai Gawra (the Great Pasha) in Istanbul by the Turks.

who reigned in the 3rd millennium BC, and many ancient stone graves can be seen here as well.

Sargalu

Sargalu is one of the Jaff Valley villages, which lies 65 km (40 mi) or 45 minutes from Sulaymani. The village has many kinds of orchards and farms. The once famous "Voice of Kurdistan" radio was broadcast from Sargalu.

Winter in Dukan

Sarsir Summer Resort

Located 36 km (22 mi) or half an hour north of Sulaymani, Sarsir Resort is surrounded by trees and several fresh water springs as well as recreational facilities attracting many tourists in the spring, summer, and fall.

Sartka Citadel / Pasha Gawra

The Great Pasha Fortress is located on a mountain

KUNAMASI

GENERAL INFORMATION / HISTORY

Not to be confused with the town of Kani Masi in Dohuk Governorate, near the city of Zakho, Kunamasi is in Sulaymani Governorate. It is also referred to as Kuna Masi, Kanamasi, Kana Masi, Kuna Masi River, or Chami Chwarta River and in Arabic Wadi Kunah Masi. It is 50 km (31 mi) or roughly forty-five minutes northeast of Sulaymani and 107 km (67 mi) or two hours east of Penjwin and is 790 m (2,592 ft.) above sea level.

HIGHLIGHTS

Kunamasi (Fish Cave) is also a nearby destination for tourists and interested explorers and archaeologists alike. The village contains several wells and springs and is a popular tourist destination

The main stream of Kunamasi is made of three streams/rivers: Maluma, Kanimew and Sangar. Each stream consists of several branches, and Kunamasi itself is a tributary of the Lesser Zab River, which flows from the foot of a mountain.

The surrounding environment is renown for its walnuts, pear, almond farms and orchards. Additionally, there are nearly forty separate species of birds that have recently been found in and around Kunamasi. The area is commercially known for its gravel mining, which has negatively affected the environment to a significant degree. As of 2012 parts of Kunamasi still had landmines due to the Iran-Iraq War (1980-1988) yet these areas seem to be well displayed in most locations and mine clearance activities are currently being conducted in this region by NGOs and the KRG. However it

Malakan

is still recommended that hikers use local Guides when in the area.

MALAKAN AND ALANA VALLEY

GENERAL INFORMATION / HISTORY

Malakan is 15 km (9 mi) east of Khalifan and Soran, near the tourist area of Korek Mt. It is 105 km (65 mi) north of Erbil (an hour and a half). The Alana village has a population of less than 1,000 and villagers use the creek/river as well as deep wells for their water supply.

These two valleys have been immortalized in orientalist writings of the early 20th century including, *Kurds, Arabs and Britons: The Memoir of Col. W. A. Lyon in Kurdistan, 1918-1945* (2002) edited by David K. Fieldhouse, *Road Through Kurdistan: Travels in Northern Iraq* (2005) by A.M. Hamilton

and, *Iraq and Rupert Hay's Two Years in Kurdistan* (2008). These books highlight the beauty of the area and its fascinating inhabitants.

Unfortunately, these two areas are also documented as being areas that were deliberately targeted under Saddam Hussein's Al-Anfal Campaign. On May 25, 1987, during "Anfal VI," Iraqi forces attacked the Malakan Valley with chemical weapons, and with mustard gas in at least one instance. One of the bombs dropped from the air landed in the spring at the top of the valley and for over three years there were no fish living in the river that stretched over ten miles. On June 11, 1987, on an airstrike on five villages in the Malakan Valley, it was reported, "thirty persons lost their eyesight." Shortly thereafter Saddam attacked the city of Halabja in a now infamous attack that left over 5,000 dead.

HIGHLIGHTS

The area is incredibly beautiful but largely undeveloped for visits by International tourists – a minus on the one hand and a plus for those seeking a more natural experience. There are several tourist attractions in Malakan albeit very basic and sparse amenities such as teashops and snack shops.

The Alana River crosses the valley in which more tourist areas have been established since 2003 and there are many crossing points between the two riverbanks. The river is small and appears more like a creek or stream though the natural beauty is perfect for picnics and tourism and locals often dip their feet in the water during hot days.

SARGALU

GENERAL INFORMATION / HISTORY

Seemingly just another quaint village nestled among streams and mountains, it is actually quite an important location both historically, culturally, religiously, and politically.

From February 26-28, 1988 there were roughly 400 families living in Sargalu. The small village had a mosque, primary school, and hospital. Over those

Malakan

two days, the Iraqi Air Force chemically bombarded much of the area. It was for a period, the headquarters of the *peshmerga* in that area and was additionally where the legendary Voice of Kurdistan Radio was broadcast during that time period.

Currently it is one of the many villages that make up the Jaff tribal area approximately 65 km (40 mi) or forty-five minutes from Sulaymani and is known to be full of rich orchards, vineyards, farms, and several fresh water sources. The surrounding area is largely mountainous with rocky ridges and steep valleys. To the south lies Daband Mountain and Halaj Mountain to the north. The small quaint villages of Sargalu and Bargalu are tucked away in the valley between both mountains.

Baha'u'llah (1817-1892), the main prophet and founder of the Baha'i faith is recorded to have journeyed to Sulaymani and to Sargalu itself during his somewhat self-imposed semi-retirement in Kurdistan. In 1854 he journeyed to Sulaymani hiding his real identity and pretended to be a dervish by the name of Darvish Muhammed Irani. His first year he lived in a cave on Sargalu Mountain, which was then a three day walk from Sulaymani. Shortly thereafter, he met the head of the famous Naqshbandi Sufi order, Sheikh Ismail who personally invited him to live in the city. They developed respect for one another and the Sheikh persuaded Baha'u'llah to move to the city.

Sargalu

For some time, he successfully cut ties with the outside world. Many Sufi Muslim mystics in the area who related closely to him favored such asceticism. The Sheikh once requested that Baha'u'llah compose an ode, known to Baha'i as the "Poem of the Dove (al- Qasidah-al-Warqa'iyyah)", which is one of his most famous poems.

HIGHLIGHTS

There are several streams originating from

Sargalu

Setak

Setak Area

the mountains and eventually all spill into the Sargalu stream. Many tourists come here in the spring and summer to enjoy the water and small waterfalls, and most recently wealthier visitors have begun building summer homes in the area. There are a few caves that have great potential archeological and historical significance and in time it is believed the area will become an important historical treasure trove.

SETAK AREA (MOUNTAIN)

GENERAL INFORMATION / HISTORY

Setak is a popular touristic area, set in the mountains next to Azmar and Goyzha Mountains, roughly 20 km (12 mi) or fifteen minutes north of Sulaymani.

HIGHLIGHTS

Many locals and tourists visit this area for picnics in the spring and summer to enjoy fresh mountain air and exquisite scenery that is now being joined by modern buildings and neighborhoods. It is an area surrounded by the peaceful noises of rustling trees and exquisite smells of various fruit orchards.

Prior to the mass interest in developing Setak, it was a simple village with mostly farmers and fruit orchards. Due to the development of the area, many wealthy and famous people have begun building homes in the area.

Currently there is an international company developing "Setak City," which is an upscale planned neigh-

borhood that will include a commercial city center, cultural and entertainment areas. In addition to the several hundred homes that will be built, hospitals, schools, and open green spaces will be provided. The complex will be made of six large skyscraper towers with an average height of 170 m (550 ft.). Each will hold 50 floors and there are to be three towers that exceed 500 m (1640 ft.). These will include offices, hotels, and luxury apartments. Future plans will include cinemas, auditoriums, and various types of museums. The project is near completion.

Cast of Bas Relief / Merquilly

MERQUILLY

GENERAL INFORMATION / HISTORY

Also known as Qimmat Mirquri or Mirquli, this site is a famous carved bas-relief dating to at 1,000 BC and rests at the top of Pira-

Piramagrun Mountain

magrun Mountain ("Old Magrun") forty-five minutes (46 km; 29 mi) northwest of the city of Sulaymani. It is an important site from the Sassanid or Parthian period. At the highest, it is 1,739 m (5,705 ft.).

The original relief has been damaged over the years but to preserve the form of the reliefs an exact replica cast was made and is now on display in the Sulaymani Museum. There is little left of the original and the site is difficult to find unless you are guided by a local or some agency that knows the area.

HIGHLIGHTS

This rock-relief, a supposed accidental discovery in 1999, is overlooking the village of

A short climb to Zarzi Cave

Zewiya. The area was excavated in 2009 revealing a small settlement, attributed to the Parthian period (247 BC-224 AD). The bas-relief portrays a man in Parthian royal dress facing the valley.

ZARZI (QUISHQIPAN) CAVE

GENERAL INFORMATION / HISTORY

Roughly 58 km (36 mi) or one hour northwest of Sulaymani is a cave that has been in use for as many as 30,000 years! Zarzi cave is 750 m (2,460 ft.) above sea level and next to Zarzi village. Its earliest inhabitants originated from the Mesolithic era. The inhabitants mostly hunted gazelle (non-existent in Kurdistan today) and archaeologists also found remnants of fox, wild goat, sheep, fish, turtle, and freshwater mollusks and crab in this incredible cave.

The Old Stone Age (Middle Paleolithic) people were found to have lived in this cave near Zarzi village, and many flint implements from the Upper Paleolithic Era were found.

Famous British archaeologist Dorothy Garrod (1892–1968) is credited with being the first to discover and professionally excavate Zarzi Cave. She found Paleolithic Era remains as early as 1928. In 1960, there was further excavations from the University of Chicago that yielded a great amount of information as well. Excavations are continuing at present, and will surely produce a great amount of information relating to prehistoric eras and the cradle of civilization.

Zarzian culture itself dates to the late Paleolithic and Mesolithic Eras that spread from

Zarzi Cave

modern day Iraq, Iran, into Central Asia. The cultural time period is approximately set at 18,000-8,000 years BC.

HIGHLIGHTS

The cave is surrounded by many Dwarf Oak and Pistachio trees and there is a pleasant stream only 95 m (312 ft.) from the cave, the Cham Tabin stream, a minor tributary of the Lesser (Little) Zab river, which itself flows into the Tigris, southwest of the city of Kirkuk.

There are only a few known Zarzian sites and this is perhaps the best preserved. Based on the types of animal remains archeologists deduced that this culture was primarily hunter-gatherer culture. Additionally intriguing is that Zarzian sites include remains of domesticated dogs as well as bows and arrows. It is believed that these were among the first people on earth to engage in the domestication of animals.

The site is so important that a near exact replica has been created and put on display in the Sulaymani Museum of Antiquities. Regardless of the precision of the replica there is no substitute for a visit to one of Kurdistan's most important archeological and historical sites.

Zarzi Cave Interior

KOREK Telecom

GROW YOUR WORLD, EXPAND YOUR HORIZONS AND DEVELOP YOUR CAPABILITIES

Enjoy a fast Internet connection on your smartphone; video calls and data download with Extra G service from Korek.

To activate any of the bundles:
• Dial *250# and follow the instructions
• Visit "Selfcare" on the following link:
http://selfcare.korektel.com

Dare to Dream

f 411

korektel.com

KAR

UPSTREAM | MIDSTREAM | DOWNSTREAM

- KHURMALA DOME
- KAR PIPELINE CO.
- ERBIL REFINERY
- KAR POWER PLANT

www.kar-k.com

Just Relax....

Ramada Sulaymaniyah is stylish and contemporary
Premise dedicated to your lifestyle and well-being
by offering highest international standards of
service with true Eastern Hospitality

Address: Sulaymaniyah, Salim Street, beside public library
Tel:+964 (0) 533 209 515   +964 (0) 533 209 516
Email : reservation@ramadasulaymaniyah-salimstreet.com
         marketing@ramadasulaymaniyah-salimstreet.com

RAMADA.
SULAYMANIYAH
★★★★★

WZA PETROLEUM COMPANY - FOR OIL AND GAS SERVICES
Providing Excellent Products & Services

www.wzapetroleum.com
info@wzapetroleum.com
00964(0)53-318-8227
House No.2, Bakhtiary Qtr.111, Sulaimaniyah, Kurdistan Region- Iraq

Bazian Refinery Project, Sulaimaniyah

Erbil 60meter street,	Slymaniah near Park Azadi
Bekhtyari main road	+964 748 155 7000
+964 750 555 000 1/2	Info@abuafif-sweets.com
Info@abuafif-sweets.com	**www.abuafif-sweets.com**
Abu Afif Sweets	abu_afif_sweets

بونیادنانـــی 15,000
یەکەی نیشـتەجێبوون
لەهەرێمی کوردستان

دەستەبەرکردنی هەلی کار بۆ
زیاتر لە 5000 کـــــارمەند

www.Bareazgroup.com
/ Bareaz Group

WHERE TO SLEEP, EAT AND SHOP IN SULAYMANI

SULAYMANI HOTELS:

ASHUR HOTEL	0770 221 4404
AZMAR PALACE	0770 191 9630
DIARY HOTEL	0770 152 4487
DOKAN PALACE HOTEL	0770 154 9300
ZAGROS MOTEL	0770 152 5505
DIM DIM HOTEL	0770 777 2483
BRAYAN HOTEL	0770 159 5468
SHERWANA PALACE HOTEL	0770 422 7757
CHRAKHAN HOTEL	0770 158 1363
SHAM MOTEL	0770 152 3464
MIHRAKO HOTEL	0770 220 0510
SLEMANI PALACE HOTEL	0770 143 3805
ABU SANA HOTEL	0770 155 0064
CAPTHORNE BARANAN HOTEL	0770 152 2222
DAWA HOTEL	053 322 5002
LALE-ZAR HOTEL	053 319 2601
RAMADA	053 320 9515
GRAND MILLUNNUM	0770 700 0000
SHKAR RESTAURANT	0770 152 1192
AZADI HOTEL	0770 155 3705

SULAYMANI RESTAURANTS

SLEMANI CULTURE CENTER	0770 771 2029
MILANO RESTAURANT	0770 157 7510
ABDULLA KABAB	0770 192 0056
SAZI RESTAURANT	0770 152 2559
OSCAR RESTAURANT	0770 155 8927
ROMA RESTAURANT	0770 155 3113
KABAB WALI	0770 146 7050
BAKHTIARY RESTAURANT	0770 253 8008
DAWA RESTAURANT	0748 015 6259
MALI CHALAK	0770 151 2976
B 2 B	0770 894 4959
PASHA RESTAURANT	0770 894 2135
TEXAS CHICKEN	0770 154 0453
KANARY RESTAURANT	0770 769 9222
CAPTAIN RESTAURANT	0770 145 8945
HAM RESTAURANT	0770 152 6006
MILANO RESTAURANT	0770 157 7510
ONE RESTAURANT	0770 101 77894
DILAN RESTAURANT	0770 151 8220
WLAT RESTAURANT	0770 522 1265
CAFE BARBERA	053 330 2930
GUSTO BLUE	0770 766 1000
SARA RESTAURANT	0770 658 4904

SHOPPING MALLS IN SULAYMANI

MAJIDI MALL
RAND GALLERY
CITY STAR SHOPPING MALL
CITY CENTER MALL
ZARA SHOPPING CENTER
KASO MALL
FAMILY MALL
METRO SHOPPING CENTER
PARK TOWER MALL

Erbil 60meter street,
Bekhtyari main road
+964 750 555 000 1/2
Info@abuafif-sweets.com
www.abuafif-sweets.com
Slymaniah near Park Azadi
+964 748 155 7000
Info@abuafif-sweets.com

Abu Afif Sweets
abu_afif_sweets

WZA PETROLEUM COMPNAY

Hiwa Foundation
Enable creativity and perfection

Non Profit Organization

Office: +964 (0) 748 061 9999
Mobile: +964 (0) 770 197 8106
E-Mail: banu@hiwafoundation.org
www.hiwafoundation.org

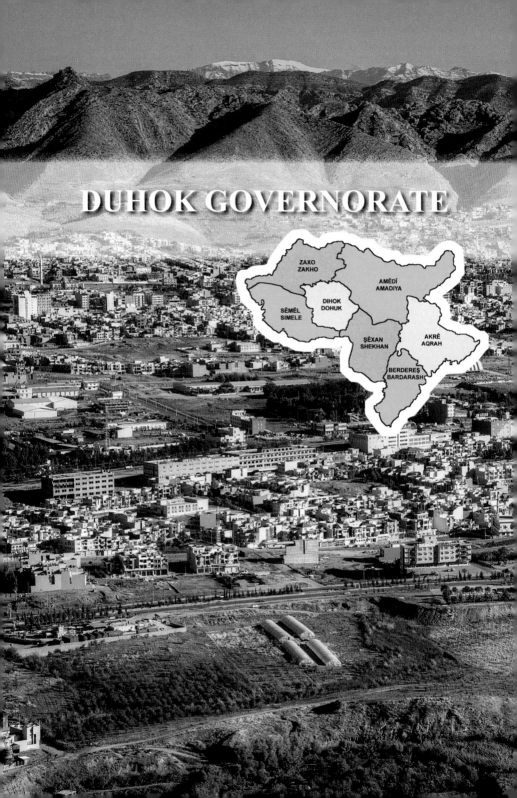

DUHOK GOVERNORATE

ZAXO
ZAKHO

AMÊDÎ
AMADIYA

SÊMÊL
SIMELE

DIHOK
DOHUK

ŞÊXAN
SHEKHAN

AKRÊ
AQRAH

BERDEREŞ
BARDARASH

DUHOK

DUHOK

GENERAL INFORMATION

Duhok (Dohuk, Dohok, Dahuk, Dihok or sometimes referred to as Nohadra by Christians) is the capital of Duhok Governorate. It is one-hour southwest of Zakho and the Turkish border, or 63 km (40 mi), one hour and fifteen minutes, or 80 km (50 mi) north of Mosul, and two and a half hours northwest from Erbil, or 160 km (100 mi). The third largest city in the Kurdistan Region, Duhok is growing rapidly as it population has steadily become urbanized since the 1990s. Mountains surround the city and an International Airport is under construction.

There is currently a population of over 350,000. It is also known as one of the richest regions in Kurdistan with considerable reserves of oil and many suspect vast minerals resources that have yet to be developed. Its proximity to the Turkish border has made it a thriving trade center and gateway for much of the imports for the rest of Kurdistan.

In 1992 the first Governor of Dohuk Abdul Aziz Tayep visited the city of Nashville, Tennessee and established a Sister City relationship. Today, Nashville boasts the largest Kurdish population in the United States. This early partnership has not been fully developed but there is a deep link between the cities as many of the refugees who settled in Nashville are from

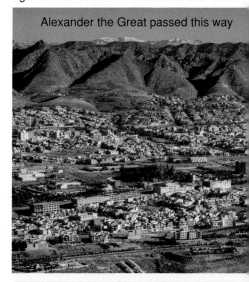

Alexander the Great passed this way

Duhok Dam

the Dohuk region. Dohuk is also partnered with the US town of Gainesville, Florida, with such stated objectives as promoting cultural exchanges, institutional exchanges, and fostering business relations.

HISTORY

The city is rich with history; once an ancient Assyrian town named Nohadra (Bet Nuhadra) it was a known stopover between Mosul and Zakho, or en route to Erbil. Alexander the Great passed through the city on his way to Gaugemela and the famous battle that made him Lord of Persia after defeating Darius III. There is a story that Alexander required the people of the town to pay a tribute of two palms, which roughly translates to "do" (two) "hok" (palms) of grain to help sustain his army. Some maintain this is where the modern name came from but there is no certain proof to support the claim. It is known that Alexander referred to the people of the region as Qarduk and some maintain this is where the modern term "Kurd" originated but there are earlier Sumerian references to Karda or Qarda thus again the Alexander attribution is suspect. One thing is certain however, the army of Alexander left its mark on the region as there are a number of blonde haired blue eyed Kurds reminiscent of the Macedonians who passed through.

GETTING AROUND

Much of Dohuk is a walkable city, though it may be much easier to take a taxi, depending on where one wants to go in the area. Taxis are plentiful, and inexpensive, costing between IQD 3,000- IQD 5,000 ($2.5-$4).

MAIN POINTS OF INTEREST

Badirkhan Public Library

Toward downtown the building consists of a reading area, rest hall, and houses nearly 120,000 books.

Bazaar

In the middle of Dohuk is the bazaar. It is not as large as in Sulaymani, and not as popular and touristy as Erbil, so there is a feel of authenticity attached to it. Like other bazaars, tourists can get food, clothing, or electronics, or just stroll down the alleys in search for something that catches your eye. The gold and silver market is a sight to see as well, since is it tucked away and separated from the rest of the bazaar. Many people shop here for wedding jewelry and tourists find it a delight to haggle as in days of old for a fine piece of locally crafted jewelry.

Chwar Stoon Cave

Chwar Stoon Cave and Sculpture

Located approximately 20 minutes from Duhok, Chwar Stoon Sculptures and Cave is also known, as the "The Four Pillars". It is a series of small caves located above the Duhok Dam. The entry to this attraction is on the right hand side when walking towards the dam and costs IQD 500 (50 cents) to enter. This area functioned as a Zoroastrian temple dating back to 600 BC and was only officially discovered in 2006. Most of the ancient aspects are hard to decipher despite many signs telling visitors what they are looking at.

Zoroastrianism also called Zarathustraism, Mazdaism and Magianism, is an ancient monotheistic Median/ Persian religion. It was once the state religion of the Medo-Persian Empire as well as the Achaemenid, Parthian, and Sasanian empires. Estimates of the current number of Zoroastrians worldwide are approximately 2.6 million.

Path to Chwar Stoon

Zoroastrianism arose in the eastern region of the ancient Medo-Persian Empire, when the religious philosopher Zoroaster simplified the pantheon of the kingdoms' gods into two opposing forces: Spenta Mainyu ("progressive mentality") and Angra Mainyu ("destructive mentality") under the one God, Ahura Mazda ("Illuminating Wisdom"). Zoroaster's ideas led to a formal religion bearing his name by about the 6th century BC.

In Zoroastrianism, the creator Ahura Mazda is perfectly good and no evil originates from him. Thus, in Zoroastrianism good and evil have distinct sources, with evil (druj) trying to destroy the creation of Mazda

(asha), and good trying to sustain it. The most important texts of the religion are those of the Avesta, of which a significant portion has been lost, and for the most part only the liturgies have survived. The lost portions are known of only through references and brief quotations in later works, primarily from the 9th to 11th centuries.

Islam gradually marginalized Zoroastrianism from the 7th century onwards. The political power of the pre-Islamic Medo-Iranian dynasties lent Zoroastrianism immense prestige in ancient times, and some of its leading doctrines were adopted by other religious systems. It has no major theological divisions (the only significant schism is based on calendar differences), but the beliefs are not uniform largely due to the fact there is no recognized universal body of coherent written doctrine or teachings.

There are 175 steps from the entrance up to the ancient cave, which contains carvings in several places. The scenery is beautiful, as you are able to see much of Duhok and the adja-

cent dam and man-made waterfall from a great vantage point. The entire visit on the mountain by Chwar Stoon should take 30-45 minutes and it is a great first stop on the way to the dam and the surrounding environs.

It is one of the first and few historical sites that have been actively controlled and maintained by the KRG/ Duhok Governorate. The small entrance fee pays for security and small enhancements such as steps making it more accessible to the public. Duhok Governorate has probably done more for the preservation of its important sites than any in the region and this is a clear evidence of this effort.

Chwar Stoon Cave Waterfall

Wall of the museum

There have been claims that Egyptian statuettes were found on the site and one such find has been under investigation to determine its authenticity. There are other evidences of Egyptian influence in the region including the Qubahani Madrassa located near Amediye, which had links to the University of Cairo in 17th Century. There is even a popular myth in the region claiming that Nefertiti was a Kurd exchanged by Pharaoh Thuthmosis III to seal an alliance with a Kurdish king named Shaustatar. There is no substantial evidence to support this claim but there is no doubt that at various times in ancient history the Egyptian rulers had some influence in the region.

Dohuk Dam

One of the main draws to the city is the large Dohuk Dam/Lake/Reservoir, which is on the northern tip of the city. The dam was completed in 1988 and 60 m (197 ft) tall. Many people come here to picnic, watch the water tucked between the mountains, and others come and sit and eat and smoke *nargilah* nearby as they people watch.

Dohuk International Film Festival

Annually since 2011 every fall this festival showcases films from all over the world and is professionally managed and facilitated. The tickets are inexpensive and much of the staff are volunteers from local universities. It is a real treat if you are in Dohuk around this time of year.

Promenade

The promenade is similar to the bazaar but more open, and leads to the Dohuk Dam if you walk in that direction. There are many restaurants, places to smoke *nargilah,* and people watch. There is also a bridge that avoids the now small trickling stream that is called the Dohuk River.

Dohuk Dam and Resort

PARKS AND NATURE

Azadi Panorama Park

Azadi Park

Originally the site of a military base during the Ba'ath regime, after the 1991 uprising, it was transformed into a public park. Near the commercial downtown and near the sports club, this park provides a wonderfully stunning view of the city and includes a garden, some restaurants, and a sculpture of a couple embracing — ironic because public displays of affections are not socially acceptable as they are in the west.

Dohuk Zoo

Not widely known to foreigners, there is a relatively small yet diverse zoo in the center of Dohuk, near the Dream City resort and amusement park. The entrance fee is nominal and though there are domesticated animals such as cats and rabbits featured in the zoo, there are also peacocks, snakes, bears, camels, wolves, jaguars, and even lions. A highlight is that someone often comes by with a baby chimpanzee dressed in baby clothes and hands her to visitors to hold. The chimpanzee is very friendly and is content to be held by anyone.

Mulla Mustafa Park (Barzani Park)

On the way to Dohuk unless you are coming from the direction of Zakho, on the outskirts of town is a park that is dedicated to the legendary Kurdish leader Mullah Mustafa Barzani, replete with a giant statue of him 'watching' over the city. It is a handsome area open to the public.

Zawita Resort

Zawita is a Christian village, and the area is known for its beautiful surrounding as well as being a place where locals come to eat chargrilled fish called *mazgouf*. Less than 30 minutes east of Dohuk (20 km; 12 mi) Gali Zawita (Zawita Valley) is between two mountains. There are tourist cabins, casinos, restaurants, and

Dream City

snack stands on both sides of the road. The surrounding area is located in a forest where many people enjoy picnics and hiking especially on weekends and holidays.

MUSEUMS

Cultural and Folklore Museum

In the center of Duhok is an old fashioned building in which hundreds of ancient antiques and artifacts are kept. The museum is a part of the Directorate of Folklore in Duhok.

Qadir Qachagh is the founder and director of the museum He has a deep interest in folklore and Kurdish culture, and will share his knowledge humbly with anyone who wants to talk about folklore. He can answer any question you pose about the museum: he knows about every single antique and artifact held there.

The museum was established in 1998, although it has been unofficially up comments and running since 1991. See the comments by Qadir Qachagh in the article titled *Artists, Poets and Writers of Kurdistan.*

Azadi Park Clock Tower

Dohuk Arts Gallery

East of the University of Dohuk near the Malta neighborhood is a small but charming art gallery with constantly changing works by local artists that are sold in the professionally run gallery.

National Museum

Inaugurated in late 2013, it is the first museum to be opened in this city by the KRG and houses over 1,000 artifacts from different historical and ancient time periods. One of the rarer pieces showcased in the museum is a round stamp used by a Mi-

Old Church (North); Church of St. Ith Llaha (Center), which is the oldest in the city and dates to the 6th century AD. It has however been completely renovated and little if any of the original structure remains.

Until the 1950s there was a sizable Jewish population. In particular there is still a village northeast of Dohuk named Sindor Yahud (Jewish Sindor) and

Ancient cunziform

tanni king believed to have ruled Duhok in 1500 BC. This empire stretched from modern day eastern Turkey and Syria to modern day Kurdistan-Iraq.

RELIGION

The town and its neighboring villages have always been known to be religiously and ethnically diverse: there is a large Yezidi minority and still a significant amount of Christians living in/around the city. There are four churches in the city Mar Gorgees (East); Mar Narse (South); Dohuk though its original inhabitants no longer live there, it was once a village entirely populated by Jews.

NIGHTLIFE

Duhok is a fairly conservative city and there is little to offer by way of entertainment at night. However, the major hotels have bars and some have live entertainment. New large five star hotels are opening in 2015, which promise more possibilities for evening entertainment. Restaurants

serving both local and International cuisine are usually at the center of an evening out.

HOSPITALS AND CLINICS

The city has at two major hospitals both located in the town center: Vajeen Private and Azadi (Freedom) Hospital.

UNIVERSITIES

American University Duhok Kurdistan (AUDK)

This is a newly established university that aspires to become a comprehensive, national and international university, and to be recognized and funded as the flagship private research university in the autonomous Kurdistan Region of Iraq.

University of Duhok (UoD)

This is a fast-growing institution in the city of Duhok. It plays a vital role in developing the community by instigating socioeconomic, cultural, and scientific as well as educational progress in the Kurdistan Region of Iraq.

The University of Zakho (UoZ)

UoZ was announced as an independent university in July 2010. Before this date, there were two colleges, Education and Commerce, which were affiliated to the University of Duhok. University of Zakho along with another three new universities were founded following the resolution made by the Parliament of Kurdistan Region to address the increased demand for higher education studies. Once the university was nominated, the colleges of Education and Commerce were reorganized into two faculties: Science and Humanities.

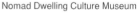

Nomad Dwelling Culture Museum

AKRE

GENERAL INFORMATION / HISTORY

Akre (Akra, Aqra) is a city and district located in Dohuk Governorate. Before 1991 Akre was part of the administrative authority of Nineveh Governorate, but after the 1991 uprising, the city officially became part of Duhok. Though Akre is an ancient city, the modern town was formed in 1877 by the Ottoman Empire and the city soon became the center of the district. Akre district has a population of around 60,000. From Erbil to Akre the trip takes about two hours (123 km) or 75 mi and from Duhok to Akre takes about an hour and forty-five minutes (108 km) or 67 mi.

A few of the many famous Akreyi's include: *Defend International* President Widad Akrawi, the Kurdish film director, Hiner Saleem, Former Israeli General and Minister of Defense Yitzhak Mordechai, and current Iraqi Minister of Finance Hoshyar Zebari.

Akre dates back at least to 580 BC in the time of the Kurdish Prince Zand. It lies on the foot of the Speelik and Kaynagal mountains. Akre is rich in historical sites, such as temples, statues, and ancient buildings, and many mineral springs can be found in or near the town. Akre has a wonderful old city, and the topography creates a beautiful townscape of terraced houses with narrow streets, mosques, bazaar and traditional shops. To the north of the city, mountains block the Zebari and Barzan areas. The Zab River winds past the mountains before Barzan. The Khazarand River lies to the West of the town, as does Sheikhan Qadha. Akre is considered among one of the oldest cities in history, dating to the Cretaceous period. Some claim Akre emerged as far back as 700 BC as a settlement created by Prince Zeid who named it Akre, derived from the Kurdish word for fire. The town is strongly connected with fire dating back to the Zoroastrian faith.

NEW AKRE

There is a "New Akre", thanks to an influx of resi-

dents from nearby villages and some returnees from abroad. The town has a teaching college, which lies before the older and more ancient parts of the city. There are new shops, restaurants, and an overall commercial area including brand new hotels.

PLANS FOR TOURISM

Roughly 180,000 tourists visited the city in 2013 and there are additional plans to build new hotels and resort areas, mostly near the waterfalls and other bodies of water.

There is a plan for a teleferic (cable car) to lift tourists to Akre's famous peaks, such a Qeli Akre Mountain, behind the old city. The municipality is planting 3,000-5,000 trees a year to restore the greenery in Akre's hills and valleys that were lost due to deforestation and war. The KRG has started to pay homeowners to renovate their homes with traditional limestone construction to give the city a more uniform 'ancient feel.' Since 2010, two hun-

Gold Bazaar

Grand Mosque

cially skin diseases and arthnitis. It is said that each mineral spring provides a remedy for a specific disease

Mimi Spring: Skin diseases (Southwest of Akre),

Ashkawti Sheikhman Spring: Rheumatism (Northeast of Akre)

Zartak Spring: Skin diseases (Northeast of Akre).

Girbish Village

Girbish is a village on the foot of Peris Mountain, 23 km (14 mi) north of Akre, and 2 km (1.2 mi) west of Dinarta village. The tourist attraction is on the top of the village. Six wells flowing under walnut trees, create beautiful shaded areas. If you want to just cool off after a nice hike up the mountain, or through the hospitable village, this is a great spot.

dred thousand USD a year has been budgeted for remodeling subsidies, awarded to citizens who voluntarily refurbish their buildings according to the style of the city's oldest structures.

Church of Akre

HIGHLIGHTS

Hiking and River Rafting

The area around Akre embodies some of Kurdistan's most scenic valleys and mountains where one can enjoy exotic flora and indigenous animals. Zarvia Dji Mountain boasts ruins of an ancient Jewish site.

Akre Mineral Springs

The mineral springs are considered a place of healing for many thousands of people who come to treat different illnesses, espe-

Grand Mosque

One of the main focal points of the old city, this whitewashed mosque towers over all other buildings in the area. Recently undergoing restoration, it makes for a spectacular view with the old city in the background.

Gundik Cave

Gundik village is 20 km (12 mi) west of Akre. The cave is 50 m (1,643 ft.) with an opening equally 50 m wide. Visitors can view ancient sculptures of two humans and animals carved on the outer wall of the cave as well as inside

Kani Zarka

A man-made swimming pool for locals, it dries up in the winter and autumn and is refilled in the spring and summer

Meriem Church

Next to the spot where youth light their torches during Newroz, it is an old Assyrian Church that is currently unused and padlocked, but a testimony to the multi-layered cultural and religious fabric of the city and its environs.

Ottoman Palace / Akre Prison

Originally built by the Ottomans, Saddam used it as a prison. After the former regime fell, much of the palace was looted. The local authorities later used it as a police station. There are plans to turn the building into a museum, much like the *Amma Suraka* (Red House) the notorious prison turned museum in Sulaymani.

Qela Akre (Castle Hill Akre) and Zervia Dji

This is perhaps the most famous attraction in Akre, particularly during the Newroz season. The Citadel lies in the northern part of Akra town, 450 m (1476 ft.). Prince Zand built it in 580 BC on top of a mountain. The citadel has four pillars, a water cistern and a room, which is called "the jail." It consists of several floors; the upper floor is known as the prince's

Akre Citadel

residence, the middle was used as food storage room, and the basement consists of a round meeting hall and a flat rock in the middle. The rooms are built in geometric shapes. The plateau behind Qela Akre Mountain is called *Zervia Dji*, (land of the Jews). This town once had a large Jewish population (some statistics show that they were 5 percent of the town in 1930). The Jewish community, which used to live in the Old City along with the Muslim Kurds and Assyrian Christians, would gather on top of the mountain for holidays and celebrations. These days it is quite accessible to climb, thanks to a set of steps winding up the slope from behind the church, which can be seen from below.

Sipa Waterfall

Shrine of Abdul Aziz Al-Jilani (Gaylani)

The shrine of Sheikh Abu Bakr Abdul-Aziz al-Jilani (Gaylani) (1137- 1206 AD) is north of Akre and is visited by thousands from all over the world every year. It is likely many of these pilgrims also pay homage to his father, Sheikh Abdul Qadir al-Jilani, who was head of the Sufi Qadiriya order. Sheikh Abdul Qadir is buried in Baghdad and is one of the most famous Sufi saints in the country and even beyond. His shrine is visited by tens of thousands of people from all over the Islamic world, said to number over 200,000 followers. The shrine of Abdul Aziz Al-Jilani is northwest of the town of Akre, in a valley full of orchards and grapes.

In 1187, Sheikh Abdul Aziz is said to have participated in conquering Jerusalem from the Crusaders, though some claim it was actually Asqalan (Ashkelon), a city in modern-day Israel, north of Gaza. He is buried in the shrine, appropriately called Geli (Valley) Abd al-Aziz in a mountain above Akre.

Though a great deal is known about his father, much less is known about Sheikh Abdul Aziz. He is mentioned by Sharaf al-Din Abu al-Barakat Ibn al-Mustawfi al-Irbili (1167–1239 AD) who was a well-known historian and native of Erbil. Sharaf al-Din describes the Sheikh as owning a Sufi lodge and was withdrawn from society for spiritual reasons. The historian recounts that the Sheikh learned and disseminated *hadith* – the Prophet Muhammad's sayings and tra-

ditions. His influence at the time stretched from Akre to Erbil and Sinjar (near Mosul), where he is said to have lived for a while, beginning in 1184 AD.

The shrine itself encompasses four buildings surrounded by courtyards: the domed burial chamber, cave and lodging rooms; the takiya (main lodge) with its reception rooms, prayer hall and library; and female reception rooms, The site also includes a burial ground, and a number of small ablution areas and a private residence for the caretakers family which is one of the many thousands of descendants of the Sheikh. Members of the Kurdish majority Qadiriyya-Wulianiyya Order live in a neighboring village a few miles southeast in a village named Rovia.

Sile Waterfall

This beautiful site is on the foot of Peris Mountain, 8 km (5 mi) east of Dinarta and 32 km (20 mi) from Akre. From a mountain gorge water flows over a 50-meter (165 ft.) high waterfall and into tall willow trees. Picnic areas are set up for tourists to enjoy the scenery.

Sipa Bjail Waterfall

This resort lies 13 km (8 mi) east of Akre, located in the center of Bjail village. The resort lies in a valley with different types of fruit trees. The waterfall is fed from several springs, which flow from mountains. There are several types of facilities such as an artificial cave behind the waterfall and many choices of restaurants.

Sipa Waterfall

This waterfall is located only 1 km (less than .5 mi) east of Akre. It is 18 m (60 ft.) high surrounded by trees and water pools, which creates a cool and refreshing and fun environment especially in the summertime and spring. There is a hotel, the first in Akre at Sipa, appropriately called the Sipa Hotel, which has 28 rooms.

Families celebrate Newroz

Zanta Valley

This famous and gorgeous resort area is only 12 km (7.5 mi) from Akre. Geli Zanta is a mountainous area with a narrow windy gorge at its southern end. There is a large valley, where the highest ridge of Pires Mt. runs northwest to southeast. There are several small streams that drain to Geli Zanta, which is covered in oak forest. It is a deep valley between two mountains and there is a large river in the middle called Bresho. Sada Mount surrounds this area from the east and Sarea Keske Mount from the west. This resort includes many springs flowing throughout the year. It is one of the more famous tourist locations in the area. Hundreds of picnickers sit alongside the river among the orchards and vineyards. Among the multitude of flora and fauna there are several dozens of bird species, including the rare Egyptian vulture.

Zoroaster Temple

The temple is located about 220m (720 ft.) at the bottom of Qeli Akre. The temple is inside a cave called Agri Temple and consists of three big rooms connected by doors. The area of each room is 12m long (40 ft.), 4m high (13 ft.) and 3m (10 ft.) wide. There is a stony chair and terrace about 7m (22. Ft.) long attached to each other in second and third rooms.

Lighting Newroz fires on Mt. Qeli

Valley of Amediye

AMEDIYE

GENERAL INFORMATION / HISTORY

Amediye (Amêdî, Amadi, Amady, Amadiya) is an ancient town perched atop a plateau which some refer to as "the city in the sky", 1,400 m (4,600 ft.) above sea level. Until modern times it was only accessible by a narrow stairway cut into the rock. It is also adjacent to a tributary of the Great Zab River in the Duhok Governorate. The city's' history dates back at least to the Assyrian Empire. From the city of Duhok it is only an hour ride 73 km (45 mi). Though there are few restaurants, it is known for some of its food, in particular the unadulterated tahini (cooked sesame seed dip) and is also known for having some of the purest honey in the region. The town is small, and currently has a population of approximately 10,000. Amediye is fed by a geothermal spring originating far below the mountain. This natural phenomenon made it next to impossible to successfully siege the city as long as there were sufficient food supplies

City in the sky

stored which was usually the case in ancient times.

HIGHLIGHTS

Aside from the breathtaking scenery, there are two main historical attractions in Amediye. The eastern Bahdinan Gate (Bab Zebar) predates the Islamic conquest and is thought by some to have been built in the 2nd Century BC. This gate is the entrance/exit to a small cave, which is a walkway that connects the top of the town to the valley below. A stunning panoramic view, it is not to be missed.

The other is the Amediye Mosque, a 15th century structure, which still has a minaret that towers over all the other buildings in the town. The minaret is 33 m (108 ft.) and was part of the mosque built for Sultan Hussein Wali (1534-1570), then prince of Bahdinan, or the Dohuk region.

Several churches are found in the town and surrounding areas as well. Outside of the town, toward Duhok, one can find an ancient Christian cemetery as well. Amediye was an important center of Chaldean astrology and astronomy. Some scholars and local folklore claim that this area is where the Biblical Magi (Three Wise Men) observed a "star" in the sky prompting their famous pilgrimage to Bethlehem to pay respects to Jesus shortly after his birth. There is actually some credence to the claim as one of the tribes that inhabited the region during that period was called Magi and the Chaldeans were ever looking to the skies for portents and signs. Whatever one believes regarding the story it is interesting to note many locals hold it to be true. The city was also an important Jewish city during the diaspora and the well-versed Jewish population had long been looking for a "sign" of the messiah to come.

Amediye Mosque Minaret

There are ruins of a synagogue in town as well but it is difficult to find if you do not know its location and directions from one of the locals or a trained guide is usually required to find it. Until recently there was an ancient door and some of the walls and part of the foundation are still in place. At one time there were reportedly two great synagogues in Amediye: the Be Hazane and the Navi Yehezqel. The Be Hazane was adjacent to the Navi Yehezqel synagogue in upper Amadiye. It is not clear which of the two the ruins represent. Historical records show that one of the Synagogues was built in two parts: the first c. 3rd

Assyrian Carving

century AD and the upper half in c. 600 AD. A few years ago a rainstorm and mudslide washed most of the Synagogue ruins away including a largely intact room where Torahs were once stored that had be-

come too worn and thus unfit to use. The Torahs were, according to the law and tradition, never destroyed. It was a tremendous loss to the archeological and historic integrity of the city and indicative of the neglect important ruins have suffered in the past. The Kurdish Regional Government has since taken a greater interest in preservation but it is usually the better-known sites that receive the most attention and unfortunately many of the "lesser" ones are being lost forever due to neglect.

Famous Jewish traveler, Benjamin of Tudela (Spain), visited Kurdistan in the 12th century:

Bab Zebar Gate

Ancient Entrance to Amediye

recorded in biblical references as well as folklore. The Kurds are descendants of the ancient Medes. The Bible states in more than one place that when the Jews were sent into exile (733 BC) they were settled in the 'cities of the Medes." II Kings 17:6 states, "In the ninth year of Hoshea, the king of Assyria captured Samaria and deported the Israelites to Assyria. He settled them in Halah, in Gozan on the Habur River (near Zakho) and in the towns of the Medes." Again, in II Kings 18:11, the biblical record states, "The king of Assyria deported Israel to Assyria and settled them in Halah, in Gozan on the Habur River and in towns of the Medes."

There is a folkloric account, from the 13th century, involving two brothers named David and Yosef who visited Amadiya from Persia as "dervishes" (influenced by Sufism) and were so taken by the town's beauty that they asked the Ottoman Pasha if they could live there. Upon learning these

in 1170 reported more than 100 Jewish communities in the Kurdistan region. But in Amadiye itself, he claimed there were 25,000 Jews who spoke the ancient biblical language of Aramaic. At the turn of the 19th century, of 6,000 people in the town, 2,500 were Kurds, 2,000 Jews and 1,500 Assyrians. While Amediye was once heavily populated with Jewish Kurds before the 1800's, due to anti-Jewish pogroms and economic hardship, by 1888 only 600 Jews were reported to be living in Amediye. In 1952 after the order for the expulsion of all Jews in Iraq, the remainder was evacuated to Israel.

The town was also the birthplace of a lesser-known Messianic figure, born centuries after Jesus, "David Alroy" or Menahem ben Solomon. In 1163 AD. Alroy, who had claimed he was the messiah led a revolt in the city. He was defeated and killed in the process.

The establishment of Jews in Amadiye is

"The Magi Journeying" James Tissot, Brooklyn Museum.

men were Jews and not traditional Muslim "dervishes", the pasha refused to let the brothers live in Amediye. As these brothers continued towards Dohuk, they supposedly used their magic powers to cast a spell upon the Pasha, so he fell ill. The Pasha reportedly sent men after the two brothers and asked them to come back to heal him and in return for a cure, he promised to give them land. Once these brothers came back, they healed the Pasha and according to legend, "asked for as much ground as the skin of a large ox could enclose," and the Pasha agreed (strips of oxhide were used as measuring tapes). David and Yosef supposedly used this land to build homes and a synagogue. While the story is without substantive proof it is indicative of the legends and folk tales that are inter-twined with this ancient city. There are many such tales surrounding the city.

The inaccessibility of the city (which somewhat resembles Masada in Israel) and its constant water supply made the city fortress almost unconquerable. Only when the city ran out of food was it in danger of being overtaken. Throughout history it has often been the case that invading armies can only sustain a siege for a year or more before troubles back home demand attention. Knowing this, the rulers of Amediye always kept more than a year's supply on hand and thus survived most attempts to starve the city out. There is a fascinating story retold by the local "keepers of lore" about a siege by Ottoman invaders that lasted longer than the food supply of the city; faced with starvation and imminent surrender the king was told of a beggar woman who claimed to be able to save the city. She asked the king for all of his remaining choice morsels of food in his palace and with basket in hand was lowered over the edge of the town during the night and was promptly captured by the invaders. When she was searched and found to be in possession of rare delicacies she told the invading commander that the city had food in abundance such that the beggars ate like princes. The story goes that the invaders left the field sure that Amediye would never fall. The story actually mirrors one told in the Bible and its authenticity is doubtful but again, locals are sure it is true.

One of the great delights of Amediye is its myths and legends, which serious scholars take with a grain of salt. Yet they are enjoyable to hear especially from the older residents of the city whose task in life seems to be to pass along colorful traditions and the oral history of the city. One should always remember that legend and myth usually have some basis in reality and one thing is sure – Amediye is an incredible city shrouded in a mystical past and a must see for any visitor the Kurdistan.

REFUGEE - IDP CAMPS

Since the fall of Mosul on 9 June 2014, to the Islamic State of Iraq Levant (ISIL or ISIS) as well as their subsequent control of large areas of Iraq's provinces (i.e. Nineveh plain, Salah al- Din and Diyala) there has been massive internal displacement of the residents of many cities: such as Tikrit, Telafar, Beiji, Quayyara, Suleiman Bek, Heet, Rashad, Hawiga, Riyadh, Falluja and Saqlawiyah. Iraq is now contending with one of the largest internally displaced populations in the world; over 2.1 million have been displaced since January last year—most of these have fled to Kurdistan. The KRG has done its utmost to accommodate this massive influx but the stress on the local economy has been crushing.

Southwest of Dohuk by less than ten min-

utes sits the largest refugee camp in the Kurdistan Region, Domiz, which houses over 250,000 Syrian refugees. Many who live in the camp work in Dohuk during the day to provide for their families.

There are a number of other refugee and internally displaced persons (IDP) camps in the Region with over one and a half million current residents comprising people who have fled from Southern or parts of northern Iraq—mostly Yezidis and Christians as well as Kurds and others from Syria. Kurdistan has a long history of providing refuge to afflicted and persecuted peoples—a testimony to the tolerant society and democratic principles that rule the region.

What does the future hold?

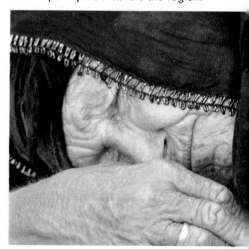

The Governor of Duhok, Farhad Atrushi, has done an incredible job of organizing the camps and providing for their occupants with the help of local and International relief agencies. However, the influx of refugees (those from outside Iraq) and IDPs (those from inside Iraq) has put a tremendous strain on the government and vastly more international help is needed.

It is significant to note that the preponderance of displaced are IDPs and not considered by the International Community to be refugees. The legal distinction is important as refugees can ultimately be given asylum in other countries while IDPs are generally not afforded this opportunity. Thus for the Kurds their "guests" present not merely an immediate issue but a long-term problem that at present seems to have no apparent solution. Many of the IDPs are being assimilated into Kurdish society and it is now quite common to see Syrian and Iraqis employed in more or less permanent situations in the major cities—especially in hotels and restaurants. While many come from tragic circumstance, it is fortunate for them that they have found refuge in a region known for its almost

American Philanthropist Foster Friess assisting refugees in Zakho

inexhaustible hospitality.

Note: A portion of the proceeds of this Guide is donated to the *America Kurdistan Friendship Association* (Akfa) based in Erbil for their work among IDPs and refugees. Projects have been undertaken in cooperation and with funding from American philanthropists who have visited the area.

There are also other very fine organizations that do great and sacrificial work to alleviate the suffering of those who have been driven from their homes by ISIS and have found a welcoming safe haven in Kurdistan. For information on these agencies or if you would like to provide assistance to the Refugees/IDPs contact: info@KurdistanIraqTours.com.

America Kurdistan Friendship Association IDP Relief Project

ZAKHO

GENERAL INFORMATION / HISTORY

Zakho (Zaxo) is located a few kilometers from the Iraq-Turkey border. The city and surrounding area has a population of over 400,000. Zakho is 58 km (36 mi) or roughly one-hour northwest of Dohuk and 92 km (57 mi) west of Amediye. Zakho is an ancient city and was an important trading city during the Greek Empire. Famous British traveler and writer Gertrude Bell was convinced Zakho was the ancient town of Hasaniyeh. The first Western Christian missionary to the region, a Dominican monk named Poldo Soldini, was buried in Zakho in 1779 and his grave is still visited by pilgrims.

The city may in fact have originally begun on a small island surrounded on all sides by the Little Khabur (Habur or Habor) River, which flows through the modern city. The Khabur flows west from Zakho to form the border between Iraq and Turkey, continuing into the Tigris. This island was one of the main neighborhoods of the well-established Jewish community, until 1952

when almost all Jews were evacuated to Israel.

There are several theories concerning the origin of the name "Zakho." Aramaic sources maintain it comes from "Zakhota" (victory), after the battle between Rome and Persia near the city, resulting in a Roman victory. Another version maintains Zakho comes from "Zey- Khowin" ("river of

Border of Kurdistan and Turkey

blood"), possibly referring to the same battle. Lastly, a third and the most likely view is that the city derives its name from two Kurdish words "Zey" (river) and "Khowak" (a curved place which blocks the water). Zakho is also known for its mineral springs which are

thought to have medicinal properties, especially for skin diseases.

Zakho was historically and is currently a trading center and stopover prior to going to Turkey. It is famous for its walnuts as well as rice, oil, sesame, wax, lentils, and fruits. Due to its strategic location, trade with Turkey is now a major factor in the local economy although recent oil exploration and exports has also contributed to its prosperity.

In 1991 the city functioned as the center of the international coalition's established safe haven during "Operation Provide Comfort" which sought to protect Kurds from being massacred by Saddam Hussein. As a result of local Kurds working with Americans, many of these largely well-educated people were able to secure

asylum abroad and caused a significant brain drain in the area. However, many of these have now returned to participate in the rebuilding of Kurdistan.

In July 2010 Zakho became the seat of the University of Zakho. In 2012 the Duhok Governorate licensed two housing projects comprising 8,000 residences worth about $525 million USD for the city. Both projects include schools, health centers, and shopping complexes.

Zakho was once well known for its large and influential Jewish population. Interestingly it was believed by the locals that the Jews were "rain makers" who were turned to when drought ravaged the land. According to local tradition they were usually successful—or at the very least were often given credit when the rains

Zakho City

finally returned. For further information on the Jews in the region a good resource is Erich Brauer's, "The Jews of Kurdistan" Wayne State University Press, 1993.

Zakho once had many synagogues and was known as "The Jerusalem of Assyria." Here the Jews spoke Aramaic, the language they spoke when they came to these areas in the 8th century BC as Assyrian slaves. The Khabur is mentioned in the Bible as one of the places where Israelites were exiled (1 Chronicles, 5:26, 2 Kings 17:6, 2 Kings 18:11). In 1891, there were a series of pogroms against the community and one of the synagogues was burnt. The next year heavy taxes were imposed, and looting Jewish stores and arresting individuals for no reason were common. This community was among the first to make *aliyah* (emigrate) to Israel. Many settled in Jerusalem and to this day the main market in Jerusalem is full of Kurdish Jewish shopkeepers whose ancestry can be traced to Zakho. Special Jewish-Zakho food is available there as well. The Jewish quarter in Zakho is still largely in its original state and

the Muslim inhabitants remarkably often remember who lived in what house and what their occupations were, etc.

In recent years much interest has arisen about the Jewish communities in Kurdistan, and from Zakho in particular. Haya Gavish's *Unwitting Zionists: The Jewish Community of Zakho in Iraqi Kurdistan* (2009) was a dissertation that incorporates folkloric tales, legends, and many interviews from Jews from Zakho who moved to Israel. Perhaps most famous is Ariel Sabar's *My Father's Paradise: A Son's Search for His Jewish Past in Kurdish Iraq* (2008). Sabar's father (Yona) was one of the last Jews to become Bar Mitzvah before leaving for Israel and is currently a professor of Neo-Aramaic language and Kurdish-Jewish Culture in UCLA.

Zakho is the seat of a diocese of the Chaldean Catholic Church and is affiliated with the ancient diocese of Adiabene (Hadyab) which was a Christian (previously Jewish) kingdom based in modern-day Erbil. Some local Assyrian bishops are mentioned as early as the fifth century AD. Today there are dozens of churches and Christian villages throughout Zakho District. Many Assyrians and Chaldeans originally from Zakho live in the diaspora and main areas include the American cities of Nashville, Detroit, San Diego, Houston, Phoenix and Washington D.C.

HIGHLIGHTS

Bahiri Cave

The cave is approximetely 45 km (27 mi) from Zakho. The inside of the cave is very large and visitors may tour the interior. There is little information concerning the historical significance of the cave but it has been used for various purposes both in ancient and modern times.

Bahnina Cave

The cavi is 25 km (15.5 mi) from Zakho and is located in the middle of Bahnina Mountain near Batufa village. This large cave contains fresh water springs. During the Kurdish struggle in the 1960s and 1970s, the cave was used as a hospital for *peshmerga* soldiers.

Barwari Resort

This is one of the more beautiful resorts surrounded by mountains and many

Bekhir Cave

streams. It is 50 km (30 mi) from Zakho. Many tourists visit this area, which is witnessing the construction of several new hotels, restaurants and other tourist facilities.

Bekhir Cave

The cave is located approximately 30 kilometers (18 miles) from Zakho. It is a beautiful and mysterious place the history of which is not yet fully known. It is a favorite destination for lo-

cals who want to get away from the city and explore the countryside.

Delal Bridge

The most famous site in Zakho is the Delal Bridge. Delal Bridge is also referred to as Pirdi Delal (stone bridge) or Pira Delal (beautiful bridge). It is an ancient bridge over the Khabur River spanning 114 m (374 ft.) and is 15.5 m (50 ft.) high. It was built using large river stones.

Outside Bekhir Cave

There is no reliable data as to the precise time of its construction and/or renovation historically. The bridge is believed by some to have been initially constructed during the Roman Era (27 BC - 476 AD). However, much of the present structure dates from a much later date in the Ottoman era (beginning in 1299 AD). There is evidence that the Bridge was constructed during the Abbasid Dynasty, which began its reign in the area around 750 AD and lasted until Mongols conquered it in 1258 AD. In the Abbasid era, the region (especially Baghdad to the South) became a center of science, culture, philosophy and invention in what was called the Golden Age of Islam during which there were many technological and architectural advances and accomplishments such as the Delal Bridge.

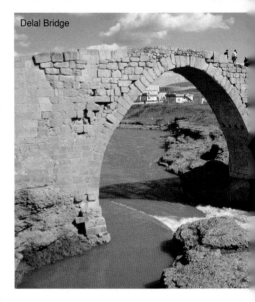

Delal Bridge

The bridge is frequently used in popular Kurdish imagery and Kurds and tourists visit the monument year round. In 2012 it was reported that the bridge is in danger

Sharanish Fall

of collapse but despite the fact thousands of tourists walk on it every week. Currently there are plans for a major preservation effort and one can now see the measurement markings across the face of the bridge used to determine the precise movements of the stones due to seismic and other natural and man induced movements.

There are many folktales about the bridge and one of the more famous tells of the actual construction itself. According to this legend, the bridge was considered such a tremendous and unique architectural feat by the ruler who had it built that the hands of the builder were amputated to ensure the bridge would remain unique. Another story is about a young man who lived on one side of the Khabur River, and the girl he loved lived on the other side, so he decided to build a bridge so they would no lowyer be separated. There are many other love stories surrounding the bridge including the tragic suicide of a young beautiful girl whose ghost supposedly haunts the bridge. Whatever the truth, one thing is certain—couples and visitors can be seen

strolling across the bridge at all times of the year and the setting amidst the fast flowing river and surrounding countryside is worth the visit.

Derabon Resort

The Resort is located in the triangle border area between Iraq, Turkey and Syria and is 16 km (10 mi) from Zakho. There is a large spring flowing from the mountains, and the area is seeing numerous tourist-related investments such as hotels, restaurants, and casinos. The area is also important to the Yezidi community, which makes pilgrimage to this site that includes the conical tomb of an important Sheikh.

Happy Theme Park

The park is a modern theme park built for young and old. There are different attractions and rides. There is a beautifully lit fountain in the middle of the lake inside the park and in addition to the rides; there is an indoor play areas, restaurants, and a cinema.

Kishani

The area is 37 km (23 mi) east of Zakho and surrounded by trees and small rivers. It is known for its low temperatures even during the summer. There are many picnic areas and provides an excellent view of lush, green valleys, streams and walnut trees.

Qubad Pasha Castle

This site is located near the ancient Zakho cemetery, and is hexagonal in shape, with six windows and an entrance gate. It lies in the city center on the western side of the river and was the governor's house during the Badinan Emirate.

Sharanish Fall

This is a beautiful waterfall 40 km (25 mi) northeast of town surrounded by many varieties of trees.

Shivana Park

The park is a beautiful area full of oak trees and wildflowers. It sits at the base of Baikhair Mt., 15 km (9 mi) south of the city. Locals visit mostly in the springtime to picnic and dance. The park is used particularly during Newroz.

Zakho Old Market

The bazaar is in the center of town Zakho (and like most other towns is in the Kurdistan Region) has a bazaar. Shop, sit, and enjoy tea and local fare with the locals.

Sharanish Fall

SERSING

GENERAL INFORMATION / HISTORY

Sarseng (pronounced Sarsenk) is an Assyrian village in Dohuk governorate. Sersing to Amediye is 26 km (26 mi) southwest of Amediye or 30 minutes and Sersing to Dohuk is 48 km (30 mi) northwest of Dohuk (45 min). The name Sersing comes from the Kurdish for above or upon the chest. The origin of the name comes from the location of the village, which is the highest altitude of a northern cliff of Gara Mountain. Sersing is moderately hot in the summer and cold in winter with a significant amount of snowfall. Spring and fall are short seasons but the fall is especially important due to the harvesting of ripe fruits. Interestingly enough, there is a Sersing Restaurant in the Greater Detroit Area!

Sersing is a tourist destination for many visiting Amediye area. Since there are currently no hotels in Amediye itself, visitors often stay in the lusher environs of Sersing and nearby Sulav. Sersing offers cottages and hotel rooms and there are many walking trails and restaurants in the area along with a large market area.

At the turn of the 20th century, 30 Assyrian families inhabited the village. A few short years later in 1928, the first private elementary school was founded, named *The Assyrian Private School of Sarsing*. Though Arabic was the primary language, Syriac and English were also taught. That same year a large church (Mar Mattai, St. Matthew – not to be confused with Mar Mattai Monastery near Mosul) was built and during the process many artifacts from antiquity were found, as the modern town was built near an old Assyrian Christian village. Among these pieces was a cross, surrounded by circles sculptured on a

stone and a baptismal stone basin as well as several Assyrian and Aramaic tablets.

A royal palace used by King Feisal (presently used as a hospital) was built in 1954 and ancient artifacts were found here as well during the process. In 1955 Mar Mattai Church was again rebuilt and residents facilitated this reconstruction both physically and financially. The Supreme Committee of Christian Affairs in Dohuk Governorate restored Mar Matti and installed Internet throughout the community. The church exists at present and is visited frequently. Another shrine was built in honor of Mar Gorgis (St. George). This monastery dates to

the fifth century and was built by royal decree. Sadly, this structure was destroyed in 1977 during the air campaign of the Ba'ath regime.

After 1991, Sersing and the surrounding valley became more developed and agriculture continued uninterrupted. Most residents of the village are farmers. Sheep and goats are the farmers' main domestic animals and main crops include grains, wheat, corn, tobacco, vegetable, grapes, nuts, and several types of fruits. In recent years, Sersing has become an established and prosperous town and many of its educated graduates occupy various high level positions in society.

HIGHLIGHTS

Sersing lies at the base of Gara Mountain, which is 2150 m. (7,054 ft.) Visitors may drive all the way to its peak, which provides a fantastic view over many villages, towns, and natural beauty. Saddam Hussein enjoyed this area for vacation and built a palace (now largely destroyed) on top of the mountain as part of a complex of ten palaces to be located throughout the valley. Several were completed prior to the 1991 Gulf War, which drove him from the region. The palace at the top of the mountain was to be linked to others by a cable car traversing the valley. The helicopter landing area next to the palace is now used for KRG police and for emergencies of other sorts.

In 1992 one could tour the palaces one of which at the foot of the mountain

boasted numerous guesthouses, which were in fact small palaces in their own right. Italian and other international craftsmen were used to complete the work with only the finest stone and marble used. There were man-made lakes and steps of sandstone along a stream leading from the bottom to the top of the mountain traversing over 6 kilometers (3.7 miles). The fence surrounding one palace is 13 kilometers (8 miles) long and is still standing. Saddam often hosted dignitaries and even movie stars at this palace and was in the process of constructing an Olympic stadium nearby in hopes of hosting the Olympics in the future. In each of the palaces all meals were prepared three times a day as no one knew when he might arrive to surprise his staff.

Saddam's Palace on Gara Mountain

Ruins of one of Saddam's Palaces

After the 1991 uprising, which placed the palaces in the hands of the Kurds, Saddam reportedly sent a message to current Prime Minister Nechirvan Barzani of the KDP who controlled the area at the time. Reportedly Saddam told the Prime Minister that his palaces would be entrusted to the PM's care until such time, as he would return. Mr. Nechirvan then announced on TV that the palaces belonged to the people and subsequently the locals took most of them apart brick by brick even going so far as to dig up the sewer pipes for sale in the local market. Almost nothing remains of the palaces today but a few shells of the buildings.

Ashawa Resort

Ashawa is 4 km (2.5 mi) west of Sersing at the foot of Gara Mountain. Tucked away behind curvy roads, Ashawa is a perfect place for a picnic or to relax in natural beauty. A long and winding water channel

Ashawa Resort

is covered with trees on both sides. Many people climb the steps that lead up to a road that many choose to hike and which offers a spectacular view of the surrounding area. Nearby there are cabins for tourists to rent and a large playground for children is available year round. It is a very popular place for tourists who visit or are en route to other tourist attractions in the area.

Enishke Cave

Enishke Cave

This fun tourist attraction is a cave located 9 km (5.6 mi) north of Sersing adjacent to Enishke village. Climbing up the stone stairs leads into the cave where water falls from the ceiling creating a natural fountain and s a cool climate inside the cave even in the hottest summers. This visit to the cave is very enjoyable, a perfect retreat especially in the hot summer days. There are a couple of nice restaurants at the cave and a wonderful view of the area is offered from every vantage point.

Swaratuka Resort

center though it lacks personnel as well as updated resources and equipment. This is soon to change due to the very recent discovery (2010) of oil throughout the village and environs of Swaratuka. HKN Oil Company (founded by Ross Perot, Jr.) recovers 10,000 barrels per day as of 2013 and the projected increase is to 50,000 bpd in 2015.

The village has several restaurants, cafes, and picnic areas. The resort is near the village and is shaded by large trees from two sides and there is a restaurant, and picnic tables as well.

Swaratuka Village and Resort

Swaratuka (Swara Tika, Swara-Tuka, Suwaratuka) is a small village in Sersing. The town lies roughly 1,400 m (4,593 ft.) above the sea level, surrounded by four mountains: Zangelo

Enishke Cave

to its east; Sare Ibrahimi to the north, and Hessen and Qopi to its west. Roughly 100 families inhabit the village; together they number less than one thousand. The village is known for its brave defense against Saddam's army in the face of insurmountable odds. On March 14th, 1991, Kurds from Duhok, Zakho, Amediye, Enishke, Sersing, and Swaratuka and surrounding areas controlled by the Iraqi armed forces repelled the army and in support of *Peshmerga* took control over all administrative offices.

Tourism is the main source of income here along with monies received from grapes harvested from the many vineyards. Cattle provide some income as well but to a much lesser degree. In the center of town is a small medical

Swaratuka

SULAV (SOLAV) RESORT

GENERAL INFORMATION / HISTORY

Sulav

From Dohuk, Sulav is approximately an hour's ride away, or 64 km (40 mi) to the northeast. It overlooks the unique and stunning plateau city Amediye and while traveling through this incredible scenic portion of Kurdistan many people choose to spend the night in Sulav or nearby Sersing. The quaint resort lies only 4 km (2.5 mi) of Amediye and is located in a densely forested valley which is known for its spectacular view of a waterfall flowing down from the mountain, which is called Sulav waterfall. There are several hotels, motels, as well as restaurants and *nargilah* bars. Flat areas around the valley include agricultural land used for tobacco (Kurdistan used to produce a great deal of tobacco).

Interesting Facts - Nashville, TN (USA) boasts the largest Kurdish community in the United States. It also has a market, appropriately called the Sulav International Market. There was also a Solav Kurdish Restaurant, in Liverpool, UK, though it has apparently closed.

HIGHLIGHTS

Sulav Resort is an area full of entertainment, with many cafés, shops, and restaurants that lie on the road from

Duhok to Amediye. Near the small river that feeds the waterfall tourists may climb up through the 1 km (.6 mi) long, cobblestone-hiking trail that leads to a small waterfall and arched stone bridge. There are smaller springs around the area as well, which can be reached by more off the beaten path trails. Near the main footpath are several hookah coffeehouses with chairs literally on top of the river — there is a good chance you will get your feet wet.

Animals

Locals have reported seeing the endangered Persian Fallow Deer. Persian Squirrels are sold here as well and are highly sought after on the pet market. There are also several species of birds in the area, including Egyptian Vultures, Bearded Vultures, and Griffon Vultures.

Bulbul Bridge

BULBUL BRIDGE (JISR BULBUL), ADNE WATERFALL AND BARWARI BALA AREA

GENERAL INFORMATION / HISTORY

Bulbul is a bridge located in the region of Barwari Bala in Duhok Governorate. It is 130 kilometers (78 miles) west of Duhok City or approximately 2 hours. It is located approximately 719 meters (2350 ft.) above sea level. The precise history of this bridge is unknown (as is the case with Delal Bridge in Zakho) but many believe it to have been built prior to or near the same time as the Delal Bridge, which could make it as old as 70 BC or as late as 750 AD.

As for the name of the bridge the root is also obscure. However the *Bulbul* is a small bird commonly found (among other places in the world) in the Kurdistan region of Iraq and the name of the bridge may refer to this species. The word bulbul derives from tha Persian meaning Nightingale. The Bulbul bird is a monogamous bird - faithfully remaining with its mate for life. There is a legend among some that the use of the word Bulbul could also denote a faithful young woman of worth.

HIGHLIGHTS

Barwari Bala is one of the more scenic regions of Kurdistan but due to its remoteness is seldom visited by International tourists and thus appeals to those who are looking for an off the beaten track experience. The areas surrounding the ruins of the bridge are some of the most beautiful in all of Kurdistan including the Adne Waterfall. There are many rivers and a vast number of orchards – apples, pears, almonds and many other varieties abound.

The precise historical background of this site may remain a mystery but the scenery surrounding this ancient bridge makes the trip well worthwhile. While there are very few foreigners that have made the journey to this area, those who have remember it as a highlight of their tour.

Barwari Bala

King Sennacharib and Assyrian Gods

HALAMATA BAS RELIEFS (CAVE)

GENERAL INFORMATION / HISTORY

This important historical cave is situated 7 km (4 mi) or twenty minutes northwest of Duhok by Kifrki and Gaverik villages. The cave consists of bas-reliefs of humans and animals are carved into the side of the mountain. They represent the victory of the Assyrian Empire in a battle during the reign of King Sennacherib (704-681 BC).

HIGHLIGHTS

Halamata Cave is found halfway up Shindokha Mountain. There are nine figures; eight facing left, and one at the front who appears to be receiving them — scholars claim this is a depiction of King Sennacherib. There are depictions of Assyrian Gods (Ashur, Anilil, Seen, Sun, Ishtar, and Adid) riding animals. The cave is more of an overhanging cliff and the bas reliefs or friezes are carved out of the rock and are shown carrying tributes – sheaves of corn, bowls, rings, and so on.

Though some of the carvings are damaged, most is still fairly well preserved and it is a cultural treasure for Assyrians and Kurds alike. Many people come here for the ancient attractions while others simply

Tourist at Jirwana

want to climb the mountain and get a grand look at the growing city of Duhok below.

One should be cautioned: the climb to Halamata requires a fair degree of physical exertion and the track is not well developed. However, for those interested in the history of the region it is well worth the effort.

JIRWANA (JIRWAN - JERWAN)

GENERAL INFORMATION / HISTORY

Sennecherib's aqueduct at Jirwana is an impressive structure with cuneiform writing on the side. Jirwana is a roughly one-hour ride east of Dohuk or 60 km (37 mi). The aqueduct carried water across a shallow valley between two hills. Water coming down the shallow valley ran under the aqueduct.

Ancient Cuneiform

How to get there? It is not easy to find unless you have a guide as the way is not marked and the road is small and sometimes impassable when it rains. There are surprisingly few people aware of or who have visited this incredible site. The aqueduct is visible on Google Earth and the coordinates are: 36.669692N, 43.393878E elevation: 407 meters.

It is located about ten minutes off the main road from Erbil to Duhok via Ruvia and Chraa. It is not visible from the main road. Coming from Erbil, the turnoff to the aqueduct, to the right, is opposite Mahad collective town, which is on the left side of the main road. A ways back from the main road, toward Mahad, there is a noticeable pinkish compound wall with white arches. There is also a large *Arcelik* billboard advertising washing machines. The dirt road opposite Mahad to the aqueduct might be muddy and deeply rutted but no problem for a four-wheel drive Land Cruiser except during the very heavy rains that sometimes deluge the area. The road goes toward low hills. Jirwana is one of the oldest if not the oldest aqueduct and bridge ruin in the world. It is over 2,700 years old (690s BC), built

by the Assyrian Emperor Sennacherib predating anything the Romans built by five centuries. The Aqueduct is part of the larger Atrush Canal built by the Assyrian king Sennacherib between 703 and 690BC, to bring waters from the Gomel Su River south to the gardens of Nineveh (45 minutes to an hour's drive south). Though it is a very well known archaeological site, only a fraction of this site has been excavated.

Many of the stones have cuneiform and ancient Assyrian carved into them—some of which are scattered around the site.

Many scholars now believe the legends referring to the *Hanging Gardens of Babylon* were actually Sennacherib's extensive gardens in Nineveh and were not located in Babylon at all. It was common in the age to refer to the region by the name Babylon and recent archeological finds are fairly conclusive. The gardens, famously known as one of the *Seven Wonders of the Ancient World*, were, according to Stephanie Dalley, an Oxford University Assyriologist, located some 340 miles north of ancient Babylon in Nineveh, on the Tigris River by Mosul (Nineveh) in modern Iraq. Dalley, whose book *The Mystery of the Hanging Gardens of Babylon* writes that earlier sources were translated incorrectly, leading to the confusion. The misinterpretation

Oldest Bridge Ruin in the World

also explains why years of excavations never yielded any credible evidence of the fabled gardens in Babylon, the capital city of Babylonia on the Euphrates River. Historians have questioned their existence for some time but have now renewed the interest leading to confirming evidence. Unfortunately the current lack of security in Mosul has made it impossible to continue this important excavation. However visitors to Jirwana can see the beginning of the aqueduct that terminated its hundreds of kilometer journey in the gardens of Sennacherib.

In the 1930s, there was an expedition from the University of Chicago to Jirwana, which studied the area and desired to reconstruct the site. The project has yet to be completed.

HIGHLIGHTS

An inscription on the Aqueduct reads: "Sennacherib king of the world king of Assyria. Over a great distance I had a watercourse directed to the environs of Nineveh, joining together the waters.... Over steep-sided valleys I spanned an aqueduct of white limestone blocks, I made those waters flow over it."

It was Sennacherib's habit to proclaim his accomplishments and elevate him to "godlike" status. Interestingly enough however, in the case of this magnificent accomplishment he also had stones inscribed that were turned inward and hidden until the aqueduct bridge collapsed centuries later. In essence these inscriptions predicted his own downfall informing readers that the exposure of these stones was proof that his empire was not eternal and that he was not a god.

Today, visitors can tour the area easily since it is a wide-open space and there are no restrictions. It is also convenient to many other historical and religious sites

Cuneiform Inscriptions

in the surrounding area such as Gaugemela and Mar Mattai Monastery (St. Matthews).

Interestingly there is a massive canal/bridge over the Elbe River in Germany that was reportedly patterned after the Jirwana Bridge—Sennacherib's kingdom may not have endured but his influence on engineering has survived the ages.

For a complete story of one of the most important archeological finds in the world you can download (free of charge) the account of the first excavations at:

http://oi.uchicago.edu/sites/oi.uchicago.edu/files/uploads/shared/docs/oip24.pdf

Entrance to Khanis

KHANIS (KING SENNACHARIB RESORT, KHANNIS, KHENIS, KHARUSA, BAVIAN, GOMEL GORGE)

GENERAL INFORMATION / HISTORY

An hour and a half east of Dohuk, or 87 km (54 mi) is one of the most well known ancient sites throughout the Kurdistan Region. The site is 13 km (8 mi) from Sheikhan and roughly 10 km (6 mi) from the Yezidi village of Lalish. Somewhat protected by the KRG and the Ministry of Antiquities, the site features a rather elaborate entrance gate which is connected to a fence that helps protect the site from unofficial guests. The site is also more secure now that there is a full time guard.

Khanis is part of an ancient Assyrian irrigation system built by Sennacharib over 2,500 years ago. It linked the palace of King Sennacharib in Nineveh to sources of water in the mountains of Kurdistan. This system also provided water to farmers in Nineveh even in the dry, scorching summer. The Aqueduct was so bountiful in its supply of water that eventually part had to be diverted en route to Nineveh into what became a swamp and the ultimate home of a number of rare species of birds and other wildlife.

Khanis is also the name of a nearby village, which evidently had been inhabited for many centuries. Families living in this

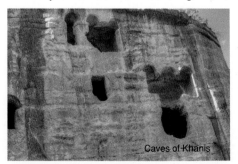
Caves of Khanis

Assyrian Carvings Khanis

lieve to have been the signet, or amulet, of Sennacherib himself is engraved with the king standing in an arched frame on the rock tablets at Bavian [Khanis]."

HIGHLIGHTS

The site holds several intricate carvings and reliefs, including many reliefs of Sennacherib (704-681 BC) carved into the rock itself.

One of the most famous aspects of the site has actually fallen into the nearby water, a large rock representing a Llamsu — a winged bull (or lion by some accounts) and other carvings partially split that are largely sunk into the shallow part of the riverbed.

Khanis is extremely popular with tourists and many visitors opt to take a swim in the water especially in the hot summer months. As of late 2013, The KRG began to build a small dam on the stream in order to retain and gather water during the rainy winter and there are plans to plant more trees and transform the area into an even greater tourist attraction. The *Duhok Governorate Directorate of Antiquities* has prepared booklets in different languages about the history of the site, which can be obtained at the entrance gate for a small fee.

area suffered under Saddam Hussein's Ba'ath regime and were displaced to nearby villages, however they were able to return after the Kurdish uprising in 1991.

There are plans by the KRG to link Khanis and Jirwana by an encircling or connected park though this has yet to come to fruition. It would be a massive undertaking but nothing compared to that Sennacharib accomplished thousands of years ago.

As was the case with the nearby site of Jirwana, The Oriental Institute (University of Chicago) traveled to Khanis in the early 1930s, and their complete findings may be found in their 1935 report: "Sennacherib's Aqueduct at Jerwan" (Jacobsen and Lloyd).

The famous orientalist Austen Layard describes Khanis in great detail in his book *Discoveries among the Ruins of Nineveh and Babylon* (1853). He writes that there were "...four cylinders and several beads, with a scorpion in lapis lazuli, all apparently once strung together. On one cylinder of translucent green feldspar (sometimes called amazon stone), which I be-

Resting place of the Llamsu

The Tombs of Lalish

LALISH TEMPLE

GENERAL INFORMATION / HISTORY

Lalish (Lalesh) is 52 km (32 mi) southeast of Dohuk, or roughly a one-hour trip. From Erbil, it is 150 km (93 mi) or a two and a half hour drive, depending on which route your driver takes you.

Best Times To Visit

The best time to visit is during holidays/festivals.
• The New Year: Certain Wednesday each April
• The Feast of Sacrifice: mid-February
• The Feast of Seven Days: (late September or early October)
• The first Friday of December: feast following three days of fasting

Cloths prayer /wish

For more information: http://www.yezidit-ruth.org/yezidi_religious_tradition

Tips

It is best not to wear blue since Yezidis generally do not wear that color though they will not be upset if you forget

If you bring outside food, do not bring lettuce, as this is against Yezidi dietary restrictions. There is a belief by some that demonic Jinn can hide between the leaves

If you are visiting in colder months, it is recommended you bring heavy socks (or wear two pairs of regular socks at once) so you do not get your feet overly cold or wet if it has rained or snowed.

Ask questions! There are a lot of misconceptions about Yezidi people and their religious beliefs.

Lalish is one of the most unique destinations in the entire Kurdistan Region. It is a cultural and religious experience, as well as a place of calming, serenity, and natural beauty. This small mountain town is the holiest place for the ethno-religious Yezidi (Yazidi) community. It is the resting place for some of the most important figures in the Yezidi faith such as Sheik Adi (1070-1162 AD), who essentially codified much of Yezidi theology from its many disparate teachings.

Yezidis are expected and encouraged to make a six-day pilgrimage to Lalish in their lifetime in order to visit the tomb of Sheikh Adi and other sacred places in the small mountain village. Yezidis living in the region attend the autumn Feast of the Assembly. The village is easily recognizable due to the famous conical struc-

Entrance to the Temple

tures (shrines).

In more recent years, and particularly since Yezidis have recently made the headlines, the holy village has become somewhat of a tourist attraction for Kurds and international visitors alike in order to understand and gain insight into this persecuted minorities' faith, culture, and traditions. There are only a few year-long residents of Lalish who are tasked with maintaining the beauty of the place, though there are many Yezidis living in surrounding towns and villages who visit often, particularly on weekends. Most are quite willing to share their religion, culture, and traditions to outsiders. Lalish is open to people of all faiths for visits and there are usually tour guides that have been officially tasked by the Yezidi community to assist and educate visitors.

Since the entire village is sacred, everyone must remove their shoes (you may wear socks). It is not a terribly large village, and the grounds are meticulously cleaned so visitors should not worry too much about stepping on anything that would be harmful. At every doorstep Yezidis believe there are angels waiting, so special care must be taken when entering any threshold—you must step *over* them.

Yezidis believe Lalish is where Noah's ark rested after the great flood and life began anew and every year thousands of Yezidis journey to Lalish to drink the holy spring water flowing throughout the village.

Ancient oil pots

There is a great deal of controversy over the actual beliefs of this colorful and mysterious people. Some mistakenly call them "devil worshippers" which is far from true. The misconception derives from writings that speak of the opposing forces of light and darkness. Yezidis do not worship the darkness and believe the light will ultimately prevail.

The teachings of the Yezidis were reportedly recorded in the *Meshef Resh* (Black Books) among others, which included accounts of

Yezidis pilgrims

the creation. It is said of these revelations that, "Outsiders may neither read nor behold them." Indeed the Yezidis in many ways are a closed society and one may neither convert to Yezidism nor marry outside of the faith. They are known as fierce warriors, which is not apparent when encountering them, as they are a gentle and hospitable people.

HIGHLIGHTS

Attached to the chamber of Sheikh Adi's tomb (the largest of the conical tombs) is the cave of the wishing rock. The legend is that if one manages to throw a piece of cloth on top of this rock, one's wishes come true. The catch is that your eyes must be closed when you throw it.

There are several smaller tombs inside the main temple, draped in brightly colored silk cloths, which are knotted. It is said that if one unties a knot (represented as a prayer) the desire of the person who originally placed it there will be realized. The visitor who unties one must retie another one, after making a wish him or herself. It is

an ancient version of "paying it forward."

Next to these tombs is a long corridor containing hundreds of clay pots that once held olive oil used to light candles in the temple as well as throughout the entire village. Adjacent to this is a small door leading to a few steps down into darkness, and one hears the faint sound of water — this is the holy water or spring of Zamzam. Pilgrims wash their hands and some even drink the fresh water, but one does not place their feet in it.

There are numerous places to visit in/around Lalish and one could spend several days there. In fact, at the entrance to the village is a hostel for just that purpose!

Deep within the temple

Lalish Temple

Mar Mattai Monastery

MAR MATTAI (ST. MATTHEWS) MONASTERY

GENERAL INFORMATION / HISTORY

The monastery is thirty-five km (22 mi) northeast of the city of Mosul and approximately 70 kilometers (45 mi) from Erbil. It is known to local Christians as *Dayro d-Mor Mattai* (The Monastery of St. Matthew) and is perhaps the most ancient religious institution in Iraq. In fact, scholars recognize this monastery as one of the oldest Christian monasteries in existence anywhere in the world.

This ancient holy site rests on Mount Alfaf close to its

Monastery Chapel

southern summit (Mount Maqloub or *Tura D'alpayeh* in Aramaic translated the thousands, meaning the multitude of his followers). In addition to Mar Mattai there are several hermitages here dating to the 4th and 5th centuries AD, including Bar Hebraeus' hermitage (named after the most respected Syriac Christian leader and thinker from the 13th century) and the "Spy's hermitage" which is at the top of the mountain and was historically used as a watchtower to warn hermits and monks of impending trouble.

The Monastery of Mar Mattai is traditionally thought to have been commissioned by Assyrian King Sinharib (Senharib) - See Marbina Qadish Koya and completed in the 4th century though this has not been validated. The monastery is one of the oldest functioning monasteries in all of Mesopotamia and holds the final resting places of many Syriac Orthodox patriarchs and scholars, including Bar Hebraeus himself, buried in the Saints' Room along with the remains of Mar Mattai, Mar Zakkai and Mar Abraham, among others.

The monastery was founded in 363 AD by Mar Mattai who became a hermit after he fled persecution in modern-day Diyarbakir (Amed). The only accurate date for the monastery actually pertains to building the church within the monastery, which was built in the mid 4th century but the monastery itself is much older. According to tradition, Mar Mattai healed, the sister of Mar Behnam named Sarah of leprosy (see Marbina Qadisha in Koya), and converted both to Christianity. Initially enraged at this act, their father, Assyrian King Senharib reportedly killed his children but later regretted this ghastly act and provided Mar Mattai Mount Alfaf as a place to establish his monastery and converted from Zoroastrianism Christianty. While there is no sure

Monastery Art

source for the story, it is widely held and an integral part of local Church history. At its peak in the 9th century the monastery was home to around 7,000 Monks.

The monastery was abandoned for unclear reasons until 1795 AD when Basil Gargis II Al-Mosuli ren-

A Christian Sanctuary for 2000 years

ovated it and built walls around its perimeter. In 1845, additional wings were added. However, church records also state that the monastery (and the Church) greatly suffered under the rule of Nader Shah (1743-1790), who was the Emperor of Persia at the time. Seeking alliances and assistance, monks established contacts with Rome in the 18th century, which brought about gradual conversion to the Syriac Catholic Church. It is also recorded that monks abandoned the monastery again in 1819 though it is unclear why this happened as well.

HIGHLIGHTS

Adjacent to the monastery is a very large cave, which contains natural spring water that drips from the caves' ceiling. Currently the monastery maintains over fifty rooms, three halls, and a church. At present the monastery is maintained by the Syriac Orthodox Church and Christians from various denominations gather in the monastery every September 18 to commemorate the day of Mar Mattai's passing. Throughout the year

Christians belonging to the Assyrian Church of the East, the Chaldean Church, the Syriac Orthodox Church, and well as other Assyrian churches frequently visit Mar Mattai for prayer and meditation.

The monastery still contains many sculptures from ancient times and there is evidence of renovations that took place in 1164 and between 1250-1261. In 1171, Muslim tribes attacked the monastery and many unique and holy manuscripts were damaged and even destroyed. The monastery was exceptionally well-known for its magnificent library and considerable collection of Syriac Christian manuscripts and as of 1298, the library contained all the writings of Bar Hebraeus — more than 35 books in addition to countless manuscripts, books, letters, and Bibles. A few remain, most in glass-enclosed cases. The monastery was also partially destroyed by the famous Mongol Emperor Timur, more commonly known in the West as Tamerlane. In the mid-14th century, another Muslim attack damaged Mar Mattai yet again. Throughout the 19th century, Muslims looted the monastery several other times and many of its precious volumes were stolen or destroyed. Thankfully many were recovered and may be currently viewed in the British Library (Cambridge) and in Berlin.

Senior Monk of the Monastery

In the modern era, the monastery was renovated in 1986, and is still visited by thousands of Christians every year. In the 20th century it was decided that all churches in the Nineveh Plains would open Sunday schools and it was permitted to use an organ during the liturgy. The Church also began to encourage young women to participate in choirs. The leadership (Synod) decided to remain on the Eastern Julian calendar, but allowed churches in America to use the Gregorian calendar, except for Easter. The Synod also forbade giving and receiving dowry. Today this massive complex is home to just six monks, a bishop and several trainee monks. After the ISIS took over and destroyed some aspects of the monastery, Christian militias and *peshmerga* wrested it back from the extremists and monks and visitors have begun returning once again to this fascinating, beautiful, and holy monastery.

Entrance to the Monastery

Tourists investigate the site

QUBAHANI MADRASSA RUINS

GENERAL INFORMATION / HISTORY

The ruins of the Qubahani School are located across the valley from the Amediye Citadel, in the Duhok Governorate. Recently a well-paved road has been built for easier access and there are plans for restoration. The road to the site is off the main highway leading to Amediya several miles before the city and there is sign indicating the turnoff. One can also hike across the valley from Amediye it self beginning from the old Amediye Gate – a great walk through the natural surroundings of the valley, which takes about 40 minutes at a leisurely pace.

The Madrassa was reportedly built in the 17th century as an extension of the famed University of Cairo during the reign of Sultan Hussein Wali (1534-1576 AD). Imams and scholars studied the Islamic religious sciences at this site for hundreds of years.

HIGHLIGHTS

The site has a number of remnants of the original walls in intact although they are in an advanced state of ruin. The site has not received a great deal of attention and little factual information is available.

Qubahan School

On Dec /22/1951 it was announced as an archaeological site, It is called "Qubahan" because there are many domes. It belongs to the (13 th) century A.D and some parts are more ancient but they were repaired by Sultan (Hussein Wali 1534-1570 A.D) in the 15th century

Directorate
Of Duhok Archaeology

Inside the Madrassa

There are plans by private individuals and the government to rectify this as it is an important part of the region's religious heritage.

Some claimed the school's library held over 2,000 volumes of books at one time. As scholars are conducting research they may soon unveil more of the story of this fascinating ruin. It is definitely worth the visit if one is traveling through the region.

RABBAN HORMIZD MONASTERY

GENERAL INFORMATION / HISTORY

This is one of the most important religious sites in Kurdistan and an ancient monastery of the Chaldean Church. It is carved out of the mountains about two miles from Alqosh, 45 kilometers (28 miles) north of Mosul. It is roughly 50 Kilometers (30 miles) from Duhok or about 45 minutes.

Founded in approximately 640 AD, it has been the official residence of the patriarchs of the *Eliya* line of the Church of the East from 1551 to the 18th century, and after the union with Rome in the early 19th century, it became a prominent monastery of the Chaldean Church.

The monastery is named after Rabban Hormizd (*rabban* is the Syriac for *monk*) who founded it in the seventh century. Because of the fame of Rabban Hormizd, the monastery he founded became extremely important for the Church of the East. It flourished until the 10th century. Before the end of the 15th century, the Rabban Hormizd Monastery served as the patriarchal burial site.

In about 1743, due to pestilence and attacks by Muslims, the monastery was left unmanned. In 1808, the Assyrian Gabriel Dambo (1775-1832) revived the abandoned monastery, rebuilt it, collected a

Road to the Monastery

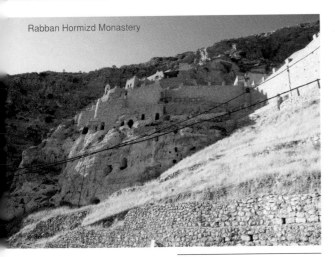
Rabban Hormizd Monastery

mountains which encloses the plain of Mosul on the north, and stands in a sort of amphitheater, which is approached by a rocky path that leads through a narrow defile; this path has been paved by generations of monks. The church is of stone and is of a dusky red color; it is built upon an enormous rock. In the hills round about the church and buildings of the monastery are rows of caves hewn out of the solid rock, in which the stern ascetics of former generations lived and died."

Today there are several monks who occupy the monastery and they are usually glad to show visitors around this amazing example of early Christian community.

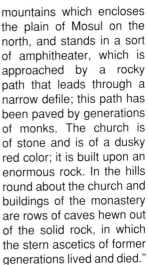

number of pupils and founded a seminary. The soldiers of Mohammed Pasha, the Kurdish Emir of Rawanduz, murdered Dambo in 1832.

The library of the Monastery of Rabban Hormizd was rich in Syriac manuscripts. In 1828, many of these manuscripts were looted and destroyed. The monks went on anyway to buy and copy manuscripts, thus forming an important library.

HIGHLIGHTS

The monastery is reached by climbing 150 steps and upon reaching the top one can see for miles across the valley below. There are numerous caves surrounding the Monastery where it is said as many as 600 monks once lived. Due to the ravages of time and looting the monastery had fallen into serious disrepair but was completely renovated in the past two decades.

E. A. Wallis Budge, who visited Rabban Hormizd Monastery in 1890, described the m o n a s t e r y thus: "Rabban Hormizd Monastery is built about half way up the range of

Sacred Cave Spring

Happy
Friday

**A LOT OF SURPRISES AWAIT YOU THIS FRIDAY
AND EVERY FRIDAY OF THE WEEK!**

Make a 3-minute phone call within the Korek network on a Friday, then
send a free text to 232 and get a free call within the network on Friday
night between 10:00 PM and 11:00 PM.
This offer is valid throughout the whole of Iraq and only on Fridays to all
korek pre-paid and post-paid subscribers.

Dare to Dream

411 ✆

korektel.com

KHURMALA DOME KAR PIPELINE CO. ERBIL REFINERY KAR POWER PLANT

KAR

UPSTREAM | MIDSTREAM | DOWNSTREAM

www.kar-k.com

Family Mall
Shopping & Entertainment Center

Erbil

Family Mall - 100m street - Erbil - Kurdistan Region -IRAQ
E-mail: info@familymallarbil.com • www.familymallarbil.com • Phone Number : 009367505618484

Suleymaniyah

Openning Soon

Family Mall - 600m street - Suleymaniyah - Kurdistan Region -IRAQ

Duhok

Openning Soon

Family Mall - Zaxo Road- Duhok - Kurdistan Region -IRAQ

KURDISTAN IRAQ TOURS

A Division of The Other Iraq Tours LLC

ALWAYS FIRST!

TRAVEL WITH THE MOST EXPERIENCED PROFESSIONALS IN THE REGION!

For information on booking a tour to Kurdistan contact:
Email: info@kurdistaniraqtours.com Tel: +964 (0) 750 339 9999

www.kurdistaniraqtours.com

Logos Brochures
Emblems Magazine
Advertisement
Catalogs
Indoor-Outdoor
Advertising
Design Magazine

 cat yayın
t a s a r ı m

info@catyayintasarim.com.tr
www.catyayintasarim.com.tr

WHERE TO SLEEP, EAT AND SHOP IN DUHOK

HOTEL

DILSHAD PALACE	062 722 7601
HAKAR HOTEL	0750 483 8581
JUTYAR HOTEL	0750 450 3289
MOTEL SHAM	0750 445 7716
HANDIREN HOTEL	0750 446 0662
HAREM HOTEL	0750 404 7047
MATIN MOTEL	0750 450 3286
KANAR MOTEL	0750 472 4527
SALAR MOTEL	0750 457 5539
MEER MOTEL	0750 450 9781
RASAN HOTEL	0750 440 7277
DUHOK PALACE	0750 459 3200
PARWAR HOTEL	0750 878 2424
SINDIBAD HOTEL	0750 445 7508
JIYAN HOTEL	0750 442 7711
NAWROZ PALACE	0750 496 2797
ZOZIK HOTEL	0750 131 9787
NAZ MOTEL	0750 450 9100
HAWAR MOTEL	0750 456 9705
MARYA HOTEL	0750 478 2351

RESTAURANT

GEVERKE RESTAURANT	07504268400
KANI RESTAURANT	07504261295
SAFIN RESTAURANT	07504508175
AMAD RESTAURANT	07504676036
AL AZAEM PALACE	07504584464
SADEER PALACE	07504902288
MALTA RESTAURANT	07504124114
FURAT RESTAURANT	07504576197
SULAV RESTAURANT	07504507603
AZADI RESTAURANT	07504454948
SHANDOKHA RESTAURANT	07504545139
SIPAN RESTAURANT	07504090627
HAREM RESTAURANT	07504589844
DUHOK STAR	07504454838
NAWROZ RESTAURANT	07504357199
MEER RESTAURANT	0750 19 9995
ZAYTONA RESTAURANT	07504172732
DYNA RESTAURANT	07504573485
HAKAR RESTAURANT	07504016038
AKITO RESTAURANT	07504740917

Geverkê Restaurant

GEVERKE

Barzan Main St., Duhok, Kurdistan Tel:+964 750 4268 400 • +964 750 4258 400

SHOPPING MALLS IN DUHOK

MAZI MALL
FAMILY MALL

GARMIAN ADMINISTRATION

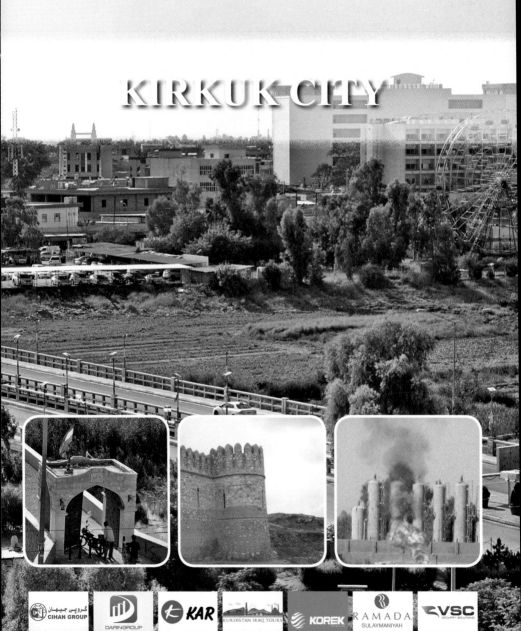

KIRKUK CITY

Kirkuk City

KIRKUK CITY

GENERAL INFORMATION / HISTORY

Kirkuk is the main city in the Garmian Governorate, which has recently been secured as part of the Kurdistan Region of Iraq (KRI). Although there are still disputes concerning its final status, the end result may now be a fait acompli as the Kurds seem determined never to relinquish this traditional Kurdish city seized by them from Saddam Hussein. From Erbil, Kirkuk is 104 km (65 mi) or one hour and a half south. Arriving from Sulaymani, Kirkuk is 124 km (77 mi) or an hour and forty-five minutes away

and 236 km (147 mi) north of Baghdad. West of the city is the Lesser Zab River, and through the city runs a small stream, the Khasa River.

Kirkuk has a diverse population made up of Kurds, Assyrians, Chaldeans, Arabs and Turkmen most of whom have claimed Kirkuk as their own at one time or another and all have their respective historical nar-

Old Kirkuk

ratives. However, for centuries the majority of the population has been Kurdish or their ancestors.

Before emigrating to Israel, Jews also featured prominently in the city. The famous Prophet Daniel and other Biblically important figures are believed buried in the city giving it a strong religious background.

At various time periods the city has been ruled by Hurrians, Assyrians, Babylonians, Medes, Ottomans, and Arabs.

Saddam Hussein undertook ruthless efforts to "Arabize" the city by relocating tens of thousands of Kurds to Southern Iraq and giving their abandoned houses to Arabs who he moved into the area. The center of the city (Citadel) is historically important to the indigenous people and

Vast Oil Reserves

in an attempt to "beautify" the site; Saddam removed at least one thousand Kurdish and Turkmen families from the citadel. Destroying these ancient homes, this campaign was part of an overall effort to depopulate Kirkuk of its Kurdish and Turkmen populations that began in the 1960s. There are still many Kurdish and Turkmen neighborhoods in this area (as well as others communities).

Kirkuk Citadel

Kirkuk contains one of the richest oil fields in the world, which has been the motivation for many to lay claim to this historic Kurdish city. However, KRG President Masoud Barzani once eloquently explained to a group of visiting journalists that the issue was one transcending economy and oil as far as the Kurds are concerned. He pointed out that Kirkuk represents one of the horrific injustices Saddam wrought on the Kurds; stealing their homes, massacring people, many of whom ended up in unmarked graves in the desert. The KRG has repeatedly demanded that all Kurds be allowed to return to their ancestral homes and those who illegally occupied houses and lands remove to their places of origin. At that time a referendum would be held to determine the final disposition of the city. No one doubts that if the issue were fairly addressed Kirkuk would be attached permanently to Kurdistan Region of Iraq (KRI). However recent events involving the defense of Kurdistan against ISIS has made the point moot. The Kurds seized the city and most other of the disputed territories and currently have no intention of relinquishing them again—at least as far as Kirkuk and clearly Kurdish areas are concerned. Time will tell but at this point Garmian Region and the city of Kirkuk are listed as a part of the KRI although formal Governorate status has not been conferred.

In the 7th century, the city and much of the surrounding area fell to the Arab Muslims and Kirkuk became part of the Islamic Caliphate until the 10th century. The Ottomans controlled much of the Middle East from the 16th century through the end of the First World War, when the British controlled modern-day Iraq including Kirkuk.

Today Kirkuk is known for its vast quantity of oil and oilfields. In 1927, oil was first "commercially" discovered in Kirkuk. However, it has been known from ancient times that oil was present and the city has long been known as *Baba Gurgur* (Father of Fire). As one drives into the city large plumes of fire can be seen—natural gas burned off in the process of pumping the oil to the surface from the vast oil fields below.

HIGHLIGHTS

Arrapha

Arrapha is another ancient name for Kirkuk, and today there is a neighborhood on the northwest part of the city named Arrapha where the *Kirkuk Oil Training Institute* is located. Due to the fact there is a great deal of infrastructure and residences, the site has not been excavated as of present, but it is certain the area holds a treasure trove of historically important artifacts.

Baba Gurgur

The site of Baba Gurgur is 16 km (10 mi) northwest of Kirkuk and is a large oil field. At first glance, this may not seem like a typical tourist attraction or a place of interest. However, this is the site of the first discovery of oil in northern Iraq (1927) and for nearly twenty years was considered the largest oilfield in the world.

This site is known for its "eternal flame" in the middle of the oil fields, and is believed by many to be the same "fiery furnace" in the Biblical Book of Daniel in which Nebuchadnezzar (c. 630–562 BCE), King of Babylon, threw three Hebrews (Hananiah, Misha'el and Azariah, or as they are known by many Shadrach, Meshach, and Abednego).

Darius reportedly cast these companions of Daniel into the furnace for refusing to abandon worship of their God in favor of obeisance to the King. According to the Biblical account they were miraculously delivered and later honored by the King for their unfailing devotion to their God. Even today the site is quite significant, as many women may be seen here asking for a baby boy, a pre-Islamic ritual that likely hearkens to Zoroastrian times.

Qalat Jarmo

This was one of the oldest agricultural communities in the world, dating back to 7090 BC, and is a settlement contemporary with Jericho in Israel/Palestine and Çatal Hüyük in modern-day Turkey. Jarmo is roughly four acres and is surrounded by oak and pistachio woodlands. The site was discovered in 1940, and first excavated in 1948. There was a great deal of evidence testifying to the agricultural nature of their society; barley and lentils were found alongside peas, acorns, carob seeds, and pistachios. Snail shells are also abundant and evidence further suggests they had domesticated dogs, goats, and sheep.

Qishla

Built in 1863 as the headquarters of the Ottoman army, the building is located in the center of the city, and is roughly six acres. In Turkish, Qishla means, "place where the army stays in the winter". There is a Turkmen non-governmental organization planning to repair parts of the structure to make it a cultural center and museum.

Tomb or Shrine of Daniel the Prophet and the Citadel

While some claim the tomb of Daniel the prophet is in Susa (Shushan), Iran, and others place it as far away as Uzbekistan, or several other locations in Iraq, the commonly held view of many scholars is that the tomb lies here in the Citadel of Kirkuk. Regardless, a famous tomb attributed to Daniel (*Hebrew*: God is my judge) is located within the Kirkuk Citadel. Originally, this site was a synagogue and later converted into a church, and lastly transformed into a mosque. This was also done to the prophet Jonah's tomb in Mosul, which was bombed by Saddam during the Anfal Campaigns and later blown up by ISIS in the summer of 2014. ISIS also tried to destroy the tomb of Daniel but were repelled by the Kurds before they could accomplish their aim. The site and the city are now firmly in the control of the Kurds.

Currently, the revered mosque includes beautiful arches, pillars and two domes in addition to three minarets, dating to the Mongolian invasion. The mosque reportedly also holds three other tombs believed to belong to the companions of Daniel — Hananiah, Misha'el and Azariah, or as they are known by many Shadrach, Meshach, and Abednego. This claim is also in dispute

Tomb of Daniel

and there will probably never be a definitive resolution of the issue. Locals however believe in the tradition of their forefathers and many scholars support this view citing its proximity to much of Daniel's deeds as outlined in the Old Testament and Torah. Believers who visit the tombs tie strips of cloth to the iron grate that surround Daniel's tomb or toss money or trinkets inside. Christian, Muslims, and Yezidi throughout Iraq engage this practice.

This area is claimed to be the first cemetery in Kirkuk and many other respected Kirkukis are buried nearby. To this day, the most popular day to visit these tombs is Saturday, a reminder that this site was originally a Jewish site.

The Citadel that houses the tombs is situated in the center of the city, towering 40 m (131 ft.) on an artificial mound near the now-mostly dried Khasa River that runs north-south through the center of the city. The Citadel is the oldest building of the city, dating to the reign of Assyrian

Father of Fire

King Ashurnasirpal II, and established between the 884-858 BC meant for a military defense citadel/fortress. Another famous aspect of the citadel is the so-called "Red Church," in which visitors may see pre-Islamic era mosaics. The famed warrior Timur (Tamerlane, C. 1405) visited the citadel in 1393 during his Mongol-led military conquests. Many of the currently standing walls date to various Ottoman periods.

The citadel once housed separate synagogues, churches and Mosques, similar to the citadel in Erbil and, like those in Erbil most of the churches and synagogues have all but been destroyed. The city is still divided demographically, as there are Kurds, Arabs Turkmen, and Christians who live in this increasingly stable area, currently controlled by the *peshmerga* of the Kurdistan Regional Government (KRG). Prior to the KRG takeover the area was considered unsafe for visitors but it has since been largely stabilized. The changing times are steadily becoming recognized by the international community, as there are currently many efforts to reconstruct

Kirkuk Citadel

the citadel. UNESCO is involved and has been actively overseeing renovations since 2010. Their objectives are to transform the Citadel and attempt to restore its former glory to a respected international standard. Post-Saddam, the Kurds (with the help of the international community) seek to restore the city and attract more tourists. There is a great deal of infrastructure that must be established before this can become a fully realized goal; including hotels and other tourist related amenities. At present however, Kirkuk is a popular day trip for those who are based in Erbil.

Other important sites of the Citadel are the Grand Mosque, and the remains of the Chaldean Church. The Qaysari Bazaar is one of the most artistic buildings in the citadel. A long corridor with two gates on both sides, it has over 300 shops to peruse. Though there are

many dilapidated areas in the citadel it is still accessible to the public and is where the Kurdish New Year (Newroz) is celebrated and offers a great vantage point of the city. On the northwest side of the citadel is the Citadel Garden, a public park, and one can still go to the cemetery and visit the tombs/shrines of Daniel and his companions.

YORGAN TEPE (NUZI)

Hurrians and Caucasus region peoples occupied this area as early as the second millennium BC. This was a center of Hurrian provincial administration, and excavations revealed government buildings with frescoes, and religious structures and shrines are elaborately decorated. Some of the 5,000 known cuneiform tablets found here began appearing in the late 1800s. Famous traveler and scholar Gertrude Bell made a note of these in 1925 when archaeological digs here were undertaken in earnest. A sprawling area, the site has fifteen separate levels. The most famous artifact found here is known as the *Nuzi Map*, the oldest ever discovered.

KALAR

GENERAL INFORMATION / HISTORY

Kalar is a city in the southeast part of the Kurdistan Region, 152 km south of Sulaymani (95 mi) (about two hours) and 77 km (48 mi) north of Khaneqin (about one hour). To its east is the Diyala River (Sirwan River in Kurdish). Only 30 short kilometers (19 mi) east of the river lies Iran (closest border crossing is Qasr e-Shirin).

Kalar is part of the twin towns of Smud-Kalar. Smud (renamed Rizgari after the 1991 uprising) was a neighborhood that became a relocation/refugee camp for Kurds. From the 1960s the village quickly grew to become a town and in 1970, the Iraqi government made it an administration in charge of neighboring villages and smaller towns.

Most of the population speaks Arabic and Persian (Farsi) in addition to Kurdish. Initially it was formed from four villages (Kalar, Hama Karim, Bingird and Gazino), The population in the district is around 250,000. In addition to another small town named Bawanoor, there are more than 100 villages in the Kalar district. There are approximately five nearby hospitals and health centers as well as over 80 schools and colleges and institutes of higher learning. The newly established University of Garmian is in Kalar as well, which functions as a sat-

ellite campus of the prestigious University of Sulaymaniyah. The university is the first local scientific center that offers both undergraduate as well as graduate courses.

Many locals are farmers that mostly grow wheat and different types of vegetables. Exporting produce to other parts of Kurdistan and Iraq provides a major source of income.

In 2006 it was reported that the city became the unofficial "capital of stolen cars" from all over Iraq. This dubious award was bestowed due to the fact that since 2003

Kalar town

Sherwana Citadel

This economic boom may be impacted negatively as around 400 families of internally displaced peoples from al-Anbar province have arrived in Kalar in 2014, most of which rented small houses, where multiple families live together to split the cost of rent.

Due to current security issues travel to the city is not advisable without escort.

HIGHLIGHTS

The city of Kalar is located on a large plain and there are many historical sites currently undergoing archaeological excavations including several different ancient and more recent time periods. Throughout the area there are many tels (mounded ancient sites) where one sees evidence of the ancient heritage of the region.

more than 8,000 stolen vehicles from Baghdad and other parts of Iraq passed through the town as well as the rest of the Kurdistan Region. There was an amnesty given after the war during which previous owners from south of Iraq could (with proof of ownership) reclaim their vehicles. After the grace period passed the vehicles were for the most part legitimized and given local licenses.

The city has been growing and developing rapidly and urban areas have begun expansion and renovation. The local infrastructure is vastly improving and the economic situation overall is one that points to confident growth. Largely attributed to its geographical proximity to Iran, Kalar serves as a conduit between trade in the Kurdistan Region and the rest of Iraq. In fact, Kalar has lately been considered one of the most expensive cities in the Kurdistan Region based on property value.

The Antiquities Department in their investigations of ancient sites in the area has also uncovered numerous mass graves left behind by Saddam Hussein during his infamous "Anfal" Campaigns in the region. One can see remains of army barracks, foxholes, and shrapnel from exploded ordinances from the Iran–Iraq War (1980-1988). There are possible landmines, though most have since been destroyed but nonetheless it is wise to have a local guide along when exploring in the area.

Folkloric Museum of Garmian

Established in 2003 by the Department of Antiquities in Kalar, the museum offers over 400 artifacts, which is part of a collection belonging to Sherwana Castle. The folklore heritage museum also includes many men and women's clothing, agricultural tools, and daily household items.

Kalar Amusement Park

In the center of Kalar, the park has many types of rides for children, and a cafeteria and picnic areas and benches are available as well.

Pasha Palace (Mahmood Pasha Jaff)

The Pasha Palace lies in Tazadai village 9 km (6 mi) northeast of Kalar in between the Aksu River and the Diyala/Sirwan River. Mahmood Pasha Jaff, the Kurdish King was supreme chief of the Jaff tribe. Once nomadic, the Jaff have more recently settled into a predominantly agricultural way of life. Total population of the tribe reaches from 1,500,000 to 3,000,000 people in both Iraq and Iran. At present, they are settled mainly in Halabja and in this region near Kalar with some residing in the Kermanshah area of Iranian Kurdistan. Saddam Hussein's chemical attack on Halabja on March 16, 1988 killed at least 5,000 people and injured or sickened 7,000 more. The majority of these victims were Jaff tribe members.

Mahmood Pasha Jaff was at one time a very influential figure in the Kurdish political scene and he was renown for being able to assemble several thousand fighters in a matter of hours when summoned to help

Pasha Palace

protect the Kurdish region. More than once the Ottoman rulers tried to depose him fearing his ever-growing power and even held him as their "guest" in Istanbul for two years at one point. Legend has it that he escaped and traveled back to Kurdistan disguised as homeless wanderer.

The remains of the building include two floors built as a mansion by Mahmood Pasha Jaff in 1895. North of the palace is a rectangular building, which was used as a storehouse and a horse and mule barn. To the south of the palace and on a high rise of land, there is a small building with a few rooms. Unlike the Sherwana Palace, and despite the fact it was newer, this palace

Kifri

is mostly in ruins and is not as frequented by tourists although historically it is a very important site.

Qoratu

Much like Qulabarz but not as congested, it is also a recreational area 25 km (15.5 mi) east of Kalar. It is famous for its beauty and greenery. Many weekend tourists come here on holidays for recreational purposes.

Qulabarz Park

This stunningly beautiful site is only 25 km (15.5 mi) north of Kalar on the Sirwan River. Many people visit the site for recreational purposes such as picnics, weddings, and on holidays and weekends. The side combines lushness, surrounded by green trees and grass

alongside a scenic river.

Sherwana Castle/Citadel (Pasha Palace)

Situated at the entrance of Kalar near the Sirwan River, the dramatic mansion, built in the 18th century, adds a nostalgic beauty to the scenery of the town. Mohammad Pasha Jaff built Sherwana Citadel for the purpose of managing local tribes as well as serving as his own residence. The castle itself consists of a basement, two floors, a large and open octagonal hall, and a small museum for excavated artifacts uncovered from the mound on which it stands is open to the public.

Mohammed Pasha Jaff, perhaps Kalar's favorite son recently had a statue made in his memory and honor in Mexico City in the summer of 2014. The statue of this national and tribal ruler was ostensibly donated to Mexico City for educational purposes to help raise Kurdish cultural and national awareness to those in Mexico as well as Latin America in general. There is a replica of the statue in his former home and famous tourist landmark, Sherwana Castle/Citadel.

KIFRI

GENERAL INFORMATION / HISTORY

Kifri is 180 km (112 mi) or two and a half hours southwest of Sulaymani and 123 km (76 mi) or one hour and forty-five minutes southeast of Kirkuk and is the seat of Kifri District. The population of the district is roughly 50,000 and is largely made up of Feylis (Shi'a Kurds), Turkmen and Arabs.

Kifri is one of the three major cities in the Garmian District. The word Garmian means, "warm country" and is the southernmost tip of the Kurdish inhabited areas in Iraq. Living up to its name the area becomes extremely hot during summer months. Until the 1970s, many inhabitants of the town and surrounding villages west of town were Turkmen while the population east of the city was almost completely Kurdish. After the 1980s enforced Arabization of the area by Saddam, many Kurds were expelled. The oldest districts, Ismail Beg, Dedeler, and Sade are the original districts mainly inhabited by Turkmen. Newer districts, namely Imam Muhammed and Awberi are almost exclusively Kurdish.

There is a great deal of Kurdish nationalist sentiment in this town, which is deeply rooted. Legendary Kurdish leader Sheik Mahmoud first made contact with the British in Kifri during the First World War. In 2012, the city celebrated its 90th anniversary of Sheikh Mahmoud's control over the town, which hearkened to the first Kurdish Government at that time. Kifri's Cultural Center and Garmian Archeology Directorate organized a two-day festival. The festival's slogan was "Kifri is the cradle of revolution and must remain alive." During the festivities, many historical and scientific research papers regarding Kifri and Sheikh Mahmoud and Garmian in general were presented, along with an art program. The festival was an attempt to draw attention to the neglected state of the town and surrounding areas.

As a result, in spring 2013, the KRG announced plans to invest 700 million IQD ($610,000) for new Tourist facilities. Much of the planned development has yet to be accomplished. In autumn 2013, there was a Kurdish poetry festival in Kifri that saw participation of 25 poets from all four parts of historical Kurdistan (Erbil, Sulaymani, Duhok and Garmian). That same year, the Independent Media Center in Kurdistan (IMCK) trained several television and radio journalists in Kifri in broadcast journalism. IMCK partnered with the local House of Culture for Children for this training.

HIGHLIGHTS

Bawashaswar Dam

It is 3 km (2 mi) north of Kifri and is frequently visited by tourists and locals who want to enjoy some quiet and relaxing time by the water.

Bawashaswar Manmade Caves

This small village and natural area is 3.3 km (2 mi) north of the city of Kifri and roughly forty-five minutes (40 km, 25 mi) northwest of the city of Kalar. In 2011-

Majeed Pasha Palace

of the 19th century. This palace has two levels, many spacious rooms as well as a guest hall. It is largely in ruin but much of the basic structure remains.

Quldar Mill of Kifri

This mill is situated due north of Kifri and north of the famous Bawashaswar cemetery. The mill has a tower with two rooms; one of them was used for grinding wheat.

2012, the KRG began built a dam at Bawashaswar, which serves as a reservoir and helps irrigate farmland as well as serving as flood control.

Bawashaswar is known for its manmade caves, which were most likely created in the early centuries AD. Graves from an unknown period are also found here, known as Bawashswar cemetery.

Kifri Qaysari

Perhaps the most famous place in Kifry is the bazaar (Qaysari) or market. The Qaysari in Kifri was built in the 19th century by the Ottoman Empire and held many shops and warehouses (Khans). Recently, many buildings have been renovated in the market though The work is not complete. The focal point for the mar-

ket is the famous arched old bazaar entrance with its recognizable Ottoman architecture and though it was largely neglected by the former regime, it is bustling and full of life at present!

Majeed Pasha Palace

Just east of Kifri, Majeed Pasha Qadir Beg established this palace at the end

Pasha Palace

Yak Mughar (Mughara)

Yak Mughar, which is 1 km (.6 mi) east of Kifri and is a famous rocky cave. This deep cave is part of Bawashaswar's famous stony hills. They are sculpted in rectangular shapes and located north and northeast of Kifri.

KHANEQIN

GENERAL INFORMATION / HISTORY

Khaneqin is 78 km (48 mi) or an hour southeast of Kalar, and 210 km (130 mi) or roughly three hours southeast of Sulaymani. This city is located at the southernmost point in the Kurdistan Region and only 8 km (5 mi) from Iran. In recent years oil has been discovered, making it a source of income for the government in Baghdad, but contested by the KRG since there are a majority of Kurds in this area. The Naft Khana oil field is capable of producing up to 16,000 barrels per day (bpd). A 20,000 bpd refinery has since been approved for construction.

Khaneqin has an estimated population of 200,000. Khaneqin is the administrative capital of the Khanaqin District, which is made of several small cities, such as Al-Sadiyah and Jalula, in addition to hundreds of villages. The city is divided in two by the Alwan River. Most of the people in the city are Fayli (Feyli) Kurds, who are Shi'a. There is also a sizable community of Shi'a Arab and Turkmen as well.

During the 1970s, Saddam Hussein's Arabization policies many Kurds, Assyrians, and Turkmen were deported from Khaneqin and surrounding areas, while Arabs were settled in their stead. After the war

Alwan (Kopre) Bridge

in 2003, the city's population swelled as many thousands of internally displaced persons returned to their homes. Famous Kurds include Leyla Qasim, one of the first female *peshmerga* murdered by Saddamıs regime in 1974 and famous PUK politician Mela Bakhtiar.

In the middle of the 19th century there were about 20 Jewish families in Khaneqin, living in the Jewish quarter, or *Jewlakan*. Less than one hundred years later that population is said to have numbered more than 700 and many spoke Aramaic in addition to Arabic. Occupationally they were known as cloth and iron merchants, shopkeepers, moneychangers, and innkeepers. The entire population left between 1950-1952 due to government pressure and social instability.

In 1911 the French school system *Alliance Israélite Universelle* established a coeducational school in the town, which was attended by almost 200 students.

Khaneqin was known as a customs station where people would stop en route to Iran. It is also situated on a main road used by Iranians on pilgrimages to Iraqi holy cities such as Najaf and Karbala further south. With the outbreak of the Iran-Iraq War (1980–88), fighting displaced many thousands and the city suffered greatly.

Current security concerns make it advis-

High Interests warned that the ancient bridge was at risk of collapse since they found some cracks in the structure of the bridge. The NGO asked both the Iraqi government and the KRG to assist in saving this historical and cultural treasure. Work has not however er begun as of yet.

able to check with authorities or your travel agent prior to traveling in the region.

HIGHLIGHTS

In autumn of 2013 the KRG announced that Khaneqin would be included and integrated into security and service plans meant for keeping the peace during tourist related events and religious holidays. It is estimated that roughly 25,000 tourists visit during Shi'a Muslim holidays.

In the spring of 2014, major tourism projects of the KRG included Khaneqin. There is currently construction of a dam on the Alwan River. Upon completion, Garmian area in general is poised to attract hundreds of thousands of tourists from both inside and outside of Kurdistan Region. Other projects related to tourism include public parks meant to revive the natural beauty in the area.

One may still see some remnants of the Jewish community and neighborhood and the Jewish cemetery (located in Al-Umal neighborhood next to the Christian cemetery) is being protected and preserved by the KRG.

Alwan (Kopre) Bridge

Perhaps the most famous site in the city is the old bridge, much like in Zakho. The Alwan (Kopre) Bridge (named after the Alwan river) that flows underneath it was constructed in 1860. It has been renovated several times by the Iraqi government as well as the Kurdistan Regional Government. In 2012, an NGO, *The Committee for Defending Khanaqin's*

Armenian Church

The church is still in use and Armenians from the city and surrounding areas come to the church here for weddings and social events though it was partially destroyed during the Iraq-Iran War.

Qalat Polish Cemetery

The cemetery was established during the Second World War in 1942 after Polish servicemen who were taken prisoner in Russia made the long journey to join British and Commonwealth fighters in Iraq. Many died en route; as a result hundred of Poles were buried in Khaneqin. Together with the 3rd Carpathian Division in the Middle East, these men formed the Polish Army in the East, remaining in Khaneqin, organizing, training, and assembling equipment. There is said to be 439 Polish servicemen buried in Khaneqin.

75%
Discount on all roaming services

Korek offers all its prepaid subscribers three roaming bundles with prices discounted by 75% on calls and text messages.

- **First Bundle:** 10 minutes talk-time and 10 SMSs for 10,000 IQD
- **Second Bundle:** 15 minutes talk-time and 15 SMSs for 15,000 IQD
- **Third Bundle:** 25 minutes talk-time and 25 SMSs for 20,000 IQD

To subscribe, dial *250# or *255# and choose the bundle that suits you.
* All bundles are valid for 10 days staring from the activation date.

For more information kindly call 411 within Iraq and +9647508000411 while abroad.

Dare to Dream

411

korektel.com

UPSTREAM | MIDSTREAM | DOWNSTREAM

KHURMALA DOME

KAR PIPELINE CO.

ERBIL REFINERY

KAR POWER PLANT

www.kar-k.com

SPECIAL
TOPICS
OF
INTEREST

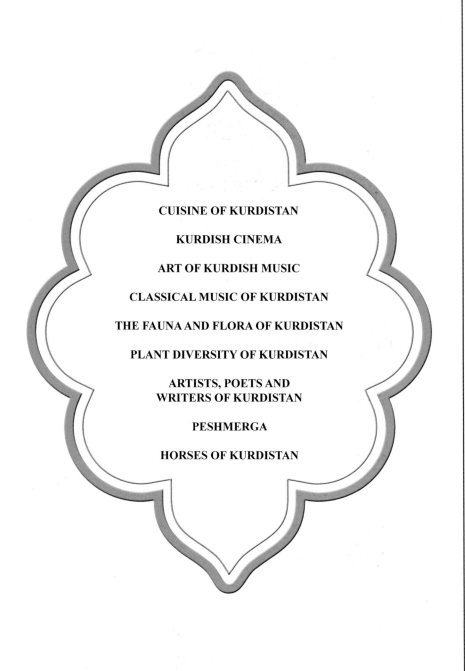

CUISINE OF KURDISTAN

KURDISH CINEMA

ART OF KURDISH MUSIC

CLASSICAL MUSIC OF KURDISTAN

THE FAUNA AND FLORA OF KURDISTAN

PLANT DIVERSITY OF KURDISTAN

ARTISTS, POETS AND
WRITERS OF KURDISTAN

PESHMERGA

HORSES OF KURDISTAN

THE CUISINE OF KURDISTAN

Ms. Chiman Zebari was born to a prominent family in Akre, which is a major city in the Duhok Governorate. Like many Kurds she has made an amazing journey witnessing not only the turmoil of her beloved land, but also the eventual emergence of a vibrant economy and democracy. After her family escaped to Iran from the regime of Saddam Hussein she eventually became a refugee in Nashville, Tennessee, which is now home to over 15,000 Kurds. She currently resides in Washington DC with her family. She speaks four languages and is an employee of the United States Government as a political analyst. Following are excerpts from her upcoming book about her life and times and passion for Kurdish cooking.

THE STORY OF KURDISH FOOD...

Kurdish food is exotically laced with flavorful spices requiring various fresh herbs with an abundance of vegetables complementing lamb and chicken—the primary meats used in the region. Sometimes we substitute fresh seafood like that caught in the many lakes and rivers that crisscross the land and which are fed by snow covered mountains generally free of pollution so common in the West. At other times beef is the dish of choice but whatever the selection—herbs and spices provide the essence of Kurdish cuisine. With proper preparation, attention to detail and a dash of passion, I am certain that you and your loved ones will enjoy eating Kurdish food as much as my family and I do.

We have learned through the generations to regard our gatherings of friends and family around a meal as the thread of a tapestry spanning thousands of years to our ancestors the Medes. Many are aware of the trying times that have faced our people at the hands of dictators like Saddam Hussein but few know that even when fleeing in the mountains of Turkey or Iran as refugees, Kurds have always taken comfort in the traditions of their food. Kurdish hot breads called *naan* can be made just about anywhere at any time. When coupled with a carefully brewed cup of chai (black tea) one can always find the strength to press on.

My grandfather was a wealthy merchant with several stores in the ancient city of Akre. He and my father were members of the Kurdish Democratic Party (KDP) and were secretly aiding the *Peshmerga* (Kurdish paramilitary forces), which were traveling through the town by supplying them with food and necessities. My grandfather had four sons and three daughters and numerous grandchildren. I remember once when we all had to

flee our beloved home as Saddam's henchmen surrounded our village firing Kalashnikovs, pillaging the town and beating even the

Fresh fish daily

elderly. My grandmother was threatened and miraculously survived. After a long trek through freezing winter snows we found ourselves in the camp of *peshmerga* who welcomed and offered to aid us on our way. However, before we could even think of departing from their

Street Vendor

camp we had, of course, to enjoy a hot meal.

Food and friends have kept us alive through the

worst of times and has also been the focus of joyous weddings (including mine). Without this treasure I wonder where we would be today. I was fortunate to be given asylum in the USA, a land I have come to love and cherish. But be sure, I have brought a little of my beloved Kurdistan along—most importantly the culinary secrets taught me by my mother who is one of the strongest and bravest women I know. Recipes from mother to daughter, generation after generation—that is the Kurdish way. It is a pleasure to share a few of these with you. Enjoy these dishes anywhere. But if you want a real taste of one of the world's great cooking delights come visit Kurdistan. I assure you that you will not return hungry for Kurdish hospitality is even more famous than its food.

Typical Meals of The Day...

Breakfast is typically flat bread called naan. We use yogurt, honey, cheese, eggs, and black tea with the *naan*. You will find the same breakfast menu on Kurd-

juices to make delicate stews that are usually served with rice or cracked wheat. In the spring and summer, salads and fresh herbs are often on the dinner table. Kurds also make many types of *kofta* and *kubba*, dumplings filled with meat.

During Newroz, the Spring Equinox New Year, Kurds celebrate by dressing in their finest clothes and setting off to the countryside for picnics, often taking a large pot of yaprakh. Also known throughout the Mediterranean as *dolma*, *yaprakh* is a dish of freshly picked vine leaves stuffed with rice, meat, herbs and garlic, simmered in a large pot.

Kurdish drinks are usually served as refreshments with the exception of *dough*, which is usually served with meals. Black, sweetened tea is Kurdistan's favorite drink. The black tea goes perfectly with *klicha*, which are date or walnut-filled cookies often prepared for religious festivals. People drink tea before meals, while shopping, when visiting friends, or after dinner. In Kurdistan, we serve tea in a piping hot small transparent glass and sip it over cubes of sugar. Alcoholic beverages are not commonly served, especially in families that are more traditional. In Kurdistan and throughout the Middle East, there are seemingly endless varieties of drinks with the delicate essence of fruit or blossoms known as *sherbet*, but fruit juice, tea and *dough* are most common drink.

The Kurdistan Region has fertile soil and a hot summer climate makes it ideal for growing grapes and orchards such as pomegranate, fig, and walnut. The Region's honey has a clear light taste and is often sold with the honeycomb. Kurdistan also produces excellent sheep, goat and buffalo dairy products, such as soft and hard cheeses, yogurt and *keshk*. These are produced in small quantities in rural communities and are sought after."

ish tables (called sofrah in Kurdish) everywhere regardless of where you are in Kurdistan. In the mountainous provinces, they prefer fresh butter, yogurt, and cheese. In the cities and urban areas, breakfast foods are often industrially processed and packaged, resembling the foods found in Western supermarkets but traditional families still make the effort to obtain locally grown fresh ingredients. Kurds usually prefer to eat handmade hot bread rather than the commercial or mass-produced breads, which are common in parts of the West. In Kurdistan, there are bakeries everywhere, and the bakeries specialize in certain kinds of bread, such as *lavash*, *dorik*, and *samon*. Each morning, these bakeries provide freshly baked bread for the customers who frequent them daily.

For lunches and dinners, savory dishes are usually served with rice or flat bread. Kebabs are a popular way to serve meat and chicken. Lamb, vegetables or beans are simmered in tomato sauce or in meat

Following Are A Few Recipes Of My Favorite Kurdish Dishes:

Stuffed Vegetable (Dolma)

- 4 cups uncooked short-grain rice such as Jasmine
1 pound chuck beef or lamb (finely chopped, washed and rinsed)
- 1 jar grape leaves (remove from jar and pour hot water over to rinse off the excess salt)
- 1 small head cabbage (prefer Chinese because the leaves are softer)
- 2 onions (makes about six once the leaves are separated)

- 2 eggplants (skinny Italian, cut in half and core each one)
- 2 zucchini (choose the long ones, cut in half and core each one)
- 2 round tomatoes (cut the

top and core inside)
- 1 cup olive oil (or vegetable oil)
- 4 cloves garlic, chopped
- 1 small can tomato paste (6 oz.)
- 1 bunch of fresh parsley, finely chopped
- 1 small onion finely chopped
- 1 cup lemon juice (or 1 tablespoon citric acid)
Salt and pepper to taste
- 3 cups water (you may need to use more to cook through)
- 1/2 pound beef ribs or skinless chicken thighs (optional to use in the bottom of the pot)

Wash rice and rinse; in a

large bowl, add chopped meat, tomato paste, parsley, onions, garlic, 1/2 cup oil, salt and pepper, lemon juice or citric acid to taste. Mix well and set aside.

I normally put ribs or chicken in the bottom of the pot that I make the dolma in. Brown both sides of your choice of meat and leave in the pot.

Cut the stem of the cabbage. Peel off the leaves and blanch in large pot of boiling water. Allow to boil until leaves are softened, but not too soft. Remove the leaves with a slotted spoon.

Place a tablespoon of the rice mixture onto 1 cabbage leaf and roll. Place in the pot (on top of the meat if you are using meat at the bottom of the pot). Continue rolling the cabbage leaves and placing in the pot until you have one layer.

Next take a tablespoon of the rice mixture onto each grape leaf and roll. Add on top of the cabbage layer in the pot. Finish until you have made one layer in the pot.

Take a tablespoon of the rice mixture and add to a layer of the onion. Roll and place on top of the grape leaves in the pot.

Continue until you've finished the layers of onions.

Stuff the eggplants with the rice mixture. Place on top of the onions in the pot. Next, stuff the zucchini and the tomatoes. If you have left over rice mixture, you can add another layer of the stuffed grape leaves or cabbage leaves. Be sure the top layer is some stuffed grape leaves or cabbage.

Place the pot onto the stove over medium-high heat. Add the remaining oil. Pour 2 cups boiling water on top. Put a flat, heavy plate on top of the vegetables to keep them from opening during the cook-

ing process. Boil for 15 minutes. Taste the water after a few minutes of boiling. If you need to adjust the salt or lemon juice, you can do so.

Reduce heat to low and allow cooking for another 20 minutes. While cooking, use the end of a fork and poke the edge of the leaves so that excess water goes downward rather than staying on top of the stuffed vegetable. Make sure you don't tear the stuffed vegetable during this process. Cook until all the water is gone. Also, check to see if the rice is cooked. If not, add more water until the rice

is ready. When cooking is complete, flip the pot upside down onto large platter. This dish is ready to serve.

This dish is common in the Middle East. Everyone makes it slightly different. This is one of my favorite dishes that I make frequently.

Kofteh in Yogurt Sauce (Dooghavah)

Dough:
- 2 cups cream of rice
- 2 cups of water (may need more)
- 1 cup cream of wheat (it should be uncooked)

- 1 pound ground beef (lean and uncooked)
- Salt and pepper to taste

Filling:
- 2 pounds ground beef (lean and uncooked)
- 1 large onion, chopped
- 1 bunch parsley, washed and chopped
- Salt and pepper to taste

Soup:
- 6 cups of plain yogurt (store-bought or homemade)
- 1 large can of chickpeas, rinsed and drained
- 1/2 cup of dried oregano
- 2 eggs, beaten
- Salt and pepper to taste
- Water (you may need to add more boiling water in the process, depending on how thick it becomes when cooking the Kofteh)

Filling: In a large skillet or pot, brown the meat. Add chopped onion and mix for about five minutes. Lastly, add chopped parsley, salt and pepper to taste. Place the meat in a colander to drain excess liquid. Set aside to cool.

Dough: Mix the cream of rice and the cream of wheat in a large bowl. Add ground beef and mix until well combined. Add water, salt and pepper to form a dough. Mix until soft, but do

not let it get too watery or it will not stick together.

Assembling: Once it is ready, shape the dough into golf ball–sized portions. With your thumb, press a hole in the middle of the ball for stuffing. The sides of the ball should be thin; remember that the dough will expand in the soup while cooking too. *Note*: I like to dip my hands in a bowl of water to keep the dough from sticking to my hands while stuffing the dough balls. This dish is similar to tirkshik above. Fill each dough ball (or shell) with the cooled cooked meat using about

the same amount per ball, or use a spoon to maintain the stuffing measurements. Close together and pat. Flatten the stuffed Kofteh into discs and put them on a baking pan. After all the balls have been stuffed, they are ready to go into the soup.

Soup: In a large non-stick pot, mix the yogurt and water together well. Mix continuously over medium high heat and bring to a boil. Once it comes to a boil, add the eggs to the mixture and continue the mixing until smooth. (The eggs prevent the yogurt from curdling). Allow this mix to cook on low heat for about 20 minutes. Add the chickpeas and dried oregano to the soup. Let it cook for 10 minutes. Carefully drop in the Kofteh that you prepared. Mix gently. Cook for 25 additional minutes on medium heat or until the Kofteh floats. When serving, remove the Kofteh with a draining spoon and put them on a platter. Pour the soup in a separate dish and serve together.

- 1/4 teaspoon pepper
- 1/4 cup olive oil
- Juice of 1 onion
- Sumac (optional)

Mix onion juice and seasonings in a bowl. Add the meat. Cover the meat completely with the mixture. Allow marinating for 2-3 hours in the refrigerator or overnight. Remove meat from the marinade and place five to six pieces onto a skewer. Broil or grill the meat, turning it frequently and sprinkling simultaneously with crushed sumac. Serve with flat bread or over rice.

Beef Shish Kabob

- 1 pound lamb or beef with some fat, cut in one-and-a-half-inch cubes
- 1 teaspoon turmeric
- 1/2 teaspoon salt

Rice Kubba (Kubba Halab)

Crust:
- 2 cup rice
- 1 1/2 cup water
- 1/2 teaspoon turmeric
- Salt to taste

Filling:
- 1 pound of lean ground beef
- 1 medium onion, finely chopped
- 1 bunch parsley, washed and chopped
- 1 teaspoon cumin
- 1 cup chopped almonds or pine nuts (optional)

• 1 cup yellow raisins (optional)

• 2 beaten eggs for the end to brush on the Kubba for a golden color

Wash rice, add salt and turmeric and bring to a boil; reduce heat to low. Allow to cook until rice is soft, but not too mushy, and definitely not crunchy. Remove the rice from the pot and into a large bowl. Allow to cool completely.

In the same pot, brown the meat; add chopped onions, parsley, almonds, salt and pepper, and cumin; mix cooked until the liquid has evaporated. Add raisins and mix again. Set aside at a room temperature to cool off.

Place the cooked rice in a food processor and mix well (or mix by hand until dough is smooth). You may have to add a bit of water as you mix.

To form the Kubba, have a bowl of water near you to wet your hands with so the dough does not stick to your hands. Take a walnut-sized ball of dough, and cradle it in the palm of one hand, use your index finger of the other hand to form a hollow in the middle of the dough/ball. Fill each one with a tablespoon of the filling, seal, and pat until you

form into an egg shape. Repeat this process until all the meat and rice is finished. Place on to a baking tray. Brush each with egg wash.

Heat the cooking oil until it is sizzling hot. Drop the Kubba in the hot oil and gently swirl the pan to allow the Kubba to turn them over as they might break because the crust is fragile.

Fry both sides until golden brown. Remove and place them on a paper towel to absorb the excess oil and serve warm with Torshi or any kind of salads or soups.

Kubba are mostly consumed in Iraq and Syria The name Halab is an ancient city in Syria.

Chicken Tikka

• 1 pound of chicken breast, boneless, cut in cube size
• 2 large tomatoes cut in cubes (or you can use cherry tomatoes whole)
• 1 large onion, quartered
• 1 large green pepper, quartered
• 1 clove garlic, minced
• 1/2 cup plain yogurt
• 3/4 cups olive oil
• 1/2 teaspoon paprika
• 1/2 teaspoon red hot pepper
• Salt and pepper to taste

Wash and rinse the chick-

en and toss it in a bowl. Add garlic, salt, paprika, yogurt and olive oil and mix well. Cover and marinate for a few hours in the refrigerator.

When ready to grill, pierce a piece of chicken, onion, green pepper, tomato onto a skewer and repeat this process until you've finished all ingredients. Grill the chicken on both sides for about 5-6 minutes. You can brush the excess marinade on the chicken as you grill to keep them moist. Serve with bread, salad and/or rice.

Mahalabia

- 3 cups whole milk
- 3 cups sugar
- 6 tablespoons cornstarch
- 1 cup cold water
- 1 tablespoon rose water
- 1 teaspoon crushed cardamom (optional)
- 1 teaspoon cinnamon
- 3 tablespoon crushed pistachio (roasted)

In a nonstick pot, boil 2 cups milk and the sugar over medium heat. In the meantime, mix the cornstarch with remaining 1 cup cold milk until smooth and set aside.

When the milk and sugar mixture has thickened, turn off heat but keep it on the stove. Add to this, the cold milk and cornstarch mixture, rose water and crushed cardamom; mix well. Pour in a glass plate (you can pour into individual ice-cream serving cups if you prefer) and allow cooling for 3-4 hours in the refrigerator.

Garnish the top with pistachio, cinnamon and if you like add a pinch of cardamom before serving. I personally like to serve in a large bowl so everyone can scoop out as much as they want.

Note: This is a great dessert to bring to a dinner party.

Baklava

3 sticks melted butter for brushing Phyllo dough
1 box Phyllo pastry at room temperature

Filling Ingredients
• 3 1/2 cups almonds, pistachios, or walnuts, finely chopped
• 2 tablespoons ground cardamom
• 1 stick melted butter
• 1 tablespoon ground cinnamon
• 1/2 cup of sugar (or sugar substitute)

Ingredients for Syrup
• 5 saffron threads
(or 1/2 teaspoon rose water extract)
• 3 tablespoons lemon juice
• 2 cups sugar
• 1 cup water
• 1 teaspoon cardamom
• 1 teaspoon cinnamon
• 1/2 cup chopped pista-

chios (for garnish)

Prepare the syrup first. Boil the water, add sugar and mix until dissolved. Add cardamom, cinnamon, saffron and lemon juice to the sugar water. Bring the mixture to a boil on medium heat. Boil for about 45 minutes to an hour until it becomes syrupy. Set it aside for cooling.

In a large bowl, prepare filling mixture. Combine nuts, cardamom, cinnamon and sugar. Add one stick of melted butter; mix well, and then set aside. Preheat oven to 350 degrees.

Spread one sheet of Phyllo dough on a large well-greased cookie sheet. Brush the entire surface with melted butter. Continue layering the Phyllo sheets and brushing using half the box of Phyllo. Spread the filling mixture evenly over the pastry dough. Layer the rest of the Phyllo sheets on top of the mixture, one at a time and coating each sheet with butter before layering the next.

Cut into squares or diamonds shape. Bake for 20-30 minutes and remove when golden brown. Remove from oven and immediately drizzle the syrup evenly over the top.

Sprinkle with almonds, pistachios, or walnuts. Allow cooling before serving. Run a knife through the previously cut grooves.

Zolobia

- 1/4 cup flour
- 1 cup plain yogurt
- 2 cups corn starch
- 2 tablespoons rosewater (you can find it at any Middle Eastern grocery)
- 1/2 teaspoon saffron, dissolved in 1 tablespoon hot water
- 1 tablespoon butter, softened at room temperature
- 1/2 teaspoon baking soda
- Canola oil (or any liquid cooking oil for frying)

Place yogurt and cornstarch in a mixing bowl; mix well. Let it sit for 5 minutes. Add flour, 2 tablespoons rosewater, butter, baking soda and dissolved saffron. Beat with a mixer until the batter is smooth (I use a hand mixer). Let it stand for 30 minutes.

Meanwhile make the syrup in a deep saucepan (enough for dipping zolobias). Combine water and sugar in a small saucepan. Bring to a boil over medium-high heat. Continue heating until sugar is completely dissolved and the syrup thickens, stirring occasionally. Add lemon; mix well. Turn off

the heat, but leave syrup on stove.

Transfer the batter to an empty ketchup bottle or similar bottle with a skinny tip. You can also use a Ziploc bag, snipping off a corner to make a 1/4-inch-wide hole

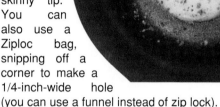

(you can use a funnel instead of zip lock).

In a deep medium skillet, heat the oil over medium-high heat. Reduce the heat to medium. Squeeze out the batter about 3-4 times in a circular motion into hot oil. Be careful, the oil may splash! Fry until golden brown on both sides, turning once. Add more oil if necessary.

Using tongs or flat spatula, carefully remove zolobia from the oil. Drop gently into syrup. Let it stand in syrup for a few minutes, while you fry the others. Place them in a colander (do not place the zolobias on top of each other while draining, just a single layer, otherwise they will get soggy).

Then transfer the zolobia to plate. Refrig-

erate before serving. This is a great dessert with tea or coffee.

Drinks

In Kurdistan and throughout the Middle East, there are seemingly endless varieties of drinks with the delicate essence of fruit or blossoms known as sherbet, but fruit juice, tea and doogh are most common drink.

Chay

Chay means tea in Kurdish. Kurds commonly serve chay at breakfast, after lunch and dinner, or for midday break. By far, the most common drink among Kurds and the rest of the Middle East is tea. In Kurdistan, tea is usually served in small transparent glasses with sugar or sipped with cubes of sugar. When guests visit, hosts serve tea regardless of time of day. Kurds always serve tea at the religious ceremonies at mosques, at national celebrations, at times of sorrow, or at times of joy, such as weddings or picnics. We serve tea in the winter to keep warm or in the summer to cool off. We invite friends over for tea.

We believe that tea calms you down and keeps you perked up as well. Kurds drink tea more than they do coffee, so a lot of attention must go into tea preparation. Cooler temperatures and taste are of vital importance. A good cup of tea is appreciated as much as a good glass of wine is in the West.

Kurds make tea in a pot called *samawar*. You may find *samawars* and *istekans*

(small tea cups) at any Middle Eastern grocery store.

First, you boil water in the samawar. You take the smaller teapot that comes with
the samawar, add loose tea leaves to the small teapot; add the boiled water from the larger samawar. Place the smaller teapot on the top of the samawar to simmer. Often, guests drink more than one cup of tea; so for replenishment, keep boiled wa-ter ready. A host will pour a small amount of the tea from the smaller teapot and then pour water from the samawar, considering one's taste and desired tea color (light or dark). Kurds use the words *kem rang* for light color, which is not very strong, or *tari* for a darker-colored or stronger tea. For

sweetener, Kurds use sugar, loose or sugar cubes in the tea; sometimes, we use rock candy too. The sweetener makes the tea very tasty.

Note: If you do not have a samawar, you can get one large kettle and one small teapot that will stand on top of the kettle top to simmer.

Drinks: Yogurt Drink (Mast Av or Dough)

- 1/2 cups water or club soda
- 1 cup yogurt
- 1/2 teaspoon crushed mint
- Salt to taste

Place yogurt in small pitcher or large glass and beat well. Add water/soda, crushed mint, and salt and stir well. Serve over ice. Makes 1-2 servings

This is a very popular drink among the Kurds for most meals except breakfast. It's very refreshing and healthy.

KURDISH CINEMA
From the Pen of Jano Rosebiani

BEST MOMENTS OF
KURDISH CINEMA IN 2014

"Kurdish cinema was practically nonexistent in the past century, save for a few films, among them the Palm d'Or winner, "Yol" (Directed by Serif Goren and Yilmaz Guney, 1982). Kurdish films began to surface in the world scene at the start of the new millennium, beginning with "A time for Drunken Horses" (Directed by Bahman Ghobadi, 2000) that received the Cannes' Camera d'Or Prize. This was followed by my very first Kurdish production, "Jiyan" (shot in 2001 and released in 2002), which premiered in Rotterdam where it was nominated for the Tiger Award. Both films garnered numerous International Awards and high critical acclaim as they made the festival rounds the world over, at times playing back to back on the same screen, and were instrumental in introducing the world to the Kurds and to the enfant Kurdish cinema.

One and a half decades later, Kurdish cinema may no longer be labeled as enfant. Since 2000 and especially after the liberation of Iraq from Saddam's grip and the solidification of the Kurdistan region's autonomy, a wave of Kurdish filmmakers from all parts of greater Kurdistan and from the diaspora came fore to turn out over a hundred films up to date. Many of these films gained international recognition and were nominated for and awarded prizes at prestigious film festivals.

The premise of the majority of Kurdish films is the suffering of the subjects under successive occupiers, and their resilience in the face of destruction and massacres of genocidal proportion. These filmmakers, some with formal education in cinema, others self-taught (myself included), have stories to tell the world with a burning desire to be heard and a passion that exceeds the artistry of the medium. As a result, one can hardly watch a Kurdish film and not shed tears. The Kurdish filmmaker in essence is the ambassador of his/her people, opening a window to the world through which one can get a glimpse of the daily life, history, culture, and suffering of the Kurds. As one film critic, David Rooney, in his *Variety Magazine* review of "Jiyan"

FIRST NEW YORK
KURDISH
A CINEMA ACROSS BORDERS
FILM FESTIVAL
OCTOBER 21-25, 2009

states, "Jiyan gives a human face to the massacre [of Halabja]."[1] Thus being the face and the voice of a nation are the driving force behind the passion for the cinematic art in Kurdistan.

As for aesthetics, Kurdistan is blessed with natural beauty; snow-capped mountains and lush valleys, stunning waterfalls from the melting snow into a surfeit of rivers and tribu-

Jano

taries, and rolling hills and plains emblazoned with spring blossom of every color imaginable. Added to this is the uniquely golden light of the sun. "The daylight of Kurdistan's sun is a cinematographer's treasured find." Stated Russian film Director Sergie Bodrov (Mongol, 2007) during his visit to Kurdistan along with a Hollywood delegation. To back such statement, during the filming of "Jiyan" in 2001, we solely relied on

sunlight, as there were no lighting equipment in the region at the time, thus the film has a natural golden tint that fills the frame with warmth. Here, it is timely to mention that the Kurds, who come from the ancient sun-worshiping Mithraic background, continue to revere the sun. Such reverence is evident in their national flag and in the shape of their Yezidi temples.

Besides the physical beauty of the land, Kurdistan is home to one of the oldest civilizations and is an incubator of great many archeological sites that are an important part of the world heritage. Additionally, the richness of the culture and the folklore that has been handed down the generations since time immemorial is yet another feature to

explore in film.

All this makes Kurdistan a fertile ground for the camera lens. Wherever the camera is directed, the captured image is as fresh and as captivating as a morning breeze. While Kurdish filmmakers have been capturing the tragedies and sufferings that had befallen their people, the time is ripe they turn their cameras to focus on the aforementioned imagery and complement it with romantic folktales of past and present. I am happy to say that I have drawn on this aspect of Kurdistan in my latest films "Chaplin of the Mountains" and "One Candle, Two Candles" (both 2014 productions). "Chaplin" is a cross-cultural road movie, and the first English language film made in Kurdistan that takes the viewer across the countryside with its magnificent mountains and authentic villages seen through the eyes of two Americans and a European. "Chaplin" may be the film to watch for any-

one planning to tour Kurdistan. "Candles", on the other hand, tackles social issues concerning the clash of generations and women's fight for equality. The film reveals an aspect of Kurdish culture where women are becoming very outspoken and modernism is catching on like rapid fire.

Kurdistan may not be spewing enough films, but the rate of success of Kurdish cinema is proportionally high in comparison with that of the other nations in the region. For instance, seven films were produced in 2014, most of which received international recognition: "One Candle, Two Candles" was chosen by HFPA as contender for the 2015 Golden Globe award[2]; "Letter to the King" (Director Hisham Zaman) received the FIBRESCI prize[3]; "Memories On Stone" (Director Shawkat Amin Korki) won the UNISCO award; and "Chaplin of the Mountains" became the New York Times Critics' pick[5]. In other words, in this past year, four out of seven Kurdish films found their place in the world film scene, as apposed to productions in other countries, including those of the United States, where only a small percentage of the films received global recognition.

Variety, Jiyan Review, David Rooney, Feb. 15 2002. http://variety.com/2002/film/reviews/jiyan-1200551290/

Foreign Language Films Compete For Golden Globe, http://www.goldenglobes.com/global/foreign-language-films-compete-golden-globe-25781

Festival del Cinema Europa, http://www.festivaldelcinemaeuropeo.com/en-2014/the-awards-of-the-15th-edition-of-the-european-cinema-festival/

IMDB,http://www.imdb.com/title/tt3954882/awards Kurdish Travels With a Tramp, The New York Times, http://www.nytimes.com/2014/02/21/movies/chaplin-of-the-

mountains-follows-iraqi-roads-less-taken.html?referrer&_r=0

ART OF KURDISH MUSIC

From the Pen of Chopy Fatah

Chopy Fatah was born in Kirkuk and was three years old when the Baathist regime in Iraq started Arabization and displacement of Kurds, and she was forced to leave her home. Later she settled in Holland along with her two brothers and parents. At age seven, Chopy sang in a choral group in Holland where she was taught the basics of music and singing and later studied at the Kurdish academy in Germany ultimately working at Med (Mede) TV. In 2004, with the help of the great artist and talented composer Burhan Mufti Zade she 'cut' her first album named "Chit naw benm" (What shall I name you?). Since then she has made many albums and risen to become one of the most popular and famous Kurdish singers holding concerts and festivals in many countries around the world.

In 2008, Asiacell named Chopy as their "Ambassador of Love." In addition to assisting in the development of the company in Beirut and Kurdistan-Iraq she has done a great deal of charity work that is still ongoing.

Tembur

"The Kurdish nation is said to be from Aryan origins, and their language has Indo-European roots. This nation is one of the most ancient nations of the region. Kurdistan today lies between the Persian (Iran), Arab states and Turkey. Some historians believe that the existence of Kurds dates back more than 5,000 years. From what has been documented in history, it is clear that Kurds exercised great power over the entire region around 700 B.C.

The beginning of the history of Kurdish music art is undetermined, but what is known is that the ancient religions of the Kurdish nation, for instance Zoroastrianism, have given a significant importance to music. That is why they have used text and melody during religious events. On the other hand, they have looked at the "Temura" (Tambura) as a holy instrument. In addition, they have written the Avesta (their holy book) attached with melodies. Zoroastrians always felt that music had a great impact on the thoughts and emotions of the people.

The long lasting wars and battles in Kurdistan, and the lack of a state named Kurdistan, have together weakened the archive of Kurdish music and songs, making them difficult to protect. Moreover, anything that has been considered Kurdish folklore, including archeology, art, and culture, have all been exposed to continuous arson and institutionalized elimination. Yet, we still have a rich folklore, with more than 20,000 original Kurdish songs that have been left for us from our ancestors, and which have always been great resources for the art of Kurdish music.

Musical instruments in the Middle East are all mixed together, and are not easily distinguished one from another regarding their origins. Some of the instruments that we Kurds are proud of are the following:

Tembur, Def, Shimshal, Dehol u Zorna, among others.

I personally believe that music is for the entirety of humanity, and borders cannot stand in its way. It has happened on many occasions that we are touched by a piece of music that has not even been written in our language, but it has still left us with great impressions. However, it is also not fair if someone were to come and claim Mozart and Beethoven's melodies to be their own. The facts have to remain as they are. Unfortunately, what is left from our folklore has been exposed to this misrepresentation, and many of our neighboring countries have distorted our folkloric songs, and claimed them to be their own.

Nevertheless, there are many parts of our music that have kept their originality. There remains a Kurdish stamp on them, and other nations have not been able to alter them. For instance: *Syachemane*, *Lawik*, *Heyran*, *Beyt* and *Hora*. There are of course many other forms, and I as an artist have tried to express myself singing *Heyran* many times, and have not neglected Kurdish folkloric songs. On the other hand, I also believe in modernization, which is why I have many modern works in both Kurdish and English.

Through my music I have been able to pass the borders of Southern Kurdistan (Iraq) to

Saz

participate in Diyarbakir, Wan, and Batman festivals (in Northern Kurdistan/Turkey), and have performed concerts in Western Kurdistan (Syria). To my great pleasure, I have also been able to conduct parties, festivals and concerts all around the world; adding to the richness of my art.

I believe that success cannot be achieved individually. Many loyal people were there to support me, in addition to my audience, which is the source of my motivation."

Def

CLASSICAL MUSIC IN KURDISTAN'

From the Pen of Adnan Karim

Adnan Karim was bornin Kirkuk in 1963 and is one of the most prominent Kurdish singers in the world. Although coming from a financially challenged family, he achieved a high level of education. Threatened by Saddam Hussein's regime and the attacks on Kurdish people in the 1990s, Adnan's family fled to Sweden in 1992. The Swedish arts communutiy embraced the gifted Adnan and in the year 2000, he performed in the famous concert hall of Stockholm. It was a highly successful and much talked about concert.

Adnan Karim uses first and foremost Kurdish classical poetry which stretches back to the 17th century. He is inspried by much-loved and well-known poets like: Mawlawi, Mahwi, Nali, Salim, etc. The authenticity of Adnan's style is admired especially by Kurdish people due to the purity of his traditional melodies and the absence of particularly modern elements. Audiences get a genuine feeling of the deep and melancholic message delivered by the songs. His soft, deep voice is accompanied by oriental instruments (some of which he plays himself) which are deeply rooted in Kurdish music. His singing in different Kurdish dialects with an excellent prosody (patterns of sound and beats in poetry) is such that every one who listens to him can be caught up in a provincial feeling to the extent that all think he is one of their own local perfromers.

"In the Middle East, the Kurds are the only people that do not have their own state although they have their own languages and a rich folklore. The beautiful nature, habits, traditions, occasions and happy and unhappy events of the Kurdish nation have been reflected in its folkloric songs. That is to say, a song is the oldest part of the Kurdish folklore arts, which have been recounted to generation after generation and kept safely through the present. To date, we depend on the Kurdish folklore art songs to distinguish our art from that of the nations to which we have been distributed.

Most of our folklore songs speak of love relationships. People of all parts of Kurdistan have created their own dances to these songs and therefore, dance is also a very rich folkloric art.

We can say that the beginning of emergence and

growth of Kurdish songs dates back to the era of Zardasht (Zoroaster) and the anthems of this holy Zoroastrian religion. The anthem of Gatas (Gasa) and Yashts mentioned in the Holy Book of Avesta is considered as the beginning of the Kurdish song in that era. The word Gata or Gasa means cry, scream and appeal, that is to say, appeals and supplications with rhythm and rhyme to Allah (God).

In each part of Kurdistan that is divided between Turkey, Iran, Iraq and Syria, there are some old Kurdish songs, which are sung only by Kurdish singers because they have such special features that they are not sung by Turkish, Persian or Arab singers. These songs are fully different from the art of those nations. Such songs are called *Hora*, *Siawchamana*, *Lawk*, *Hayran*, *Bayt*, *Chamary* and *Sozy Garmian*.

The Kurds have often been expelled from their homeland or their homeland has been occupied. So, because of war and life sufferings, the Kurds have at times lost their music archives. Thus, the oldest Kurdish recorded music dates back to 1929 when the gramophone companies came to the east and west of Kurdistan and recorded the songs of the famous Kurdish singers: Said Ali Asghar and Hamdi Afandi. After 1940, the famous singers Ali Mardan, Shamal Saib, Mohammed Arf Jazeeri,

Tahir Tawfiq and several other singers recorded their Kurdish music and songs on Qawan (recording label). In the 1960s, the Kermashan Orchestra Music Group recorded many Kurdish songs for famous singers such as Hasan Zeerak, Mazhari Khlaiqi and several other singers in the voice studio in the City of Kermashan in the East Part of Kurdistan (Iran). Famous musicians like Hasan Yousif Zamani, Hasan Kamkar and several other musicians composed the music of those songs. This stage is considered as the beginning of composed Kurdish songs. In the years of 1970s, several music groups were formed in the cities of Sulaymani, Erbil and Duhok. The most famous Kurdish music group that has introduced itself to the world with its composed folklore songs and music works including all Kurdish beautiful rhymes to date is the *Group of Kamkaran*. Today, many Kurdish youths have engaged themselves worldwide with music studies and many music composers have emerged who are introducing Kurdish music around the world."

Adnan Kareem
25/1/2015

THE FAUNA AND FLORA OF KURDISTAN

FAUNA

Kurdistan was once a densely forested and flowered land filled with various species of animals and birds. While eons of civilization and a lack of conservation have diminished its former glory, the region still presents a magnificent opportunity to observe many species of animals and birds as well as plants. The Kurdistan Region boasts several dozen kinds of birds, mammals, and reptiles—some rare or unknown anywhere else. As the area is now open to researchers from all over the world, new species are being discovered.

Approximately 100,000 years ago people at Barda Balka (near Chamchamal on the Lesser Zab River) appear to have consumed rhinoceros and elephants, which once roamed Kurdistan's forests and plains in plenty. Remains found in Hazar Merd Cave (a group of Paleolithic cave sites first excavated by Dorothy Garrod in 1928 – translated "Cave of a Thousand Men") near Sulaymani further reveal that 25,000 years ago people ate deer, gazelle, and goat. The Dark Cave as it is referred to (or Ashkawty Tarik in Kurdish) has a single lofty chamber 11 by 12 m (36-39 ft.) wide containing many hearths, burnt flints and bones. The bones are from wild goat, red deer, gazelle, field mice, mole rats, hare, bats and several birds of woodland and scrub habitat.

The ruins of Jarmo (6700 BC) near Kirkuk revealed bones indicating there was systematic domestication of dogs such as Salukis also known as the Royal Dog of Egypt or Persian Greyhound, one of the oldest known breeds of domesticated dog. There were also remains of domesticated goats and pigs raised by ancient peoples for food.

BIRDS

The national bird for Kurdistan is the Kew, a red-legged Partridge with a red bill. Its chin and throat are white, surrounded by a black line or streak, which goes to its brow and nostrils, to its eyes and continues to the lower neck. The body is striped black and light blue.

There are four designated locations of this bird throughout the Kurdistan Region: 1) both of the lakes of Dukan and Derbendikhan as well as Bekhma Dam (between Duhok and Erbil governorates), 2) Benavi (20 km/12 mi NW of Amediye), 3) Dori Serguza (north of Amediye), and 4) Ser Amadiye.

Eastern Imperial Eagles, Red Kite, Eurasian Siskins, Common Starlings, Upcher's Warblers, Eastern Orphean Warbler, Peregrine Falcons, Kurdish Wheatears, Barbary Falcons, Singing Eastern Bonelli's Warbler, the endangered Saker Falcon, Great Reed Warblers, Sedge Warblers, Eastern Mourning Wheatears, European Rollers, Eastern Cinereous Buntings, Little Swifts, Alpine Swifts, Desert Finches, White-winged Snowfinch, Golden Eagle, Lammergeier, Winter Wren, and Black Redstarts. Specific to Ser-Amediye are Orphean Warblers, Alpine Choughs, Red-Billed Choughs, and Ortolan Bunting.

EXTINCT ANIMALS ONCE INDIGENOUS TO KURDISTAN

According to *Nature Iraq* (2010), 138 species of birds have been identified in Kurdistan including nearly three percent of the world population of Lesser White-Fronted Geese. Here one will also find Bearded and Egyptian Vultures, Eurasian Griffons, Radde's Accentors, White Storks, Partridges, White-Throated Robins, Eastern and Western Rock Nuthatches, Syrian Woodpeckers, Sombre Tits, Masked Shrikes, Red-Fronted Serin. Pine Buntings, Little Bustards, Great Black-headed Gulls, Alpine Accentors,

The following once roamed the region but have been hunted to extinction: Rhinoceros, Bison, Water Buffalo, Elephant, Wild Cattle, Stag, Beaver (Khabur River in Zakho), Oryx (last one was known was in 1914), Lion, (last was killed between 1916-18), Fallow Deer and Onager (Wild Ass).

VULNERABLE AND/ OR NEAR-EXTINCT SPECIES

Many animals that are known to be vulnerable include: European Roll-

er, Semi-collared Flycatcher, Golden Jackals, Beech Marten, Weasels, Marbled Polecats, Red Foxes, Grey Wolves, Indian-Crested Porcupines, Eastern European Hedgehog, Eurasian Badgers, Brown Hares, Wild Boar, Jungle Cats, Wild Cats, Persian Squirrels, Beavers, Jerboas, Mongoose (Common Gray and Small Asian Mongoose as well as Indian Grey), Syrian Brown Bear, Urmia Rock Lizard (Piramagroon Mountain), Wild sheep, Wild Goat, Roe Deer, Gazelle, Lynx, Honey Badger, Marten, Sind Ibex, and Persian Squirrel as well as Gazelle, Persian Leopards and a variation of the Azerbaijan Newt.

The Persian leopard is listed as endangered by the *International Union for Conservation of Nature (IUCN)*. However there are no official figures for how many remain in Iraq and Iran, and thieves stealing equipment used to track the animals have hampered independent efforts. The IUCN estimates this population around one thousand, though most are said to live in Iran. Before

2008, when two leopards were found in Diyala governorate of Iraq they were considered extinct from this area. Landmines have killed some, while many others have been shot by hunters/poachers.

The Kurdistan Region in particular has reported at least three sightings of Persian leopards in recent times: Asos Mountain (2009), Bradost Mountain (2008) and Ahmed Awa

(2002). At a certain time these majestic and feared creatures were spread throughout the Caucasus but are now relegated to the harsh mountains along the Kurdistan Iraq-Iran border. Though millions of landmines have been planted by Iraq and Iran during their war (1980-1988) and pose a general threat to wildlife, landmines also have become a kind of protection for leopards, as they discourage poachers from entering certain areas.

Jaguar, like leopards have become increasingly rare and usually when they are found, are hunted and killed. In some cases jaguars have been found killed by snakes or the victim of landmines.

Striped Hyenas have also been sighted near Dukan Lake and Bradost and Sakran Mountains.

Eurasian Otters, also recognized as a near-threatened species by IUCN have been found at Dukan Lake as well as Derbendikhan Lake as well as Aweisar, Bradost, and even as far west as the Khabur River in Zakho.

Eurasian Lynx have been spotted around Derbendikhan.

Brown Bears have been sighted in several areas including Ahmed Awa and Sakran Mountain in recent years.

PRINCIPAL AREAS
FOR ANIMAL WATCHING

Bradost

There are a wide variety of bird species in the Bradost area. The fauna also include many wild goats that spend their time on the mountainous areas, Golden Jackals, Grey Wolves, Indian Crested Porcupines, Syrian Brown Bears, Striped Hyenas, and Wildcats. Rivers, particularly near Rawanduz, contain several kinds of fish that are used by locals.

Derbendikhan

There are over fifty distinct species of birds while the Lake boasts twenty-six species of fish and one hundred and twenty five species of plants. The lake is home to the threatened Eurasian Otter, Golden Jackals, and Eurasian Lynxes. Incredibly, and only on rare occasions one may be able to find endangered species like Egyptian Vultures or even Persian Leopards.

The surrounding environment is biologically diverse for wildlife and listed as an "Important Bird Area" by *BirdLife International*. Today Derbendikhan is largely a tourist destination, and surrounded by a great deal of wildlife and gorgeous natural settings including several mountains such as Baranan, Bashari, Zmnako and Zawaly. Many people take walks or picnic next to the lake or rivers. Derbendikhan's main feature is the large freshwater reservoir generated by the Derbendikhan Dam; two historical rivers feed the dam, the Tanjero in the north and the Sirwan (Diyala) in the east. The area is unique ecologically as numerous distinct species vital to the ecosystem can be found in the immediate environs.

Dukan

The area boasts hundreds of species of birds, several hundred plant species, dozens of reptiles and mammals such as the near threatened Eurasian Otter and Striped Hyaena. There have also been reports of wolf attacks on local animal herds recently.

Haji Omran

Haji Omran is known for many kinds of animals: there are more than sixty

species of birds, and in recent years there have been several sighting of Brown Bears, Grey Wolves, Golden Jackals, Eurasian Otters, Diadem Snakes, and Lemon-Yellow Tree Frogs.

Mergapan

The area is known for its flora and fauna; there are over 120 species of flora and numerous animals such as wild goats, tortoises, and over 130 species of birds, including vultures and falcons. However previously documents Persian Leopards are considered no longer present in this area. The site offers a full

opportunity for ecotourism and wildlife education tourism!

Qashqoli Resort

Northwest of the city of Sulaymani by 55 km (35 mi) or 45 minutes, Dukan (Dokan) is one of the better known tourist destinations in the Kurdistan Region is 70 km (44 mi) or one hour southeast of Rania. Aside from the main attraction, which is the man-made reservoir-dam (the largest in the Kurdistan Region), which includes a hydroelectric power station. Dukan Dam is located on the Lesser Zab River, a tributary of the Tigris River. The area boasts hundreds of species of birds, several hundred plant species, dozens of reptiles and mammals such as the near threatened Eurasian Otter and Striped Hyaena. There

have also been relative recent reports of wolf attacks on local animal herds.

Rawanduz Gorge (Kharand), Bekhal Falls, Jundyan

Thirteen species of birds can be found here including the near-threatened Eastern Cinereous Bunting. A Ray Finned Fish was found along with Levantine Scraper and a local kind of catfish.

Safeen Mountain (Shaqlawa)

Birds: Egyptian and Griffon Vultures, Imperial and Golden Eagles, Several types of Owls, Dove, Kesttral, Woodpeckers. All together there are over twenty species of birds in/around Safeen Mountain.

Mammals: Asian Jackal, Squirrel, Common Red Fox, Weasel, Wild Goat, Roe Deer, Brown Hare, Euphrates Jerboa, Striped Hyaena, Wildcat, Wild Boar Red Sheep, Indian-Crested Porcupine, Badger, Otter, Common Lynx, Several types of bats including Long Eared Bat.

Reptiles: Several species of snakes including the "Kurdistan" Viper that lives in the mountains, Whip Snake, Water Snake, Montpellier Snake, Green Lizard, Scorpions, Geckos, Spiders, Frog, Banded Newt, Caspian Terrapin, Keeled Rock Gecko, Fat-Tailed Gecko and Cave Gecko.

Sulav

Locals have reported seeing the endangered Persian Fallow Deer, Persian Squirrels, which are highly sought after on the pet market, and there are several species of birds in the area, including Egyptian Vultures, Bearded Vultures, and Griffon Vultures.

Zanta Valley

Among the multitude of flora and fauna there are several dozens of bird species, including the Egyptian Vulture.

CONSERVATION

Animal Markets and Animal Trade

Within the KRG, anyone spotted with a hunting rifle in a nature reserve is immediately disarmed and turned over to the local magistrate, though these same people are not easily dissuaded and often reappear.

According to the conservation NGO *Nature Iraq*, uncontrolled hunting and trade are the main reasons for the decrease of rare species as these animals are often hunted and/or sold and used for their fur, hides, and even meat — either for food or in traditional medicinal potions such as in the case of the Indian-Crested Porcupine, believed to treat high blood pressure, or the Eurasian Magpie Pica, which supposedly cures typhoid disease. The Eurasian Badger is used for lowering blood cholesterol.

Animal hunting and trade is a recurring issue and many endangered or rare species are hunted in these regions and transported throughout the country. Persian Squirrels are hunted in large numbers and transported to markets for sale as pets. Though the Kurdistan Regional Government (KRG) and its police force have tightened control over markets, hunters and wildlife traders have continued activities in areas with weak police jurisdiction. As such there is extensive hunting in the Kurdistan region despite legislation prohibiting hunting within certain areas such as conservation parks in Barzan and Halgurd-Sakran Park.

General Conservation Concerns and Recommendations

There are numerous threats for various species and habitats throughout the Kurdistan Region. Some of this is due to lack of education among locals, while in other instances building and infrastructure affects

rivers and other natural areas while developers face no consequences. Threats include but are not limited to livestock over-produc-

tion/grazing, agricultural issues (clearing of fields, unsustainable water usage, runoff of agricultural chemicals and/or pesticides), over-hunting or ignoring

already existing laws, sewage and garbage, and activities related to tourism, roads and general constructions (gravel mining, dams), industrial ground and water pollution, oil development, and the millions of landmines that have yet to be cleared. Unfortunately the majority of sites in the Kurdistan Region are threatened in varying degrees.

Halgurd Sakran National Park and Sakran Valley

Halgurd Sakran National Park (HSNP) will be the first National Park in mountains of Kurdistan and the whole of Iraq. HSNP and is situated in Erbil Governorate, 120km (75 mi) northeast of the city of Erbil and only a few minutes away from the town of Choman. HSNP will be the largest protected mountain area in Kurdistan, expected to cover more than 1100 km2 (425 sq. miles), with a height up to 3,609 m (11,841 ft.) at Halgurd Peak, the second highest mountain in Iraq after Cheekha Dar, which is 3,611 m (11,847 ft.). Officially opened in 2012, the main objectives revolve around nature conservation and recreation. One area of the park will be completely forbidden to construct or build. Officially opened in 2012, the main objectives revolve around nature conservation and recreation.

Halgurd Mountain is located among wonderful districts such as Galala, Haji Omran, Roost, and Sidakan. The peak of the mountain is covered with snow throughout the whole year. There are many springs and lakes around the mountain that give an additionally beautiful view to the area. Halgurd and Hasara Roost Mountain Chains are included in the Halgurd-Sakaran National Park. The National Park extends from Sakran Mountain to Haji Omran and Sidakan district. Tourists from all over Iraq and other countries spend enjoyable time in adventure and hiking in Halgurd-Sakran National Park. There are also various herbs that can be used as medicine found in this area and locals will be happy to share their knowledge with guests.

The great diversity of natural habitats in the envisaged Halgurd Sakran National Park enables the many species of animals and plants that are rare, or near extinct elsewhere, to survive and re-generate in the environment in which they originated. Accordingly, there are over three-dozen species of birds that have been found in and around Sakran Mountain and its valley.

In addition to Barzan's conservation reserve (partially based on Sheikh Abdul-Salam Barzani's belief in environmentalism as well as that of the current President Masoud Barzani) as well as Halgurd Sakran National Park, there are organizations throughout the Region that have been making inroads at bettering the conditions for animal species as well as educating the public on the importance of conservation and not killing off entire species of animals simply for sport or folk/traditional medicine. There are several online groups involved in spreading awareness about the plight of animal cruelty and trading and hunting endangered animals. *Kurdistan-Iraq STOP Animal Cruelty* seeks to raise awareness of animal-rights related issues and has nearly 1,000 members. The most popular conservation organization is *The Kurdistan Organization of Animal Rights Protection (KOARP)* which is a local NGO affiliated with the *International Organization for Animal Protection (OIPA),* which is an affiliate of the *United Nations Department of Public*

Information and UN Economic and Social Council. KOARPs main objectives are to protect and maintain animal rights and providing veterinary care. Primarily focused on dogs and cats this organization seeks to educate owners and the public about how to care for their pets and decrease the population of unwanted, stray domesticated animals. KOARP also encourages the public not to hunt particularly endangered and threatened/vulnerable animals. Every October 4th, KOARP commemorates *World Animal Day,* which raises awareness about the importance of animal safety and their positive contribution to the environment.

FLORA

Flowers have always played a valuable and central role in the different cultures of modern-day Kurdistan. This has been true of the past as well as the present. Ralph Solecki, the famous archaeologist who was the first professional to excavate the Shanindar Cave in the 1950s, wrote a book in 1971 entitled *Shanindar, the first Flower People in Kurdistan.* The 'people' he was referenc-

ing were not hippies who went "off the grid" to live in a cave in the middle of the Kurdistan Region during the "Flower Power Era," of the 1960s, but in fact Neanderthals who settled in the cave and the surrounding area some 40-60,000 years ago. Among their remains and soil samples were found several skeletons that had apparently been interred with flowers. Archeologists found a great deal of pollen from several flowers, including Ephedra (also known as Joint Pine or Woody Horsetail), a modern herbal remedy and Yarrow, Cornflower, Bachelor's Button, St. Barnaby's Thistle, Ragwort or Groundsel, Grape Hyacinth, and Hollyhock—plants known for their diuretic, stimulant, astringent and anti-inflammatory properties. It seems—contrary to previously held views in the scientific world—that Neanderthals were very much as we are today—lovers of nature, nurturers of the wounded and mournful of their loss of loved ones. While some of the conclusions remain controversial, the discovery changed scholarly thinking concerning this era or at the very least prompted a debate inconceivable prior to this discovery.

Kurdish-Iranian biologist Abu Hanifah Ahmad ibn Dawud Dinawari (828–896 AD) is largely considered the founder of "Arabic" botany and his *Book of Plants* details over 600 species. One might more accurately state he was the founder of "Kurdish" Botanical Studies and appropriately so as it was in the prehistoric regions of modern day Kurdistan where many plants and flowers found a beginning. This was not only the cradle of civilization for man, but due to climatic conditions for much of the plant world as well.

In Kurdistan, flowers have been traditionally used in making dyes for tribal carpets as well as traditional medicines and in some cases for clothing. The most famous names for women in Kurdish are names of flowers and there are hundreds of such appellations. References to flowers are popular in traditional as well as contemporary music and literature.

Among the many flowers in Kurdistan are Tulips, Hyacinths, Pussy Willows, Joint Pine, Goat's Beard, Primrose, Yarrow, Cornflower, Bachelor's Button, St. Barnaby's Thistle, Ragwort or Groundsel, Hollyhocks, Several types of Iris, Poppy Anem-

one, and Saffron Crocus. Discovered in 2014 by a member of *Nature Iraq*, a local NGO, a species of Perennial Herb with yellow flowers (*Ferula shehbaziana*-Apiaceae) was found exclusively in a small sub-alpine area of the Rangin Mountain in the Hawraman region.

Tulips and their importance to Kurds and Kurdistan

It is believed there are over 150 kinds of Tulips making up a rainbow of colors and that the origin of many stem from Kurdistan. Spring in Kurdistan is naturally when flowers bloom and vibrant colors and wonderful smells emanate from all over. Any trip to the mountains or sweeping valleys will provide plentiful evidence that many

varieties of tulips grow here naturally. The native Lilliput Tulip (Kur, *Lîloz*) is an early-blooming tulip with fire engine red petals and a violet base topped off with a golden ring. It normally grows four to six inches (11-15 cm) with three or four petals. Popular perception would have us believe that Tulips are indigenous to Holland but in fact they were imported from Kurdistan. The Ottoman Empire sold tulips to Europe, which they cultivated in and exported from Kurdistan. The symbolism of the tulip in Kurdish culture goes back to at least the 17th century, as it is referenced in the tragic Kurdish love story Mam and Zin (Mem û Zîn), a true life Kurdish Romeo and Juliet tale, written by Kurdish poet and scholar Ahmad Khani (1650-1707). The couple was eventually laid beside each other in the city of Cizere in Kurdistan of Turkey (a few kilometers from Zahko in Iraqi Kurdistan). According to legend at the place of their internment, a bush sprouted and eventually became a faced-down tulip.

Many of the most common and popular flowers in the West today found their origin in Kurdistan. For example, Daffodils are the first flower of Kurdistan's spring. It is common practice to de-

liver large bouquets of this beautiful heavily scented flower to friends as early as late January. Throughout Kurdistan this speaks of great things to come and best wishes for the year ahead.

Nergiz (Nergis) is also known as a Pinkster Lily, Narcissus, Poet's Daffodil, Pheasant's Eye, or Findern Flower. Regardless of the name, Nergiz are ubiquitously used in Kurdish culture and is a popular name for females. It is often used as a symbol of love, beauty, and softness. Referred to in many poems, it represents: blood of martyrs, the land itself, and love and softness. The Lily blooms and blossoms in spring and from March through May, and are seemingly everywhere. A favorite poem tells of the flowers import in Kurdish Culture:

I smell Nergiz, it's telling me spring is here
I love spring, it's started by

Nawroz [Kurdish New Year]
I love Nawroz, it's the story that shows me the road to liberty

Kurdistan Botanical Foundation (KBF)

The KBF strives to study, collect, identify, record and preserve native plants via scientific research within as well as outside of the Kurdistan Region. This organization compiles lists and studies plants and flowers and educates the public on their importance. In 2011, a delegation from the Kurdistan Botanical Garden Committee visited the Jepson Herbaria at the University of California-Berkeley. Thereafter in 2014 KBGF initiated their Plant Survey, where fieldwork in Kurdistan at Azmar and Goyzha Mountains in Sulaymani were conducted. Findings revealed nearly 3,000 samples in over seventy designated areas and were collected and stored in the

KBF Herbarium where they are to be identified and codified to their scientific families, genus, and species. Another objective of the KBF is to train and educate agriculture and biology students about indigenous flowers in Kurdistan. Moreover, an ambitious program of the KBF is to establish the Kurdistan National Herbarium at the University of Sulaymani as well as a Botanical Garden in Sulaymani.

See the following article by the President of the Kurdistan Botanical Society, Dr. Sarbagh Salih.

"PLANT DIVERSITY OF THE KURDISTAN REGION OF IRAQ"

From The Pen of Dr. Sarbagh Salih President of the Kurdistan Botanical Foundation

In May 2014 the American University of Iraq-Sulaymaniyah (AUIS) joined with the Kurdistan Botanical Foundation and sponsored a course in advanced systematic botany. Students participated in many activities and learned about several related subjects, including botanical nomenclature, evolution, herbarium organization and management, among others. The President of the Kurdistan Botanical Foundation is Dr. Sarbagh Salih, who earned her

Doctorate from the University of Bath (UK) and worked for over a decade for USDA/ Agriculture Research Service. Additionally, she has published over fifteen papers specializing in plants and flowers. She is also the wife of former Prime Minister of the Kurdistan Regional Government, Dr. Barham Salih.

"Mesopotamia, also known as the land of the 'Twin Rivers', has contributed to the development of human civilization in many ways. It stands as the place where the origin of agriculture, writing, and urban development were first practiced. Mesopotamia, within which part of Kurdistan falls, is also referred to as the 'Fertile Crescent' and is commonly considered the cradle of the earliest known civilizations.

The Kurdistan Region of Iraq is also exceptionally diverse botanically, as it is the home of many important germplasms of wheat, barley, and other crops. The Zagros Mountain chain is considered one of the world's top twenty hot spots of species biodiversity thanks to its rich topography. Forty-five of the eighty-two Important Plant

Areas (IPA) in Iraq are located in Kurdistan. An IPA is the site that contains threatened species and/or botanically threatened rich habitats.

Iraq has about 3,300 species of vascular plants, the vast majority (approximately 90%) of which grow in Kurdistan. Of that total, 250-300 species are endemic, and many others are economically important as medicinal plants, wild ornamentals, or valuable genetic resources.

Iraq is divided into four topographic regions: the Mountain Region, Upper Plains and Foothills Region, Desert Plateau Region, and Lower Mesopotamian Region, and the vegetation of the Kurdistan Region is divided into the following zones:

Dry - steppe Zone: This area is located at elevation of 100-350 m and is dominated plant species such as Artemisia herba-alba, Scrophularia deserti, Pteropyrum aucheri, Achillea conferta, Poa bulbosa, and Carex stenophylla.

Moist - steppe Zone: This falls at altitudes between 500–800 m and is dominated by Pistacia eurycarpa, Gundelia tournefortii, Ephedra foliata, Narcissus tazzetta, and Anemone coronaria, along with many grasses that are important genetic resources (e.g., species of grass genera such as Hordeum, Aegilops, Avena, Bromus, Triticum, and Lolium).

Forest Zone: Elevation is between 500-1750 m, and it is dominated by three native oak species (Quercus aegilops, Q. infectoria, and Q. libani) and associated with some herbaceous plants like Tulipa systola, Euphorbia, and Hyoscyamus. This zone is very important for commercial wild plant families like Orchidaceae, Rosaceae, and Liliaceae.

Timberline Zone: This is a narrow transitional belt above the Forest Zone from 1750 to 1900 m and is dominated by Daphne mucronata, Lonicera arborea, Astragalus spp., and Rheum ribes.

Thorn-cushion or Subalpine Zone: This zone occupies elevations of 1900-3000 m, and it is dominated by Cousinia, Dionysia, Acanthophyllum, Acantholimon, Primula, dwarf and thorn bushes of Astragalus spp., and Sarcopoterium spinosum, along with the very rare Tulipa kurdica and T. buhseana that grow on Halgurd Mt. at 2900 m.

Alpine Zone: This discontinuous zone comprises the higher mountain peaks above 2800 m and is dominated by some plant species of the families Brassicaceae, Asteraceae, Labiatae, and Caryophyllaceae.

The Kurdistan Region of Iraq is one of the richest centers of endemic plants in the Middle East and includes 250-300 species that grow nowhere else. This is particularly true in mountains such as Hawraman, Qaradagh, Piramagroon, Qandil, Helgurd, Sakri Sakran, and Sinjar for species such as Allium arlgirdense, Alyssum penjwinense, Alyssum sinjarense, Astragalus gudrunensis, Centurea gudrunensis, Cousinia algurdina,

Cousinia kopi-karadaghensis, Cousinia kurdica, Cousinia qandilica, Galium qaradaghnense, Hedysarum singarense, Hyoscyamus kurdicus, Onosma hawramanenses, Onosma qandilicum, Scrophularia sulaimanica, Stipa kurdistanica. Most of the endemic species are very rare and based on the IUCN red-listing criteria, are highly threatened or critically endangered.

The earliest botanical explorations in Kurdistan were conducted by European botanists like Pierre Edmond Boissier (1810-1885), Heinrich Carl Haussknecht (1830-1903), Michael Zohary (1898-1983), J. B. Gillett (1911-1995), and Carl Heinz Rechinger (1906-1998),

and by native botanists Ali Rawi and Ihsan A. Al-Shehbaz. Most of their collections are currently deposited outside Iraq. In 2013, Saman A. Ahmad conducted an exploration of the flora of Hawraman Mountain and collected 1085 species belonging to 90 different families. Ahmad also discovered four species new to science (Ferula shehbaziana, Onosma hawramanensis, Petrorhagia sarbagiae, Scrophularia sulaimanica), and 18 species new to the flora of Iraq.

The traditional use of wild native plants in the Kurdistan region has a long history, as people use plants for medicine, food, building materials, dyes, tools, and ornamentals, among other things. For example, the various parts of the pistachio plant (Pistacia eurycarpa) are used as follows:

(i) The stems exude a bitter gum (bneshtatall in Kurdish) that is produced by injuring the stem and using the gum as for treating gastrointestinal problems.

(ii) Local chewing gum (bnesht in Kurdish) is made from bneshtatall by boiling it in water.

(iii) Fresh unripe fruits are used in late spring as a condiment and eaten fresh.

(iv) Holes are bored into both sides of the dry ripe fruits and converted into necklaces and worship beads (tazbeh in Kurdish).

The Kurdistan Botanical Foundation (KBF), Kurdistanbotanical.org, is a non-profit organization. It was established in 2013 to study, collect, identify, record, and preserve the botanical wealth of Kurdistan in an effort counter the grave and irreversible factors that threaten of its current biodiversity.

The KBF is supporting two ongoing programs in the city of Sulaimani: the establishment of the Kurdistan National Herbarium at the University of Sulaimani, and the creation of the Botanical Garden of Sulaimani in Hawari Shar Park. It is also conducting intensive botanical explorations of Azmer Mountains and Qaradagh and plans to do the same for other botanically rich parts of Kurdistan. Furthermore, it has been heavily involved in the training and capacity building of young botanists throughout Kurdistan and the rest of Iraq and will continue to do so in the future."

ARTISTS, POETS and WRITERS of KURDISTAN

From the Pen of Douglas Layton

With Comments by Qadir Qachagh

Douglas Layton is a Master Designer of Jewelry Art working primarily with antiques and relics of antiquity, which he has collected throughout his world travels. Upon discovering a rare and usually damaged element, he restores it and creates a new piece while retaining the intent and aura of the original artist. He is an avid patron of the arts—especially Kurdish Art—and owns a collection of rare canvases and artifacts from a number of well-known Kurdish artisans and craftsman.

THE ART AND ARTISTS OF KURDISTAN

So He waited there with a watchful eye, with a love that is strong and sure

And His gold did not suffer a bit more heat than was needed to make it pure!

Author Unknown

"I first visited Kurdistan in January 1992 and was immediately amazed and surprised by the treasures I discovered. One somehow expects a desert but is confronted suddenly with awe and art inspiring snow-covered peaks and flower bedecked mountains—rivers, lakes and no end of colorful culture—an artists dream!

One comes to Kurdistan having heard plenty about *peshmerga* and the struggles of the Kurdistan Region both past and present. But as an artist in search of those with similar passions I quickly found the land abounding with brilliant painters and sculptors as well as accomplished

Woman with Flowers by Kelho

poets and writers. I have traveled to over one hundred countries and savored the art of the nations—both modern and classic. I never dreamed I would find in Kurdistan a most amazing well of talent and quickly became one of the largest collectors of Kurdish art in the world. Unknown to most, the Kurds have produced some of the greatest artists, poets and writers—both of our time and of eras long past.

My first encounter with Kurdish art was through a man named Abdul Rahman Kelho. I saw one of his paintings hanging in the home of the first Governor of Duhok, Abdul Aziz Tayep in January of 1992. I inquired about the creator and in short order found myself escorted to the humble abode of a man who had painted from childhood. Before the meeting was over I openly wept. He was a truly great man who had—along with all of his people—suffered terrible tragedy. His story was not unlike that of many if not most artists of the region. Saddam Hussein in his effort to annihilate Kurdish society took particular pains to destroy its culture. For many enemies of his State there was imprisonment, torture and execution but for the artists he reserved a particularly painful torment. Often, rather than kill or incarcerate them (although some ultimately did endure long stretches in prison and some were executed) Saddam's secret police (the Mukhabarart) would drag the artist from his home and burn all of his work before his or her eyes. For many it was a more terrible type of torture than any physical pain they might endure— watching a lifetime of work enveloped by flames.

In the case of Abdul Rahman, he lost most but managed to secret away a few of his finest works from different periods. He was also unwilling to let a tyrant destroy his passion for painting. As the Nobel Prize winning teenager

Antique Kurdish Tribal Restoration and Design
Douglas Layton

Malala Yousafzai recently said, "They can shoot your body but they cannot shoot your dream." Abdul Rahman like hundreds of thousands of others became a homeless IDP (Internally Displaced Person) after the Gulf War in 1991. The US Army under the auspices of Operation Provide Comfort (of which my brother was then Deputy Commander), supplied thousands of tents to these homeless Kurds to insure their survival through the winter. While perusing the pieces Abdul Rahman lay before me on the floor of his sparse apartment, I noticed a number were painted on what appeared to be tent canvas. I wondered if perhaps Rahman's tent had disappeared square-by-square slowly transformed from the abode of the body to that of the soul. He had also painted on cardboard or any other item he could find—limited only by his short supply of paint. When I saw his work I immediately asked how much he wanted for each. He sheepishly said, "$100?" To which I replied, "How about $150?" I bought a dozen pieces and took them to a Washington DC gallery owned by a friend of mine and asked if he thought they were any good. After studying them

The Wedding by Kelho

M'orraq by M. Ghiassi

carefully he replied, "Douglas, this is most assuredly investment quality art!" He was right.

Soon after I curated a show in Nashville, TN where there is a large number of resettled Kurdish refugees (the largest in the US) and a number of sympathetic Americans. I quickly sold all the pieces I had—except for one. I then bought rolls of canvas and barrels of paint and returned to Kurdistan bearing gifts for the artists who had for so long been without the basic elements of their craft—things Western artists oft take for granted. The issue for us in America is, "Which brand of oil or what brush to use." For a Kurd in those days the question was, "How long will my painting survive if rendered on cardboard?" Each time I visited Kurdistan (countless trips in the past twenty-two years) I would often buy works from various artists, sell them, keep one and return with more supplies with which the artists could pursue their craft. Abdul Rahman Kelho went on to become the Director of the University Fine Arts Academy in Duhok and other cities in Kurdistan and today,

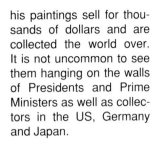

The Carpet Merchant by Jean-Léon Gérôme in M'orraq by Ghiassi

his paintings sell for thousands of dollars and are collected the world over. It is not uncommon to see them hanging on the walls of Presidents and Prime Ministers as well as collectors in the US, Germany and Japan.

I was once invited to address the *Kurdish Artist's and Writer's Union* in Duhok. I was never more humbled in my life. A fairly well known writer accompanied me from the United States. After my lecture, he began chatting with a very frail old artist with shoulder length snow-white hair and beard and sad but piercing eyes. He asked if the man had any of his paintings to view to which he replied that Saddam had destroyed them all. BUT... he did have some picture post cards of his paintings and asked if my friend would like to see them. As this 'important' American writer thumbed through them he remarked, "This is reminiscent of Picasso". The old man without giving the slightest hint of it being a bit unusual replied, "Why yes, I stayed with Picasso for some time many years ago." While never attaining the fame of his one time mentor the aged artisan was ultimately collected the world over—especially in Germany and other parts of Europe.

At work in Sulaymani Gallery

Another time I was lecturing at the Khanzad Resort Hotel near Erbil and passed an exhibit by an artist who worked in the ancient Persian Art form called *M'oarraq* (wood Inlay and miniature painting). His name is M. Ghiassi born in the Kurdish part of Iran. Upon inspection of one of his pieces it appeared seamless yet was crafted from hundreds of hand cut tiny pieces of wood of varied colors and types from exotic locales such as Borneo and Malaysia. I was enamored with one work and asked how long it took him to create it. "Two years," he replied. I immediately purchased it for what seemed a paltry sum and visited his studio in the mountains the next day. I immediately saw why it took him two years. He had no electricity and only a small coping saw with which to cut the wood by hand. I asked if I were to supply him with a proper studio, power tools and electricity how long would it take. "Oh!" he replied, "I could do it so quickly—maybe six months." Ghiassi is perhaps one of the five or six truly great masters of the art form alive today. By the way, you can no longer purchase his work for a paltry sum. But take heart; there are many more amazing Kurdish artists to discover.

If you are privileged to vis-

it the Kurdistan Region of Iraq, your visit will be not be complete without taking time to peruse the galleries and speak with those who know little or nothing of waging wars but know more than we can imagine about stirring the soul and what it means to preserve a dream in the face of almost insurmountable adversity and the searing heat of the refiner's fire.

ON THE POETRY AND LITERATURE OF KURDISTAN

Qadir Qachagh

Qadir Qachagh is the founder and curator of the Cultural and Folklore Museum in Duhok. He is one of the more knowledgeable curators in the Kurdish Region as well as a passionate poet.

"If literature is a garden, its shiniest flower is a poem. The very beginning of recorded humanity dates to the Gilgamesh epic, which started with a poem (written c. 2100 BC in Mesopotamia – modern day Iraq). The Greeks and other ancient civilizations have all had poetry as a foundation of their civilization and like other Middle-Eastern nations; Kurdistan has given great importance to literature and poetry since the beginning of their history.

According to ancient records, Kurdish history is older than many of its neighboring nations. Evidence also shows that the most ancient poetry documents uncovered were written in Hawrami (a Kurdish dialect used by people of Hawraman), which dates to the 6th century BC. It is regarded as the most archaic of the Gorani group. It is mostly spoken in western Iran (Iranian Kurdistan) and northeastern Iraq (Iraqi Kurdistan). The key cities of this region are Pawe in Iran and Halabja in Iraq. As an Indo-Iranian language Horami is related to Avestan, the language of the ancient religion of Zoroastrianism.

Similar to the other nations all around the world, Kurdistan has its own literature. However, Kurds are especially known for poetry. The history of its beginning goes back to "Baba-Tayari Hamadani's" poems, who lived from 935 AD to 1010 AD. In modern Kurdistan, the rise of poetry dates to 1850 AD and the great Kurdish poet "Mawlawi" who was primarily influenced by:

The stunning environment and nature of Kurdistan
Division of Kurdistan, and restrictions to the freedom of travel of its citizens
Absence of a defined political entity
Deprivation of Kurds by their occupiers

İbn Al-Mustafi

Absence of land roads, seaway and skyway to connect Kurdistan to the outside world
Depriving Kurds of basic human rights and democracy

Political art in Suly Park

Destruction of the wealth and treasure of Kurdistan by the neighboring countries by the attacks of ancient empires
Suppression of Kurdish females by religion and tribalism."

SOME FAMOUS POETS AND WRITERS OF KURDISTAN...

Mubarak Bin Ahmad Sharaf-Aldin Abu al-Barakat Ibn al-Mustawfi

("Mawlawi" - 1169-1239 AD), a famous Kurdish historian of Arbil, was born in the ancient Citadel of Arbil. He wrote in several areas: history, literature and language. His masterpiece is a four volumes book of titled "History of Arbil."

Ibn Khallikan said about him in his book Wafayat al-Ayan, "He was a dignified person, he had great humility, broad generosity. Every virtuous person who visited Arbil hastened to visit him, as he had great virtues, and was knowledgeable of many arts."

He studied the science of language and literature, and rhetoric.

He was a poet and Minister in Erbil, in the era of Muzaffar al-Din Abu Sa'eed

Poet Naly

Poet Kurdi

Poet Salim

al-Kawkaboori and Governor of Erbil in the reign of Sultan Saladin. In the year 1236 AD Ibn al-Mustawfi moved to Mosul after the Tatars occupied Erbil and lived there until his death in 1239 AD.

Ahmad Khani
(1651-1707)

He was one of the early proponents of Kurdish Independence and wrote what is considered the épopée of Kurdish literature titled *Mam and Zin* (Mem û Zîn). It is a Kurdish classic love story written down in 1692. It is based on a true

Tomb of Mem and Zin

story, passed down from generation to generation by oral tradition. The content is very similar to the story of Romeo and Juliet written one hundred years before by Shakespeare. However, the oral tradition for the tale most likely predates the work of Shakespeare. For Kurds, Mam and Zin are symbols of the Kurdish people and the land of Kurdistan, which are separated and have been tragically forbidden from joining together. The Mem-u Zin Mausoleum is located in Cizre, Turkey just across the border from Zakho.

By Reshad Naef

PESHMERGA, ORIGIN AND DUTIES

From the Pen of Muhsin Khalidi
Senior Peshmerga and author

The first written account of Kurds being mentioned in a major battle was 358 BC by the Greek mercenary and historian Xenophon in his book detailing the Greek army attack against Persia. He briefly described some legions called "Kardokhi" an early name given to the Kurds. By this reference we understand that Kurds throughout history used brave legions in defense of their land helping to insure their protection and survival.

Origin of Word "Peshmerga" in Modern Kurdistan

During the short-lived Kurdistan Republic Of Mahabad (1946), President Qazi Mohammed held discussions with his leaders seeking to find an appropriate word for their armed forces. According to a well-known account Ahmed Kahveci (the servant that serves tea) suggested the title "Peshmerga" and the name was adopted and remains to this day. It is an ancient and symbolic word for 'sacrifice' and was used in times past to refer to someone whose life would be brief due to his willingness to sacrifice it.

Meaning of Peshmerga

The struggle of *peshmerga* has a significant meaning in Kurdish history. The word "peshmerga" consists of two parts "pesh" literally meaning "takeover" and "merg" meaning death". Together the meaning indicates "a person taken over by death" or in another sense "someone who sacrifices himself to protect other people without getting any benefit or profit from that sacrifice." The philosophy of the peshmerga has lead to enormous self-confidence and has gained the trust of the Kurdish People for their armed forces. The last 70 years of sacrifices by the *peshmerga* has led to what is oft referred to as the "blood, emotional, and cultural" relationship between all Kurdish communities. In fact the word peshmerga among Kurdish people has become synonymous with the freedom for Kurdistan.

A history of protecting Kurdistan

Being a *peshmerga* is not only about being armed and participating in struggles & fights for freedom but in the last couple of decades the thousands of people who became peshmerga have been educated to promote a nation that is environmentally friendly and respectful of human rights. Peshmerga view their role as a guardian of the dignity of the people. For them being a peshmerga is more than being a freedom fighter; it is also a style of life and philosophy.

Looking at Kurdish history in the last century; specifically from the Kurdistan Republic of Mahabad till today, not only in Iraq, but Iran, Syria and Turkey as well, these "national guards" have never given in when they have aimed their weapons at the would be conquerors and betrayers of Kurdistan. This is what makes a man or woman a *peshmerga*.

Both men and women serve as Peshmerga

Current Peshmerga Duty

After many years of the *peshmerga's* sacrifices in Kurdistan the peshmerga secured the region in 2003. After that the *peshmerga's* task changed from mountain fighting into new tasks in cities. The task of many commanders was altered to one of management responsibility and the "Ministry of Peshmerga" was formed. Rather than being a loosely knit group of freedom fighters living off the land and support of the locals, the *Peshmerga* began to be paid like any other government employees, protecting the regions borders and cities as their primary role.

For the past 22 years despite many ups and downs and dishonest treatment by the Central Government of Baghdad, Kurds have worked to establish a stable government. Recently however, a Jihadist

rebel group with the aid of some regional countries has once again threatened Kurdistan. This predator organization is named Islamic State of Iraq & Levant (ISIL). After controlling Mosul (70km - 42 miles from Erbil) they threatened the areas under control of Peshmerga's forces. After a predatory attack on Shengal and Yezidis near the border area ISIL increased its attacks to include areas from Shengal to Khaneqin, which led to a difficult task for the *peshmerga*.

Baghdad has not assisted the Kurds in any way and to date the *peshmerga* does not own any up-to-date weapons while ISIL is well armed having captured many modern weapons from the Iraqi army. Yet, despite all these difficulties the peshmerga again sacrificed to protect Kurdistan.

The Peshmerga with the support of their people and coalition countries un-

der leadership of United States become the first force in the world to effectively fight against this unrivalled terrorist organization. The peshmerga have had frequent success and achievements over the last couple of months and have once again secured the borders of Kurdistan.

Peshmerga and the Future

We believe the military and politic leaders of the world should see the reality and view the peshmerga in a different way.

Peshmerga can be a stabilizing force for the political situation in the region.

Coalition countries should consider that the situation of Baghdad and Iraq's interior issues and problems are not helping the situation and should send weapons to the peshmerga directly as most of the arms intended to fight ISIL are not

reaching the only people (the peshmerga) who are effective against this predator

The coalition countries should increase their training for *peshmerga.*

To accept the reality that the *peshmerga* fight against ISIL is as a representative for the world. Therefore the coalition countries should support the *peshmerga* in every manner, supplying weapons, training, even living expenses.

The peshmerga are ready to sacrifice as always and to become an instrument of peace and a guardian force to protect all nations and religions in the Middle East without any discrimination. It is the only regional armed force that can protect against and neutralize ISIL. The *peshmerga* have proved themselves. Now it is the world's turn to prove themselves.

HORSES OF KURDISTAN

The Mission and Vision of the Ketin Horse Club

From the Pen of Karwan Barzani

Due to the beauty, physical stature and their overall value, horses have often been cherished by human beings and seen as priceless creatures. From ancient times, horse riding and chivalry have both been associated with the traditions of the Kurdish society. Raising horses for individual entertainment, or using them as a means of transportation in the past, or in weddings all attest to the fact of human attachment to this magnificent creature. They have been highly valued as they symbolize courage and are a source of inspiration. Their presence alongside our war heroes cannot be overlooked.

Amongst famous Kurdish families and peoples, horses have been considered symbols of resistance in whose eyes they saw victory. The late Immortal Mullah Mustapha Barzani paid special attention to horses, and alongside the *Peshmergas*, horses played a vital role in the Ailul (September 1961) Revolution, and generally in the Kurdish Freedom Movement. The Immortal Barzani did not value horses merely as God's beautiful creatures, but he viewed them with integrity and believed that the success of the Kurdish movement could never be detached from the role of horses played in the heroic achievements of the Kurds.

Accordingly, it is indispensable that this tradition of horse breeding should be honoured and more attention be paid to the commemoration of it. Therefore the *Ketin Horse Club* and our associates are sponsoring horse exhibitions and festivals to remind people and to teach the new generation about the significant role of horses in the history of our people.

Moreover, I believe this tradition should also become part of the nation's educational program so that the new generation can better understand the meaning and values of horses in our culture. This will contribute to their understandings of the very meaning of our land and nation. We at the Ketin Horse Club are committed to assist in this educational process in any way we can.

DOING BUSINESS IN KURDISTAN

Kurdistan is experiencing an incredible economic boom and there are opportunities for investment in every sector. Following is a very brief overview with contacts for further information.

ECONOMY

A new, liberal foreign investment law was ratified in June 2006 providing incentives for foreign investors such as the possibility of owning land, up to 10-year tax holidays and easy repatriation of profits.

To rapidly benefit from its oil and gas resources, the KRG has signed dozens of production sharing contracts with companies from 17 countries.

INVESTMENT IN THE KURDISTAN REGION

For investment enquiries please visit the website of the Kurdistan Region Board of Investment. The Kurdistan Region Investment Law outlines the Region's policy for direct investment, and has been instrumental in promoting economic growth.

Kurdistan Investment Board Head Office Erbil City

In front of the Council of Ministers Building, 30 Metre Street
Tel: +964 (0) 66 253 1559 / 253 5010
Email:
info@kurdistaninvestment.org
Slemani Branch Slemani City - Hammdi Street, Kani Askan District
Tel: +964 (0) 53 312 3907 / 312 3918
Email:
suli@kurdistaninvestment.org
Duhok Branch Duhok City - 1st Shubat Street
Tel: +964 (0) 62 7627175 / 7627 013
Email:
duhok@kurdistaninvestment.org

THE KURDISTAN REGION: INVEST IN THE FUTURE

This is a publication produced by the KRG providing an overview of investment opportunities in many sectors. The PDF versions can be viewed and downloaded from these links:

Investment guide 2011: The Kurdistan Region, Invest in Democracy

Investment guide 2009: The Kurdistan

Region, Invest in the Future

Investment guide 2008: The Kurdistan Region, Invest in the Future

CHAMBERS OF COMMERCE

Erbil Chamber of Commerce President:
Mr. Dara Jalil Khayat
Website: www.erbilchamber.org
Email:erbilchamberofcommerce@yahoo.com
Tel: +964 (0) 66 2222014,
Tel: +964 (0) 66 2222162,
Tel: +964 (0) 66 2230671
Visiting address: Aras Street, Chamber of commerce BLDG., Erbil, Kurdistan Region, Iraq

Slemani Chamber of Commerce
President: Mr. Sirwan Mohamed Mahmood
Website: www.sulcci.com
Email: info@sulcci.com; sulaimanychamber@yahoo.com; / info@sule-chamber.org

Tel: +964 (0) 53 312 3293 / 3772 / 6845.
Fax: +964 (0) 52 312 6985
Visiting address: Sulaimany Salim St, Opp. Sulaimany Museum, SCC Building, Kurdistan Region, Iraq

Duhok Chamber of Commerce President:
Mr. Ayad H. Abdul Halim
Website:
www.duhokchamber.com
Email:
info@duhokchamber.com;
ayad@duhokchamber.com
Alternative email:
abdulhalim_h@yahoo.com
Tel:+964 (0) 750 471 7827

Mr. Abdulsalam Salih al-Doski - Adviser,
Tel: +964 (0) 62 722 1647

Mr. Mustafa Ramazan Ahmed - Manager,
Tel: +964 (0) 62 722 4633

KURDISTAN CONTRACTORS UNION

The Union represents local contracting companies
President: Mr. Ahmad Aziz Rekani
Website:
www.balendaran.com
Email:
balendaran@yahoo.com
Tel: +964 (0) 53 321 0496
Tel:+964 (0) 770 143 3333
Tel:+964 (0) 770 143 5822
Tel:+964 (0) 750 112 6969

IMPORTERS AND EXPORTERS UNION OF IRAQ

The Kurdistan branch of the Importers and Exporters Union represents local compa-

nies that trade internationally.
Chairman: Mr. Mustafa Abdulrahman Abdullah
Website: www.ieku.org/English.aspx

TRADE AND INDUSTRY

For trade enquires please contact the Ministry of Trade and Industry Trade Missions. The KRG welcomes inward trade or investment missions. Companies and trade associations can contact the KRG for advice on visiting the Region and exploring business opportunities. Contact the KRG Department of Foreign Relations at dfr@krg. org or your nearest KRG Representation.

The KRG regularly welcomes and assists inward business delegations from many countries, including from the Czech Republic, France, Germany, Italy, Japan, Jordan, South Korea, Lebanon, Spain, Turkey, the US and the UK. Please contact your country's trade ministry or trade associations to enquire about their missions to the Kurdistan Region.

REGISTERING A COMPANY OR BRANCH IN THE KURDISTAN REGION

Note: It is strongly advised to seek appropriate local legal assistance Requirements for incorporating a limited liability company in the Kurdistan Region and documents/ actions needed.

RESERVATION OF NAME OF PROPOSED COMPANY AT CHAMBER OF COMMERCE

• Completed application form;

• Draft company statement/company contract (similar to a memorandum of association);

• Certificate of incorporation;

• Articles of association/charter;

• Board resolution approving incorporation of a subsidiary in the Kurdistan Region;

• Power of attorney in favor of a Kurdistan Region lawyer to undertake Incorporation procedures;

For each corporate shareholder or each individual shareholder:

• Passport copy;

Power of attorney in favor of a Kurdistan Region lawyer;

• Lease of premises in the Kurdistan Region;

• Evidence of residency of proposed managing director in the Kurdistan Region;

• Deposit of initial share capital (minimum one million Iraqi dinars);

• Appointment of statutory lawyer;

• Appointment of statutory accountant

All documents submitted to the Companies Registry must be in Kurdish or Arabic or accompanied by a translation. Documents signed outside Iraq must be notarized and legalized at the nearest KRG Representation Office or Iraqi Embassy.

REQUIREMENTS FOR REGISTERING A BRANCH OFFICE OF A FOREIGN COMPANY IN THE KURDISTAN

• Region and documents/actions needed:

• Completed application form;

• Certificate of incorporation of foreign company registering branch office ("Parent Company");

• Articles of association/ charter of Parent Company;

• Power of attorney in favor of a Kurdistan Region lawyer to undertake registration procedures;

• Certificate of incorporation of each corporate shareholder in Parent Company;

• Articles of association/ charter of each corporate shareholder in Parent Company;

• Copy of passport of each individual shareholder in Parent Company;

• Audited financial statements of Parent Company;

• Letter from Parent Company authorizing registration of the branch office;

• Letter from Parent Company undertaking to assume liabilities of the branch office;

• Lease of premises in t he Kurdistan Region;

• Evidence of residency of proposed chief management official in the Kurdistan Region;

• Appointment of statutory lawyer;

• Appointment of statutory accountant

All documents submitted to the Companies Registry must be in Kurdish or Arabic or accompanied by a translation. Documents signed outside Iraq must be notarized and legalized at the nearest KRG Representation Office or Iraqi Embassy.

A local lawyer and accountant can undertake most of the procedures outlined above.

WORKING IN THE KURDISTAN REGION OIL & GAS SERVICES SECTOR

Please visit the KRG Ministry of Natural Resources website. http://mnr.krg.org/index.php/en

LONG TERM STAYS IN KURDISTAN

For those wishing to reside in Kurdistan long term the procedure is relatively simple if employment is obtained with a known company or investment is made in an approved development project. Inquiries can be made at the Foreigners Registration Office located at 100 Meter Road, next to Erbil International Airport.

KURDISTAN RESOURCES NATGEO, BOOKS, FILMS, VIDEOS, PHOTOS

Updated 26 October 2014

National Geographic

National Geographic magazine began publishing in 1888. The first issue with an article on Kurdistan was published in 1909, **The Mountaineers of the Euphrates**. Since then, NatGeo has published more than ten articles with direct reference to Kurdistan. National Geographic Magazine issues from 1888 to 2010 are available on DVD-ROM or external hard disk with 'search' and other helpful functions for about $50.

Here is an excerpt, in the idiom of those times, over a hundred years ago...

"The lineal descendants of the Carduchi who opposed the march of Xenophon are the Kurds – a sturdy, strong-featured race of Mohammedan Aryans, allied to the Persians on the one hand and to the Armenians on the other. Their home is the southern part of the Armenian plateau, among the headwaters of the Euphrates and Tigris rivers, and in the Zagros Mountains, which run southeastward from Lake Van to the Persian Gulf and form the boundary between Turkey and Persia."

Iraq – Where Oil and Water Mix - October 1958

They visited Slemani and remarked, "The Kurds are a remarkable and thoroughly lovable people." They relate a story about a "Kurdish bandit chieftain who terrorized all northern Iraq before he was brought to justice." When sentenced to hanging, he was granted one last wish. Gleefully he said to the judge, "I should like to be hanged with a red-and-green rope." (The colors of the Kurdish Flag)

We Who Face Death - March 1975

Article on the Peshmerga is particularly important because, though it was written earlier that year, it was published the same month as the Algiers accords between Saddam Hussein and the Shah of Iran that led to the collapse of the Kurdish revolution that began in 1961. Many thousands fled their homeland in Iraq to Iran and other neighboring places, and then to many parts of the world, particularly Europe and North America.

Struggle of the Kurds - August 1992

Focuses on the plight of Kurds following mass exodus into the wintry mountains along the Turkey and Iran borders - text by Christopher Hitchens, with photos by Ed Kashi who also produced the photos for the January 2006 NatGeo article.

The Dawn of Humans: Neandertals - January 1996

Among this article's features is the Shanidar Cave, about a 2-hour drive from Erbil, where 50,000-year old Neandertal skeletons were found buried according to ritual, with flowers, the earliest indication of human-like beings (hominids) having feelings for each other.

The Kurds in Control - January 2006

Features "The Other Iraq". It's all there in black and white text, and convincing color photographs by Ed Kashi.

West from the Khyber Pass - July 1958 by Supreme Court Justice William O. Douglas

This is part 1 of a road trip, which began in Karachi (Pakistan) and on to Istanbul via Afghanistan, Iran and Iraq passing through Khanaquin to Baghdad.

Station Wagon Odyssey: Baghdad to Istanbul - January 1959 by Supreme Court Justice William O.

Douglas

Part 2 of a road journey from Karachi (Pakistan) to Istanbul via Afghanistan, Iran, and Iraq – from Baghdad to Kirkuk, Mosul, Hatra, Yezidis – Baidhra and Lalish, Tel Kayf, Erbil, Hamilton Road to Hajj Omran, and back into Iran to Turkey

---

BOOKS

The Kurdish National Movement: Its Origins and Development by Wadie Jwaideh (Syracuse University Press, 2006); based on a PhD dissertation submitted to Syracuse University in 1960. Jwaideh was a Christian born in Basra who served the Iraqi Government in Iraqi Kurdistan during the 1940s.

Mustafa Barzani and the Kurdish Liberation Movement (1931-1961) by Masoud Barzani (Palgrave MacMillan, 2003). Excels not only for its observations and insights, but also for the publication of numerous documents.

Kurdistan: In the Shadow of History by Susan Meiselas (University of Chicago Press, 2008) Available in hardback & paperback both beautifully illustrated with old and more recent photos, 472 pages.

Journey Among Brave Men by Dana Adams

Schmidt (Little, Brown, 1964) Another treasure. From an obituary in The New York Times: "Mr. Schmidt was with The Times from 1943 to 1972. He won the Overseas Press Club's George Polk Award in 1963 for "the best reporting requiring exceptional courage and enterprise abroad" for a series of articles on the Kurdish rebels in Iraq.

After Such Knowledge, What Forgiveness by Jonathan Randal (Farrar, Straus and Giroux, 1997) Stories of Kurdistan's failures in becoming a nation-state and the role of international powers, including their betrayals. Based on firsthand observations by one of the earliest correspondents to Iraqi Kurdistan.

Invisible Nation: How the Kurds' Quest for Statehood is Shaping Iraq and the Middle East by Quil Lawrence (Walker & Company, 2008). An account of the effects of the Kurdish struggle for statehood since the collapse of the Ottoman Empire in 1918 to the events of 1991 with the formation of the Kurdistan Region of Iraq, and the continuing pursuit since 2003 of autonomy in post-Saddam Iraq.

Road Through Kurdistan: The Narrative of an Engineer in Iraq by Archibald Milne Hamilton (Tauris Parke Paperbacks, 2005) First published in 1937 this book is about what today is still called the 'Hamilton Road', one of the world's great drives, through the deepest canyons in the Middle East and up through the highest mountains in Iraq, built in 1928-1932 to connect the British and Persian Empires.

The Kurdish National Movement by Chris Kutschera (e-book, Amazon Digital Services, Inc., 2012) Good detail, notably around the period of the breakup of the Ottoman Empire.

The Long March of The Kurds: 40 Years of History in the Making by Chris Kutschera (pdf download: JePublie, 2012) http://www.numilog.net/142436/The-Long-March-of-The-Kurds--40-years-of-history-in-the-making.ebook

The Cradle of Mankind: Life in Eastern Kurdistan by WA and ETA Wigram (A & C Black, 1914) download: Google 'archive.org ı eBook and Texts ı California Digital Library'

The Jews of Kurdistan by Erich Brauer Wayne State University Press (August 1, 1993) The Jews of Kurdistan is a unique historical document in that it presents a picture of Kurdish Jewish life and culture prior to World War II. It is the only ethnological study of the Kurdish Jews ever written and provides a comprehensive look at their material culture, life cycles, religious practices, occupations, and relations with the Muslims.

My Father's Paradise: A Son's Search for His Family's Past by Ariel Sabar (Algonquin Books, 2009) Also available in Turkish. A delightful book about the Jews of Zakho!

Folk Literature of Kurdistany Jews by Yona Sabar (Yale University Press, 1984)

My Father's Rifle: A Childhood in Kurdistan by Hiner Saleem (Picador, 2006)

A People Without a Country: The Kurds and Kurdistan by Gerard Chaliand (Interlink Publishing Group, 1993)

When the Borders Bleed: The Struggle of the Kurds by Ed Kashi and Christopher Hitchens (Pantheon, 1994)

Journeys in Persia and Kurdistan: Travels on Horseback in 1890 Volume One by Isabella Bird (Long Riders' Guild Press, first published 1891) and

Journeys in Persia and Kurdistan II by Isabella Bird (Virago Press Ltd., 1989)
To improve her health, intrepid Isabella Bird traveled from Britain, alone, by ship and on horseback during the late 19th century to Australia, "to Hawaii where her health miraculously improved", the Rocky Mountains, Japan, Malaya, Morocco, Turkey, Tibet and Ladakh, Korea and China, and Persia and Kurdistan. She was the first woman inducted into the Royal Geographical Society in London.

A Thousand Sighs, A Thousand Revolts: Journeys in Kurdistan by Christiane Bird (Random House, 2005, paperback) The author traveled around Kurdistan avoiding the usual places and people by staying with families to observe and absorb Kurdish culture. (No relation to Isabella Bird.)

Iraq and Rupert Hay's Two Years in Kurdistan by Paul J. Rich (Lexington Books, 2008) Detailing two years (1918-1920) in the life of a British political officer charged with establishing and maintaining British rule in the Kurdish district of Arbil in Iraq.

To Mesopotamia and Kurdistan in Disguise by Ely Banister Soane (Cosimo, Inc., 2007)

The Kurds: A Concise Handbook by Mehrdad R. Izady (Taylor & Francis, 1992). Well researched by an academic of tribes, political parties, and much more.

The Kurds: A National Denied by David McDowall (Minority Rights Group, 1992)

A Modern History of The Kurds by David McDowall (IB Tauris, 1997)

Kurds Turks and Arabs: Politics, Travel and Research in Northeastern Iraq 1919-1925 by CJ Edmonds (Oxford University Press, 1957)

Kurds, Arabs and Britons: The Memoir of Col. W. A. Lyon in Kurdistan, 1918- 1945 by David K. Fieldhouse (IB Tauris, 2002)

The Kurds of Iraq by Michael M. Gunter (St. Martin's Press, 1992)

The Kurdish Predicament in Iraq: A Political Analysis by Michael M. Gunter (St. Martin's Press, 1999)

Historical Dictionary of the Kurds by Michael M. Gunter (The Scarecrow Press, 2004)

The Kurds Ascending: The Evolving Solution to the Kurdish Problem in Iraq and Turkey by Michael M. Gunter (Palgrave MacMillan, 2008)

The A to Z of the Kurds by Michael M. Gunter (Scarecrow Press, 2009)

Understanding Turkey's Kurdish Question edited by Fevzi Bilgin and Ali Sarihan with contributors including Hugh Pope, Michael M. Gunter, Cengiz Cander and others (Lexington Books, 2013)

Blood and Belief by Aliza Marcus (New York University Press, 2007)

A Poisonous Affair: America, Iraq, and the Gassing of Halabja by Joost R. Hiltermann (Cambridge University Press, 2007)

Iraq's Crime of Genocide: The Anfal Campaign Against the Kurds by Human Rights Watch (Human Rights Watch, 1994)

Bernard Wittmann: Letters from Kurdistan 1954-1963 (in English: Verlag Hans Schiler, Berlin, 2008)

Erbil in the Cuneiform Sources By John MacGinnis (KRG Ministry of Culture & Youth, 2013)

Kurdish Identity: Human Rights and Political Status edited by Charles G. MacDonald and Carole A. O'Leary (University Press of Florida, 2007)

The Emergence of Kurdish Nationalism and the

Sheikh Said Rebellion, 1880- 1925 by Robert Olson and William F. Tucker (University of Texas Press, 1989)

The Kurdish Nationalist Movement in the 1990s: Its Impact on Turkey and the Middle East Robert Olson, Editor (The University Press of Kentucky, 1996)

The Kurdish Question and Turkish-Iranian Relations: From World War I to 1998 by Robert W. Olson (Mazda Publishers, 1998)

The Goat and The Butcher: Nationalism and State Formation in Kurdistan-Iraq since the Iraqi War by Robert Olson (Mazda Publishers, 2005)

Blood, Belief and Ballots: The Management of Kurdish Nationalism in Turkey, 2007-2009 by Robert Olson (Mazda Publishers, 2009)

The Kurdish Nationalist Movement in the 1990s: It's Impact on Turkey and the Middle East by Robert Olson (Mazda Publishers, 2011)

The Kurdish Nationalist Movement in Turkey 1980 to 2011 by Robert Olson (Mazda Publishers, 2011)

The Kurdish Nationalist Movement: Opportunity, Mobilization and Identity by David Ramano (Cambridge University Press, 2006)

Kurdistan: Crafting of National Selves by Christopher Houston (Indiana University Press, 2008)

The Kurdish Question in Iraq by Edmund Ghareeb (Syracuse University Press, 1981)

Humanitarian Intervention Assisting the Iraqi Kurds in Operation Provide Comfort, 1991 by Gordon W. Rudd and US Army Center of Military History (Military Bookshop, 2012)

Martyrs, Traitors and Patriots: Kurdistan After the Gulf War by Sheri Laizer (Zed Books, 1996)

Kurdish Culture and Identity edited by Philip Kreyenbroek and Christine Allison (Zed Books, 1996)

Kurdish Culture: A Cross-Cultural Guide by Denise L. Sweetnam (Verlag fur Kultur und Wissenschaft, 1994)

Kurdistan – a Nation Emerges by Jonathan Fryer (Stacy International, 2010)

Kurdistan on the Global Stage: Kinship, Land, and Community in Iraq by Diane E. King (Rutgers University Press, 2013) "Anthropologist Diane E. King has written about everyday life in the Kurdistan Region of Iraq which covers much of the area long known as Iraqi Kurdistan"

How to Get Out of Iraq with Integrity by Brendan O'Leary (University of Pennsylvania Press, 2009)

The Future of Kurdistan in Iraq by Brendan O'Leary, John McGarry, and Khaled Salih (University of Pennsylvania Press, 2006)

The Kurds of Iraq: Building a State Within a State by Ofra Bengio (Lynn Rienner Pub, 2012)

The Kurdish Quasi-State by Denise Natali (Syracuse University Press, 2010)

A Fire in My Heart; Kurdish Tales by Diane Edgecomb, Mohammed MA Ahmed, Cetel Ozel (Libraries Unlimited Inc., 2007)

Elvis Is Titanic: Classroom Tales from Iraqi Kurdistan by Ian Klaus (Vintage, 2008)

Love in a Torn Land: Joanna of Kurdistan: The True Story of a Freedom Fighter's Escape from Iraqi Vengeance by Jean Sasson (Wiley, 2007)

Jewish Subjects and Their Tribal Chieftains in Kurdistan by Mordechai Zaken (BRILL, 2007)

The Kurds: A People in Search of Their Home-

land by Kevin Mckiernan (St. Martin's Press, 2006)

Turning Enemies into Friends: Change in Turkey's Relations with KRG: How Iraqi Kurds became Turkey's best ally in the Middle East by Minhac Celik (Lap Lambert Academic, 2013)

Iraq Since the Gulf War: Prospects for Democracy edited by Fran Hazelton (Zed Books, 1994) with contributions by Ahmad Chalabi, Ali Allawi, Dlawer Ala'Aldeen, Falaq al-Din Kakai Laith Kubba, Kanan Makiya, Ann Clwyd, and others.

On Current Affairs: The Kurdish Question, Problems of Development, The National Front, Facing Imperialism and Counter-Resolution by Saddam Hussein (Ath-Thawra Publications, 1974). Speeches by Saddam Hussein delivered between September 1973 and April 1974.

The Future of Iraq: Dictatorship, Democracy or Division? By Gareth Stansfield and Liam D. Anderson (Basingstoke: Palgrave Macmillan, 2004)

Iraq by Gareth Stansfield (Polity Press, 2007) Background history and politics of the KRI

The Kurds and Iraq by Gareth Stansfield (Rouledge, 2014)

The Kurds in Iraq: The Past, Present and Future by Kerim Yildiz (Pluto Press, 2007)

The Kurds of Iraq by Michiel Hegener (Mets & Schilt, 2010)

The Kurds of Iraq: Ethnonationalism and National Identity in Iraqi Kurdistan by Mahir A. Aziz (Tauris Academic Studies, 2011)

Hell Is Over: Voices of the Kurds after Saddam, An Oral History by Mike Tucker (The Lyons Press, 2004)

The Militant Kurds: A Dual Strategy for Freedom by Eccarius-Kelly (Praeger Cloth A Titles, 2010)

The Kurds: Nationalism and Politics by Faleh A. Jabar and Hosham Dawood (Saqi Books, 2007)

The Passion and Death of Rahman the Kurd: Dreaming Kurdistan by Carol Prunhuber (iUniverse, 2010, also Kindle Edition)

The United States, Iraq and the Kurds: Shock, Awe and Aftermath by Mohammed Shareef (Routledge, 2014)

The Kurds (Genocide and Persecution) by Noah Berlatsky (Greenhaven Press, 2013)

The Kurds: A Nation on the Way to Statehood by Jamal Jalal Abdullah (authorhouse, 2012)

Iraqi Kurds and Nation-Building by Mohammed MA Ahmed (Palgrave Macmillan, 2012, also Kindle Edition)

The Kurds and US Foreign Policy: International Relations in the Middle East since 1945 by Marianna Charountaki (Routledge, 2010, also Kindle Edition)

The Kurdish Republic of 1946 by William Eagleton (Oxford U P, 1963)

An Introduction to Kurdish Rugs and Other Weavings by William Eagleton (Interlink Pub Group, 1988)

Agha, Shaikh and State: The Social and Political Structures of Kurdistan by Martin van Bruinessen (Zed Books, 1992) free download: https://www.academia.edu/2521173/Agha_Shaikh_and_State_The_Social_and_Political_Structures_of_Kurdistan

A Kizilbash Community in Iraqi Kurdistan: The Shabak By Martin van Bruinessen www.hum.uu.nl/medewerkers/m.vanbruinessen/.../Bruinessen_Shabak.pdf (National Geographic Magazine, October 1928, published The Kizilbash Clans of Kurdistan.)

Selected papers by Martin van Bruinessen available to download, free: https://universiteitutrecht. academia.edu/Martinvan-Bruinessen

Kurds: Through the Photographer's Lens by Mark Muller, Kerim Yildiz, and 6 more including Susan Meiseles (Trolley Books, 2008)

No Friends but the Mountains: The Tragic History of the Kurds by John Bullock and Harvey Morris (Oxford University Press, 1993)

Kurdistan: Region Under Siege by Karl Bodnarchuk (Lerner Publishing Group, 2000)

Primitive Rebels Or Revolutionary Modernisers? The Kurdish Nationalist Movement in Turkey by Paul J. White (Zed Books, 2001)

Ghosts of Halabja: Saddam Hussein and the Kurdish Genocide by Michael J. Kelly (Praeger, 2008)

Kurds and Kurdistan by Arshak Safrastian (The Harvill Press Ltd., 1948)

Fire, Snow and Honey: Kurdistan by Gina Lennox (Halstead Press, 2001)

Life for Us by Choman Hardi (Bloodaxe Books, 2004)

Gendered Experiences of Genocide: Anfal Survivors in Kurdistan-Iraq by Choman Hardi (Ashgate, 2011)

Iraqi Federalism and the Kurds: Learning to Live Together by Alex Danilovich (Ashgate, 2014)

The Man in Blue Pyjamas: Prison Memoir in the Form of a Novel by Jalal Barzanji (University of Alberta Press, 2011)

The Idea of Kurdistan: The Modern History of Kurdistan Through the Life of Mullah Mustafa Barzani By Davan Yahya Khalil (CreateSpace Independent Publishing Platform, 2014)

The Kurds of Iraq: Nationalism and Identity in Iraqi Kurdistan By Mahir A. Aziz (I.B. Taurus, 2014)

Strategic Priorities for Improving Access to Quality Education in the Kurdistan Region of Iraq By Georges Vernez and Shelly Culbertson (Rand Corporation, 2014)

Improving Technical Vocational Education and Training in the Kurdistan Region – Iraq By Louay Constant, Shelly Culbertson, et al (Rand Corporation, 2014)

Capacity Building at the Kurdistan Statistics Office Through Data Collection By Shmuel Abrmzon, Nicholas Burger, et al (Rand Corporation, 2014)

An Assessment of the Present and Future Labor Market in the Kurdistan Region – Iraq: Implications for Policies to Increase Private-Sector Employment By Howard J. Shatz, Louay Constant, et al (Rand Corporation, 2014)

Stategies for Private-Sector Development and Civil-Service Reform in the Kurdistan Region – Iraq By Michael L. Hanson and Howard J. Shatz (Rand Corporation, 2014)

Teachers' Use of English Language Learning Materials in Kurdistan By Zana Hassan (CreateSpace Independent Publishing Platform, 2014)

The Impact of Training on Employee Performance in Public Organizations: A Case Study of the Municipality of Erbil –Kurdistan Region of Iraq by Karokh Hamad (CreateSpace Independent Publishing Platform, 2014)

Iraqi-Kurdistan. Does the Kurdistan Regional Government have a Foreign Policy? By Anonym

(GRIN Verlag GmbH, 2014)

The First Dissident: The Book of Job in Today's Politics by William Safire (Random House, 1992) This book is dedicated to Mustafa Barzani who William Safire says was the most Joban character he ever met.

Nineveh And Its Remains Vol. II by Austen Henry Layard (Kessinger Publishing, 2007)

Shanidar: The First Flower People by Ralph S. Solecki (Alfred A. Knopf, 1971) "A personal narrative of one of the most important and exciting archaeological discoveries of recent years."

The Old Social Classes and the Revolutionary Movements of Iraq: A Study of Iraq's Old Landed and Commercial Classes and of its Communists, Ba'thists and Free Officers by Hanna Batatu (Princeton University Press, 1978)

KURDISTAN DOCUMENTARIES, VIDEOS

GWYNNE ROBERTS **'Frontline' interview, transcripts, films** http://www.pbs.org/frontlineworld/stories/iraq501/audio_index.html

Anfal - The Kurdish Genocide vimeo.com/39764719

Saddam's Road to Hell www.pbs.org/frontlineworld/stories/iraq501/video_index.html

1998-March: Saddam's Secret Time Bomb vimeo.com/2721112

KURDISTAN FEATURE FILMS

Chaplin Of The Mountains – 2014 Director: Jano Rosebiani Charlie Chaplin films. Trailer: http://www.youtube.com/watch?v=SIRTZFPf8rs

Letter To The King (Brev Til Kongen) – 2014 Director: Hisham Zaman

One Candle, Two Candles – 2014 Director: Jano Rosebiani - Nominated for Golden Globe 2015

Before Snowfall (For Snoen Faller) – 2013 Director: Hisham Zaman

My Sweet Pepperland – 2013 Director: Hiner Saleem

Babamin Sesa – 2012 Directors: Orhan Eskiloy, Zeynel Dogan

Bekas – 2012 Director: Karzan Kader Writer: Karzan Kader

De Fyra Sista – 2010 Director: Karzan Kader

Before Your Eyes (Min Dit) – 2009 Director: Miraz Bezar

The Legend Of Kawa, The Blacksmith – 2009 Directors: Stuart Palmer, Havi Ibrahim - CGI-animated developed and produced by a community project in Hull, England English Voices by: John Ainsworth, Andrew Rolfe, and Dom Heffer

Winterland – 2007 Director: Hisham Zaman

Beritan - 2006 Directors: Halil Uysal, Jinda Baran, and Dersim Zeravanr

Half Moon (Nive Heyve) – 2006 Director: Bahman Ghobadi

Kilometre Zero - 2005 Director: Hiner Saleem

Turtles Can Fly (Kusi Ji Dikarin Bifirin) – 2004 Director: Bahman Ghobadi - won the main prize at the San Sebastian Film Festival

Colourful Dreams (Xewnên Rengin) - 2003 Directors: Mano Khalil Cast: Hasa H. Inan, David Imhoof, Max Rüdlinger, Sandra Forrer, and Rezan Cetin Switzerland. 60 minutes.

Vodka Lemon (Vodka Leymun) - 2003 Director: Hiner Saleem Cast: Romen Avinian, Lala Sarkissian, Ivan Franek France-Italy-Switzerland-Armenia.

Jiyan - 2002 Director: Jano Rosebiani

Marooned In Iraq - 2002 Director: Bahman Ghobadi

Tirej - 2002 Director: Halil Uysal Editor: Ozgur Reyzan

Tall Mirror (Eyna Bejnê) - 2002 Director: Halil Uysal

A Time For Drunken Horses - 2000 Director: Bahman Ghobadi

Beyond Our Dreams - 2000 Director: Hiner Saleem

The Photograph (Fotograf) - 2000 Director: Kazim Öz

Ax (Land) – 1999 Director: Kazim Oz Turkey

Long Live The Bride... And The Liberation Of Kurdistan - 1997 Director: Hiner Saleem

A Song For Beko (Kelamek Jib O Beko) – 1992 Director: Nizamettin Aric

Yol (The Journey) – 1982 Directors: Serif Gören, Yilmaz Güney

The Herd (Sürü) – 1978 Director: Zeki Ökten / Yılmaz Güney

KURDISTAN PHOTOS

Gulan-Uk Collection
http://www.gulan.org.uk/kurdistan-photography.html

Anthony Kersting photos at The Courtwald Institute of Art, London

Christians Of Kurdistan
http://www.gulan.org.uk/archive-anthony-kersting-christians-of- kurdistan.html

Jews Of Kurdistan
http://www.gulan.org.uk/archive-anthony-kersting-jews-of-kurdistan.html

Kurdistan-Photo Library Kurdish History In Images http://kurdistan.photoshelter.com/

Chris Kutschera
http://kurdistan.photoshelter.com/gallery/Chris-Kutschera-Archives-Kurdish- leaders-in-the-XX-and-XXI-century/G0000m2RBTD8eRsw/

Photo Book:
Stories Kurdistan Histoires by Chris Kutschera of many Kurdistani personalities. Published by Aras Press in Erbil.

Francois Xavier Lovat http://kurdistan.photoshelter.com/gallery/Francois-Xavier-Lovat-Kurdistan- Iraq-1960s/G0000eJ17J3szqzs/

Photo books on the religions of Kurdistan and other topics are available through:
http://www.kurdistanmemory.com/site/english/commander.html

Susan Meiselas In addition to her wonderful, treasurable photo book, don't miss her website: http://www.susanmeiselas.com/archive-projects/kurdistan/#id=intro

William Carter http://bywilliamcarter.wordpress.com/2012/04/19/plight-of-syrias-kurds- breaks-into-the-news/

Photos From The 1960's: http://www.wcarter.us/php/eng/public/381.php

Talk By William Carter available on YouTube:
Part 1:
https://www.youtube.com/watch?v=nSJtDIUMM70
Part 2:
http://www.youtube.com/watch?v=gWaY2V918og&feature=youtu.be&t=3m46s

Wilfred Thesiger Wonderful photos at the Pitt Rivers Museum at Oxford University. See volumes 16 (pages 40 to 60) and 17 (pages 56 to 72). http://web.prm.ox.ac.uk/thesiger/index.php/thesigers-albums.html

Saeed Mahmoudi Aznaveh Website: http://www.aznaveh.ir/enn.swf

Photobook: Kurdistan, The Green Pearl by Saeed M. Aznaveh (Gooya Art House)

SINGLE PHOTO ATTRIBUTIONS:

- Jacob Russell . EIH Airport and women in airport meeting
- Jeffrey Beall . Erbil International Airport / Wikipedia Commons
- "Montage of Slemani" by Myararat83, Slemanibob, Thomas Brechmann, Rawauploaded89 - Photo by Myararat83, CC BY-SA 3.0Photo by Slemanibob, CC BY-SA 4.0Photo by Thomas Brechmann (https://www.flickr.com/photos/128516062@N05/15780745191), CC BY 2.0Photo by Rawauploaded89, CC BY-SA 3.0. Licensed under CC BY-SA 4.0 via Wikimedia Commons - http://commons.wikimedia.org/wiki/File:Montage_of_Slemani.jpg#mediaviewer/File:Montage_of_Slemani.jpg
- "Sulamani-kurdistan (3)" by Myararat83 - Own work. Licensed under CC BY-SA 3.0 via Wikimedia Commons - http://commons.wikimedia.org/wiki/File:Sulamani-kurdistan_(3).jpg#mediaviewer/File:Sulamani-kurdistan_(3).jpg
- "Sharaf Khan Bidlisi Statue at Slemani Public Park" by Slemanibob - Own work. Licensed under CC BY-SA 4.0 via Wikimedia Commons - http://commons.wikimedia.org/wiki/File:Sharaf_Khan_Bidlisi_Statue_at_Slemani_Public_Park.jpg#mediaviewer/File:Sharaf_Khan_Bidlisi_Statue_at_Slemani_Public_Park.jpg
- "Aram Gallery" by Rawauploaded89 (talk) - I (Rawauploaded89 (talk)) created this work entirely by myself.. Licensed under CC BY-SA 3.0 via Wikipedia - http://en.wikipedia.org/wiki/File:Aram_Gallery.jpg#mediaviewer/File:Aram_Gallery.jpg
- "Kurdishflagslemani" by Rawauploaded89 - Own work. Licensed under CC BY-SA 3.0 via Wikimedia Commons - http://commons.wikimedia.org/wiki/File:Kurdishflagslemani.jpg#mediaviewer/File:Kurdishflagslemani.jpg
- By Osama Shukir Muhammed Amin FRCP(Glasg) (Own work) [CC BY-SA 4.0 (http://creativecommons.org/licenses/by-sa/4.0)], via Wikimedia Commons
- Zagros Mountains "Oshtoran Kooh" by Wiki66 - Own work. Licensed under CC BY-SA 3.0 via Wikimedia Commons - http://commons.wikimedia.org/wiki/File:Oshtoran_Kooh.jpg#mediaviewer/File:Oshtoran_Kooh.jpg
- Mem o Zin Shrine - "Gora Mem û Zîn" by Gomada - Own work. Licensed under CC BY-SA 3.0 via Wikimedia Commons- http://commons.wikimedia.org/wiki/File:Gora_Mem_%C3%BB_Z%C3%AEn.JPG#mediaviewer/File:Gora_Mem_%C3%BB_Z%C3%AEn.JPG
- "Hawler Castle" by jan kurdistani - kurdistan Arbil .irak -Hawler. Licensed under CC BY-SA 2.0 via Wikimedia Commons http://commons.wikimedia.org/wiki/File:Hawler_Castle.jpg#mediaviewer/File:Hawler_Castle.jpg
- "Franso Hariri Stadium" by Kushared - Own work. Licensed under CC BY 3.0 via Wikimedia Commons - http://commons.wikimedia.org/wiki/File:Franso_Hariri_Stadium.JPG#mediaviewer/File:Franso_Hariri_Stadium.JPG
- "Persepolis The Persian Soldiers" von Arad - Eigenes Werk. Lizenziert unter CC BY-SA 3.0 über Wikimedia Commons - http://commons.wikimedia.org/wiki/File:Persepolis_The_Persian_Soldiers.jpg#mediaviewer/File:Persepolis_The_Persian_Soldiers.jpg
- "Persepolis stairs of the Apadana relief" von Phillip Maiwald (Nikopol) - Eigenes Werk. Lizenziert unter CC BY-SA 3.0 über Wikimedia Commons - http://commons.wikimedia.org/wiki/File:Persepolis_stairs_of_the_Apadana_relief.jpg#mediaviewer/File:Persepolis_stairs_of_the_Apadana_relief.jpg
- By James (Jim) Gordon [CC BY 2.0 (http://creativecommons.org/licenses/by/2.0)], via Wikimedia Commons
- "Sherwana Castle" by Orientepop2012 - Own work. Licensed under CC BY-SA 3.0 via Wikimedia Commons - http://commons.wikimedia.org/wiki/File:Sherwana_Castle.jpg#mediaviewer/File:Sherwana_Castle.jpg
- "Battle of Gaugamela (Arbela)" by Tapestry after a work by Charles Le Brun, court painter to the Sun King (Louis Quatorze) - Image taken by User:Mathiasrex Maciej Szczepa czyk. Licensed under CC BY 3.0 via Wikimedia Commons - http://commons.wikimedia.org/wiki/File:Battle_of_Gaugamela_(Arbela).PNG#/

- media/File:Battle_of_Gaugamela_(Arbela).PNG
- "MacedonEmpire" by Generic Mapping Tools - created by user. Licensed under CC BY-SA 3.0 via Wikimedia Commons - http://commons.wikimedia.org/wiki/File:MacedonEmpire.jpg#/media/File:MacedonEmpire.jpg
- "Vulpes vulpes Kurdistanica (cropped)" by Vulpes_vulpes_Kurdistanica.jpg: Dûrzan cîranoderivative work: Mariomassone (talk) 16:23, 17 December 2011 (UTC) - Vulpes_vulpes_Kurdistanica.jpg. Licensed under CC BY-SA 3.0 via Wikimedia Commons - http://commons.wikimedia.org/wiki/File:Vulpes_vulpes_Kurdistanica_(cropped).jpg#/media/File:Vulpes_vulpes_Kurdistanica_(cropped).jpg
- "Mêşa Rîçalê" by Dûrzan cîrano - Own work. Licensed under CC BY-SA 3.0 via Wikimedia Commons - http://commons.wikimedia.org/wiki/File:M%C3%AA%C5%9Fa_R%C3%AE%C3%A7al%C3%AA.jpg#/media/File:M%C3%AA%C5%9Fa_R%C3%AE%C3%A7al%C3%AA.jpg
- "Hesp û Cahnûk" by Dûrzan cîrano - Own work. Licensed under CC BY-SA 3.0 via Wikimedia Commons http://commons.wikimedia.org/wiki/File:Hesp_%C3%BB_Cahn%C3%BBk.jpg#/media/File:Hesp_%C3%BB_Cahn%C3%BBk.jpg
- "Chukarhuhn Weltvogelpark Walsrode 2010" by Olaf Oliviero Riemer. Licensed under CC BY-SA 3.0 via Wikimedia Commons - http://commons.wikimedia.org/wiki/File:Chukarhuhn_Weltvogelpark_Walsrode_2010.jpg#/media/File:Chukarhuhn_Weltvogelpark_Walsrode_2010.jpg
- "Alectoris-chukar-001" by Mdf - Originally from en.wikipedia; description page is (was) herefirst upload in en.wikipedia on 17:18, 12 May 2005 by Mdf. Licensed under CC BY-SA 3.0 via Wikimedia Commons - http://commons.wikimedia.org/wiki/File:Alectoris-chukar-001.jpg#/media/File:Alectoris-chukar-001.jpg
- KIBBEH
"Kibbeh3" by Basel15 at the English language Wikipedia. Licensed under CC BY-SA 3.0 via Wikimedia Commons - http://commons.wikimedia.org/wiki/File:Kibbeh3.jpg#/media/File:Kibbeh3.jpg
- "Xwarin-shingal1" by Bablekan at the English language Wikipedia. Licensed under CC BY-SA 3.0 via Wikimedia Commons - http://commons.wikimedia.org/wiki/File:Xwarin-shingal1.jpg#/media/File:Xwarin-shingal1.jpg
- "Armeniadoma" by Original uploader was Artaxiad at en.wikipedia - Transferred from en.wikipedia; transferred to Commons by User:Vriullop using CommonsHelper.. Licensed under CC BY-SA 3.0 via Wikimedia Commons - http://commons.wikimedia.org/wiki/File:Armeniadoma.jpg#/media/File:Armeniadoma.jpg
- "Napoli BW 2013-05-16 16-25-06 1 DxO" by Berthold Werner. Licensed under CC BY-SA 3.0 via Wikimedia Commons - http://commons.wikimedia.org/wiki/File:Napoli_BW_2013-05-16_16-25-06_1_DxO.jpg#/media/File:Napoli_BW_2013-05-16_16-25-06_1_DxO.jpg
- "Battle Gaugamela decisive" by Frank Martini. Cartographer, Department of books, United States Military Academy - The Department of History, United States Military Academy [1]. Licensed under CC BY-SA 3.0 via Wikimedia Commons – http://commons.wikimedia.org/wiki/File:Battle_gaugamela_decisive.png#/media/File:Battle_gaugamela_decisive.png
- "Pair of dafs" by Olaf - http://flickr.com/photos/gradin/50928484/. Licensed under CC BY-SA 2.0 via Wikimedia Commons http://commons.wikimedia.org/wiki/File:Pair_of_dafs.jpg#/media/File:Pair_of_dafs.jpg
- "Tambur" by I, Allauddin. Licensed under CC BY-SA 3.0 via Wikimedia Commons - http://commons.wikimedia.org/wiki/File:Tambur.jpg#/media/File:Tambur.jpg
- "Merton College library hall" by Tom Murphy VII - Taken by user (Tom Murphy VII). Licensed under CC BY-SA 3.0 via Wikimedia Commons - http://commons.wikimedia.org/wiki/File:Merton_College_library_hall.jpg#/media/File:Merton_College_library_hall.jpg

MY TRAVEL NOTES

MY TRAVEL NOTES

MY TRAVEL NOTES

MY TRAVEL NOTES

MY TRAVEL NOTES

MY TRAVEL NOTES

MY TRAVEL NOTES

KAR

UPSTREAM | *MIDSTREAM* | *DOWNSTREAM*